# WOMEN'S RIGHTS

Recent Titles in
A World View of Social Issues Series

Crime and Crime Control: A Global View
*Gregg Barak, editor*

# WOMEN'S RIGHTS

## A GLOBAL VIEW

Edited by Lynn Walter

**A World View of Social Issues**
*Andrew L. Cherry, Series Adviser*

**Greenwood Press**
Westport, Connecticut • London

**Library of Congress Cataloging-in-Publication Data**

Women's rights : a global view / edited by Lynn Walter.
    p.   cm.—(A world view of social issues, ISSN 1526–9442)
    Includes bibliographical references and index.
    ISBN 0–313–30890–X (alk. paper)
    1. Women's rights.  2. Women—Social conditions.  I. Walter, Lynn, 1945–  II.
Series.
HQ1236.W6527   2001
305.42—dc21      00–027632

British Library Cataloguing in Publication Data is available.

Library of Congress Catalog Card Number: 00–027632
ISBN: 0–313–30890–X
ISSN: 1526–9442

First published in 2001

Greenwood Press, 88 Post Road West, Westport, CT 06881
An imprint of Greenwood Publishing Group, Inc.
www.greenwood.com

Printed in the United States of America

The paper used in this book complies with the
Permanent Paper Standard issued by the National
Information Standards Organization (Z39.48–1984).

10 9 8 7 6 5 4 3 2

This book is dedicated to Alice,
Sue Ann,
and Roseanna Lynn

# CONTENTS

# SERIES FOREWORD

Why are child abuse in the family and homelessness social conditions to be endured or at least tolerated in some countries while in other countries they are viewed as social problems that must be reduced or eliminated? What social institutions and other factors affect these behaviors? What historical, political, and social forces influence a society's response to a social condition? In many cases, individuals around the world have the same or similar hopes and problems. However, in most cases we deal with the same social conditions in very dissimilar ways.

The volumes in the Greenwood series A World View of Social Issues examine different social issues and problems that are being faced by individuals and societies around the world. These volumes examine problems of poverty and homelessness, drugs and alcohol addiction, HIV/AIDS, teen pregnancy, crime, women's rights, and a myriad of other issues that affect all of us in one way or another.

Each volume is devoted to one social issue or problem. All volumes follow the same general format. Each volume has up to fifteen chapters that describe how people in different countries perceive and try to cope with a given problem or social issue. The countries chosen represent as many world regions as possible, making it possible to explore how each issue has been recognized and what actions have been taken to alleviate it in a variety of settings.

Each chapter begins with a profile of the country being highlighted and an overview of the impact of the social issue or problem there. Basic policies, legislation, and demographic information related to the social issue are cov-

ered. A brief history of the problem helps the reader better understand the
political and social responses. Political initiatives and policies are also discussed, as well as social views, customs, and practices related to the problem
or social issue. Discussions about how the countries plan to deal with these
social problems are also included.

These volumes present a comprehensive and engaging approach for the
study of international social conditions and problems. The goal is to provide
a convenient framework for readers to examine specific social problems, how
they are viewed, and what actions are being taken by different countries
around the world.

For example, how is a problem like crime and crime control handled in
third world countries? How is substance abuse controlled in industrialized
countries? How are poverty and homelessness handled in the poorest countries? How does culture influence the definition and response to domestic
violence in different countries? What part does economics play in shaping
both the issue of and the response to women's rights? How does a national
philosophy impact the definition and response to child abuse? These questions and more will be answered by the volumes in this series.

As we learn more about our counterparts in other countries, they become
real to us, and our worldview cannot help but change. We will think of
others as we think of those we know. They will be people who get up in
the morning and go to work. We will see people who are struggling with
relationships, attending religious services, being born, and growing old, and
dying.

This series will cover issues that will add to your knowledge about contemporary social society. These volumes will help you to better understand
social conditions and social issues in a broader sense, giving you a view of
what various problems mean to different people and how these perspectives
impact a society's response. You will be able to see how specific social problems are managed by governments and individuals confronting the consequences of these social dilemmas. By studying one problem from various
angles, you will be better able to grasp the totality of the situation, while at
the same time speculating as to how solutions used in one country could
be incorporated in another. Finally, this series will allow you to compare
and contrast how these social issues impact individuals in different countries
and how the effect is dissimilar or similar to your own experiences.

As series adviser, it is my hope that these volumes, which are unique in
the history of publishing, will increase your understanding and appreciation
of your counterparts around the world.

Andrew L. Cherry
Series Adviser

# PREFACE

This series, A World View of Social Issues, is based on the premise that addressing social problems is advanced by historical and comparative perspectives; so too are the courses I teach in anthropology and women's studies. For example, I always begin my introductory cultural anthropology class by arguing that our common humanity is to be found in our particular histories and cultures. Throughout human history and around the globe we have faced the common problems of life and have come up with different ways of addressing them. We have always and everywhere shared those ways with our neighbors, whether they were the family next door, the village down the road, the tribe over the river, or the country across the border. Too often, what we did not share with our neighbors, we fought over. And who are our neighbors today? Our "neighbors" are now connected in cyberspace and in the global marketplace and in the United Nations. For better or worse, the world has become a neighborhood. Sharing solutions to common problems is more important and easier now than it has ever been, and the consequences of not sharing are more far-reaching and frightening.

Women's rights advocates have been among those social activists most eager to share their ideas with international sisters in struggle. I well remember that, in 1975, I went to an international panel of non-Western women grass-roots activists, organized by the new women's movement in Madison, Wisconsin, eager to hear how the sisters around the world addressed their problems. One after the other, the panelists said that "women's liberation," as we called it then, did not mean anything to them, that it was just the concern of privileged, white, Western, middle-class women. That was the beginning of my education on the necessity of addressing women's rights in ways that took cultural, class, and racial differences among women into account. Since then, I have had many more years and many more occasions to think about it, and I bring those years of teaching, writing, and discussing with women from many cultures to this volume. I wish I could say that it got easier, but all I can say is that I have learned a great deal and that I continue to learn more every day from the experience of listening and trying to understand many different cultural perspectives on the question of women's rights. I hope the readers may benefit from my experience and those of the other authors in this volume, as I have benefited from my many teachers.

I would like to thank some of them. First, I am grateful to all of the contributors for their work and a level of professionalism that has made my job that much easier. I would also like to thank Emily Birch at Greenwood and series adviser Andrew L. Cherry for their ideas and supportive responses. My colleagues and students in the Women's Studies Program at the University of Wisconsin–Green Bay have, over twenty-some years, been the inspiration for much of what I know about women's rights, and I am happy to have this opportunity to publicly thank them. My colleagues in Social Change and Development I thank for the shared view that justice, equity, democracy, and the development of human potential should be the mission of an academic program. I also owe a deep intellectual and personal debt of gratitude to my friends and colleagues in women's studies in Denmark, especially Bente Rosenbeck at Copenhagen University and Anna-Birte Ravn at Aalborg University.

# INTRODUCTION

In the late 1950s my highly qualified cousin Patricia applied to many different medical schools but was only admitted to one—a women's medical college—because, said the others, they could not take the risk that she would get married, have children, and waste the education they gave her. When I was in college in the early 1960s women students had to be in the dorms by 11:00 P.M., but men had no curfew, because, they said, women needed to be protected from the men. When I went to graduate school in 1967 only two doctors in town would prescribe birth control pills to unmarried women students because it was against the law to do so; the thinking was that birth control for unmarried women would encourage their promiscuity—men could buy condoms with no questions asked. When a single friend of mine, a professor of microbiology, wanted to buy a house in the mid-1960s, banks did not want to lend money to a woman. These are just a few of the incidents of gender inequality in the United States that came to mind as I joined the new women's movement that arose around the world in the 1970s. At that time most of us in the U.S. movement were young middle-class women who thought we had discovered women's rights for the first time in history and that, once discovered, it would not be long before we would solve all these problems. I can only plead the arrogance of youth and relative privilege.

It is nearly thirty years later, more than twenty of them spent teaching women's studies, and now I know that the cause of women's rights owes a debt to our foremothers that goes back at least two centuries and that many of the problems women face are deeply entangled in economic, political, and familial power structures. From the work of women around the world whose efforts to define and achieve women's rights in their own countries raised questions I would not have thought to ask, I learned that understanding the roots of women's inequality and strategies for achieving women's rights must be an international endeavor.

*Women's Rights: A Global View* examines some of the ways women's rights have been defined, denied, and achieved. The fifteen cases presented here were selected from five continents to represent different cultural practices and historical processes: from Hinduism to Judaism, from post-industrial capitalist to socialist economies, from national to international political systems, from colonialization to globalization, and from democratic to theocratic governments. Given so much variation it is not surprising that "women's rights" means different things to different people; what *is* surprising is that women from such diverse backgrounds have been able to arrive at important international understandings about what we mean when we say "women's rights."

This volume is about the disagreements and the agreements. It is written for people whose work, as students, activists, and engaged citizens, could benefit from knowledge of women's rights around the world. The subject of women's rights internationally raises difficult theoretical and political issues; and, in every case, the contributors have tried to do justice to that complexity without getting mired in it.

Deciding what aspects of women's rights to present in each case drew upon our individual disciplinary, theoretical, and cultural knowledge. However, commonalities in our approach to the issue facilitate comparisons across the various cases. First, each author examines how women's rights have changed over time, focusing her historical analysis on the nineteenth and twentieth centuries, when the development of nation-states and international organizations brought women's rights into the political arena. All of the exemplars are states with the important exceptions of the Ojibwe Nation and the European Union; the latter help us to think comparatively about how forms of political organization might affect women's rights. Second, all of the authors explore how women, and men, have struggled for the establishment of women's rights and what kinds of opposition they confronted. This meant analyzing the ways women's rights have been promoted or impeded by social movements, especially women's movements. Third, we examine how socioeconomic class, religious, ethnic, and racial differences in the experiences of women have shaped their understanding and practice of women's rights. Lastly, we have defined the concept of women's rights broadly enough to include not only such rights as the right to vote, but also the right to a decent standard of living and a secure future.

## CONCEPTUALIZING WOMEN'S RIGHTS

### Types of Women's Rights

To understand how women's rights are addressed in various countries and within ethnic groups and international organizations, it is helpful to think in terms of different types of rights. Marshall (1964) divided rights into three types—civil, political, and social. Civil rights are necessary for individual freedom. Under individual freedom he included personal liberty (as opposed to slavery, debt peonage, or serfdom); freedom of speech, thought, and faith; the right to own property and conclude valid contracts; and the right to justice. Political rights are the rights to be included in political decision-making, as in a democracy, and social rights are the rights to a decent standard of living comparable to others in society, to reasonable security, and to health care, education, and welfare.

In the fifteen cases presented in this volume, the concept of rights is applied broadly to encompass civil, political, and social rights. Defining women's rights as including adequate living conditions recognizes that class differences in economic opportunity affect women's understanding of justice and equity. Focusing on class difference among women also makes it easier to account for difference in the goals of women's rights movements between relatively prosperous and relatively poor countries. For example, Desai (Chapter 8) argues that women in India see sustainable development as a fundamental basis of women's rights. Sustainable development provides for the well-being of the present generation without sacrificing the quality of life for future generations. For women this means going beyond equal access with men to poverty and insecurity, to equal access to a decent standard of living and a secure future for their children.

### Women's Rights in the Family

Women's rights are complicated by the fact that they include not only rights associated with women's participation in the public sphere or civil society—the arena of formal education, the mass media, the market economy, and political participation—but also the presumedly private sphere of family. Patriarchal family practices related to sexuality, the authority of the head of the family, inheritance rules, and child custody, often sanctioned by religious beliefs, come into conflict with the ideal of the rights of women as individuals. Domestic violence, for example, is the most common form of violence faced by women around the world. Yet, it was not until the latter half of the twentieth century that freedom from domestic violence became an international human rights issue.

In many places rape is considered a crime against the victim's husband and family. Women raped during the wars in Bosnia and Kosovo were reluctant to report it for fear of the perceived dishonor to themselves and their families. In Italy it was not until 1996 that the law changed to recognize rape as a criminal felony against the victim as opposed to a moral offense against the honor of her family, and to eliminate the former possibility that the perpetrator could escape punishment by agreeing to marry his victim (Stanley 1999).

## Women's Rights: Equal to and Different from Men's Rights

The distinction between what might be labeled an equal rights perspective on women's rights and an approach that goes beyond equal rights to equal results is important in understanding what women want from a women's rights agenda. A narrowly constructed concept of equal rights might propose, on the one hand, that women and men are similar enough to be treated exactly the same under almost all circumstances. Most would argue, on the other hand, that women and men are different enough to require that some provision be made for special treatment in order to promote substantial equality. The latter interpretation of equal rights recognizes that there are significant differences between men and women. An obvious example is the right to choose whether or not to have a child. The women's rights position is that the woman has a greater right to decide whether to become pregnant than the prospective father does. The reverse was true in feudal China (Chapter 3) and in most other places with patriarchal family forms in which the husband had more control over sexual relations and procreation than the wife did.

Other differences between the rights of women and men reflect efforts to rectify the effects of past discriminatory practices by establishing affirmative action programs, called "positive discrimination" in Denmark (Chapter 5). The 40 percent sex quotas that several Danish political parties have established for their lists of candidates for elected and appointed political positions are one example.

Most women's rights scholars agree with Scott (1988) that women and men can be different *and* equal; and whether presumed gender differences are used to support equality or to rationalize inequality depends upon specific historical and cultural contexts. In the nineteenth century women's rights campaigners in many places in the world applied what has come to be called a "separate spheres model" of women's role in society in order to advance the cause of women's rights. For instance, elite women in India used a separate spheres model of women's rights in their nineteenth century campaign to promote better education for women, arguing that education would make women better wives and mothers. Poupart (Chapter 13) argues that precolonial Ojibwe women had greater political and economic power than they do today and that part of their power was based on the high value placed on motherhood among Ojibwe. Precolonially, the western Igbo of Nigeria had a dual political system in which women wielded authority over markets, women's crops, marital disputes, and other aspects of life deemed of most concern to women (Tashjian, Chapter 12). Such conceptions of women's rights call for the significant differences between women and men not to make a difference in terms of their quality of life, status, authority, and power.

## THE HISTORICAL DEVELOPMENT OF WOMEN'S RIGHTS

The work to stop domestic violence and to control one's own body and sexuality is relatively recent in the history of women's rights legislation and activism. First came women's rights in the public sphere, such as the right to appear in court as legally recognized adults, to retain their own wages, and to vote. These rights were articulated in the contexts of eighteenth, nineteenth, and twentieth century struggles that overthrew the divine right of kings and established the rights of citizens in new nation-states.

### Concepts of Natural Rights and Equal Rights

For example, the United States was founded on the notion that "life, liberty and the pursuit of happiness" are *natural rights*. The idea that ordinary men had such rights inherent in their very nature as human beings was a quite radical notion at a time when the hierarchy of king and subject was just being openly challenged. The long campaign to abolish slavery and the bloodiest war in U.S. history were defended, in part, by appeals to the notion that natural rights of men applied equally to all men, including those then in slavery. Thus, the idea of the *equal rights* of men was built upon the concept of natural rights. In mid-nineteenth century America, the idea that women too should have such rights was so radical as to seem preposterous. Nevertheless, as Kalny (Chapter 14) points out, in 1848, at a time in U.S. history when women were not allowed to vote or hold political office, to enter most of the professions and trades, to attend college, or, if married, to claim their own wages or property, the participants in the first women's rights convention resolved to work for all of these rights and more. Their declaration of rights drew explicitly upon the rhetoric of equal and natural rights (see Appendix 2).

Equal and natural rights for African Americans and other people of color were not established in all states and under federal law until late into the twentieth century, and then not without a long civil rights struggle. Through two centuries the United States women's rights campaign has followed a course that paralleled, often in cooperation and occasionally in opposition, the movement for equal rights for African Americans. This intertwining of American histories calls upon those of us who work on women's rights in the United States to consider how our efforts are connected to other struggles for justice and equity. This calling is necessarily an international one since nowhere is the *ideal* of the equal and natural rights of women nourished by the suppression of others.

## The Impact of Colonialism on Women's Rights

The eighteenth and nineteenth centuries saw the beginnings of the realization of equal and natural rights for men and women. However, as Poupart (Chapter 13) underscores, this was also an era marked by the suppression of the rights of the indigenous peoples of the Americas and other colonized regions; and this fact has shaped their conception of women's rights.

American Indians lost their lives, liberty, and land in the same historical period that saw the establishment of the ideal of the natural rights of Anglo-American men. Poupart argues that, in addition to the loss of rights by all American Indian people, American Indian women lost power and status relative to American Indian men. She attributes some contemporary problems, such as domestic violence, to their history of colonial oppression.

Taking internal ethnic, racial, national, religious, and class differences into account in the national histories of women's rights is vital to understanding why women disagree about what constitutes women's rights. It also counters the uncritical assumption that "women in China" or "Argentine women" constitute a single, unified category. In her study of women's rights in Bolivia (Chapter 2), Smeall points out that indigenous women think of their rights in terms of ethnicity and class and rarely as a dimension of gender. Tashjian (Chapter 12) notes the difficulty of generalizing about women's rights in Nigeria, a country with more than 250 different ethnic groups located within boundaries drawn by the colonial powers.

The nineteenth and twentieth centuries saw the height of European colonial power and economic control over much of Africa, Asia, and the Americas and the success of independence movements in those regions. The revitalized nationalism and religious fervor of postcolonial nation-building have often been correlated with debates over the position of women in those societies. In the context of shaping opinion about what the women's rights agenda should be, some argue that the whole idea of women's rights is Western-inspired and insensitive to the needs of ordinary women in postcolonial societies, that is, that the idea of women's rights is tainted by the same kinds of ethnocentric thinking that supported colonialism in the first place.

In her study of women's rights in Egypt, Sherif (Chapter 6) criticizes some Western women's rights advocates for their uncritical assumption that Islamic ideals are necessarily worse for women's rights than Western ones are. She argues that the appeal of Islamist messages to women and men in Egypt should be understood in the larger picture as a response to economic hardship and the search for a postcolonial identity. Mir-Hosseini (Chapter 9) reports on the drastic methods used by the Iranian police in the 1930s to attempt to enforce a governmental ban on women wearing the *hejab*, the women's covering. Public reaction against the police actions contributed to the veil becoming a symbol of the violence and decadence of secular government. In the postcolonial context, as Mir-Hosseini states, Iranian women who promote their own indigenous women's agenda have faced difficulties not confronted by women from the dominant cultures in the West—that is, they are criticized for adopting foreign attitudes, while also being criticized by Western women for their supposedly backward ways regarding women.

Add national differences to cultural and religious diversity, class divisions, and a history of slavery and colonialism, and one can readily understand why any international agreement about what constitutes women's rights took so long to achieve. It came first in the form of the concept of *universal human rights*.

## Universal Human Rights and the Universal Rights of Women

In 1948 the United Nations adopted the Universal Declaration of Human Rights (see Appendix 3). Coming after the Holocaust and a devastating world war, it declared that the ideal of equal and natural rights should be applied internationally and that the UN should do all in its power to promote the progress of universal human rights. Article 1 states, "All human beings are born free and equal in dignity and rights. They are endowed with reason and conscience and should act towards one another in a spirit of brotherhood." Among the rights it recognized are life, liberty, and security of person; freedom from slavery, torture, and cruel and degrading punishment; and recognition as a person before the law with the rights to equal treatment under the law. With this document the assembled nations of the world proclaimed that these and many other rights were universal and, as such, beyond the moral authority of any state to deny.

The United Nations reiterated the universality of human rights in Article 2, which states that everyone is entitled to human rights "without distinction of any kind, such as race, colour, sex, language, religion, political or other opinion, national or social origin, property, birth or other status." The inclusion of "sex" as one of the prohibited bases of discrimination made it clear that *internationally*, human rights were to include women's rights.

In 1979 the United Nations reaffirmed the principle that human rights were women's rights by adopting the Convention on the Elimination of All Forms of Discrimination Against Women (CEDAW) (see Appendix 4). This convention recognized that women were still not equal in practice and, furthermore, that women confronted problems that were different enough from men's to require special attention. It called for action programs in each country to address forms of inequality not easily addressed simply by passing anti-discrimination laws. For example, CEDAW recognizes that motherhood can adversely affect a woman's right to employment and her ability to earn a decent wage. Therefore, Article 11 of CEDAW calls for maternity leave and daycare to address this problem.

For many women around the world, CEDAW and the several UN conferences and action programs for women are important to the promotion of women's rights in their country. Of the authors in this volume, Smeall (Chapter 2) focuses most directly on the importance of CEDAW in pushing the Bolivian government to institute changes called for by the convention. The United States, in contrast, has yet to ratify CEDAW. Mayer (1996), in her analysis of why this is so, argues that the mistaken belief that U.S. law is superior to any international human rights conventions, its failure to ratify the Equal Rights Amendment, and recent trends toward more conservative interpretations of the U.S. Constitution have combined to set back women's rights in the United States, relative to international women's rights declarations.

Just as the establishment of natural rights paralleled the development of modern independent, democratic states, the concept of universal rights arose along with the establishment of international organizations with enough moral and political clout to make universal rights practicable. The United Nations, established in 1945, is the most important of the international organizations promoting women's rights. Since 1975 the UN has organized a series of four international women's conferences, the last one in Peking in 1995. White (Chapter 11) notes that women in Japan are using the action program from the Peking conference to pressure their government for more equality.

Another powerful international organization affecting women's equality is the European Union (EU), which was founded in 1957. Shea (Chapter 7) focuses on the role that the EU has played in advancing women's rights in Europe, where it has taken the lead in promoting maternity leave and childcare provisions. Danish women (Chapter 5), whose rights are greater than in many other European nations, feared that Denmark's entry into the European Union would be a setback for women's rights. Their worst fears have not materialized.

## Globalization

However, such fears are not unfounded, because, like other small, less powerful nations, Denmark feels it must join the progressively more powerful international organization that is the European Union in order not to be left out in the cold in the process of the globalization of the world economy. Thus, the EU and its programs for women represent one facet of a larger process that includes the increasing concentration of capital in transnational corporations, the weakening of national sovereignty, and the movement of labor-intensive jobs to areas of the world where corporations can take advantage of very low-wage workers, many of whom are girls and women.

The globalization of the economy ties the problems of Third World poverty to the wealth inequalities between the rich and poor countries—with women in poorer countries being employed in jobs under abusive working conditions with the lowest pay, no benefits, and no job security. For them, the most critical women's rights are a decent standard of living, humane working conditions, and real economic opportunities. Tied to the lack of economic options and power is the trafficking of girls and young women into forced prostitution reported in Thailand, Burma, Bangladesh, and Pakistan by Human Rights Watch Women's Rights Project (1995) and also in China by Hom (Chapter 3).

## COMPARATIVE PERSPECTIVES ON WOMEN'S RIGHTS

For many reasons it is critical to examine how different societies approach the issue of women's rights. First, the concept of rights develops within specific cultural traditions, and the universality of specific rights may be called into question by the different culture histories. Furthermore, what rights *should* be universal women's rights is not always as clear as international declarations make it seem, especially in cases where proposed universal rights collide with one another. For example, Hom (Chapter 3) argues that labor laws meant to protect Chinese women during menstruation and pregnancy may also prevent them from being hired in the first place. Second, if any universal women's right is meaningful, it must be more than an international declaration; it must be enforced at the local and national level. Thus, we need to pay attention to how existing laws are applied in specific countries. Finally, issues of importance to women arise out of women's lives, experience, and actions. To understand how women come to define and work for women's rights and what barriers they confront to the realization of those rights requires an examination of the issues within the historical and cultural contexts of their societies.

### Universal Rights Versus Cultural Practices

A comparative approach to women's rights is vital to the international process of defining what rights should be universal (or at least international). However, the internationalization of women's rights can infringe upon cultural practices whose claim to great worth is deeply felt and grounded in indigenous religion and morality. What we need are approaches that avoid cultural relativist excuses for oppression, as well as ethnocentric forms of universalism. Some differences between universal and cultural practices of women's rights can be interpreted by seeing the latter as a cultural manifestation of a problem that is international. For example, women in India are protesting the rising costs of dowries and the corresponding increase in the number of brides being murdered by their husbands' families for their dowries (Jaising 1995). These "dowry deaths" are an Indian manifestation of the international problem of domestic violence. However, in order to address the specific problem of dowry deaths, one must understand both its specific cultural context and the fact that it is an example of a violation of women's universal right to live free from the terrorism of domestic violence.

Another approach to confronting the tension between universal and cultural rights is to examine how particular issues are entangled in a web of other problems tied to specific traditions and to ask which of the many threads is most critical. For example, it is often the case that a woman's economic dependence upon her husband leaves her defenseless in the face of other problems, such as how much control she has over her own body. Demanding the universal right of a woman to control her own body without considering how reproductive controls are tied to her economic dependency may lead her to face dire poverty and disgrace.

Both Sherif (Chapter 6) and Tashjian (Chapter 12) discuss this point with regard to female circumcision, which is practiced in Malaysia, Indonesia, parts of the Arabian Peninsula and certain African countries (Gunning 1992). The severity of the practice varies from surgical removal of the clitoral hood (prepuce) to removal of the clitoris, labia minora, and labia majora. Efforts have been made by human rights advocates and public health workers around the world to end this practice, including, most importantly, women from the societies that practice it. In her study of women's health educational campaigns in the rural Sudan, Gruenbaum (1991) found that ideologies of ethnic superiority and religious conservatism have contributed to the continuation of female circumcision despite its illegality there since 1945. Furthermore, it must be noted that this practice occurs with the support of women whose hope for their daughters is that they be able to marry and have a family and a decent life, and who see no chance for any of these things to happen if their daughters are not circumcised. Focusing on the underlying male power structures rather than the specific practice is a way to address this issue. For example, despite much Western attention to this particular custom, African women's rights lawyer Florence Butegwa (1997) sees the major women's rights issues in Africa as domestic violence, violence against women in war, health care, and property rights.

## STRUCTURAL BARRIERS TO WOMEN'S RIGHTS

Women's primary responsibility for childbearing and rearing, the greater attention paid by law to the public sphere, male control over the political and judicial system, cultural and religious traditions that place women in roles of service to men, wealth inequalities, inadequate health care and education, and racial and national hierarchies are just some of the *structural barriers* to women's rights. Anti-discrimination laws cannot achieve equality between men and women until such barriers to women's equality are removed. For example, Frankfort-Nachmias (Chapter 10) maintains that the legal equality of women, which followed the establishment of the state of Israel, will not be a practical reality until there are significant structural changes in the family and the military. And White (Chapter 11) notes that in contemporary Japan, the ancient Confucian values of filial piety, hierarchy, gender inequality, and male-centered households still hold sway and limit the effective enforcement of current laws to guarantee women's equal opportunity in employment.

The impact of macroeconomic structures on women's lives is discussed by several of the authors. In her analysis of Cuba's approach to women's rights, Alonso (Chapter 4) examines whether the structural changes associated with the shift from capitalism to communism are sufficient to promote women's rights. From the official Cuban perspective, capitalism itself is a structural barrier to women's rights. The Chinese government makes the same argument, as do many democratic socialist parties throughout the world. While Alonso sees the Cuban Revolution as having led to important improvement in women's education and health, she argues that women's rights in Cuba remain partial and that race and class divisions still affect women's lives. Hom (Chapter 3) examines the lived realities of Chinese women hidden behind the ideology of egalitarianism and the "market socialism" of China today. She looks especially at Special Economic Zones (SEZs) where many young women from the countryside come to work in the cities in labor-intensive industries with difficult working conditions, poor housing, low pay, and long hours. She notes with some optimism that these young women are not like those of feudal China; they are angry at injustices they experience and do not suffer in silence.

Economic policies within wealthy capitalist economies to promote long-term private sector development and the export sector in poorer countries have negatively affected the lives of poor women. Smeall (Chapter 2) reports that the structural adjustment policies (SAPs) demanded by international lending agencies have led to violence and unrest in the countryside and migration to the cities. Indigenous women find only menial jobs there with low wages and abusive working conditions, sometimes including sexual abuse. Sherif (Chapter 6) reports similar effects on poor women in Egypt under Anwar Sadat's Open Door Policy, which helped the economy at the macro-level but led to cutbacks in social services, including health care for low-income women and children.

While the ability of human rights/women's rights campaigns to effect structural changes in world economies is very limited, it is encouraging to women's rights advocates that the Universal Declaration of Human Rights includes the right to "a standard of living adequate for . . . health and well-being." Working within the framework of humanitarian conceptions of universal rights, which include the right to well-being, gives them a certain amount of moral clout with which to raise the issue of economic justice domestically and internationally.

CEDAW includes mostly anti-discrimination clauses with only a few to address structural barriers. An important example of the latter is found in Article 5, addressing patriarchal culture. It declares that "States Parties shall take all appropriate measures . . . [t]o modify the social and cultural patterns of conduct of men and women, with a view to achieving the elimination of prejudices and customary and all other practices which are based on the idea of the inferiority or the superiority of either of the sexes or on stereotyped roles for men and women." Article 5 raises questions that demand to be addressed in those most intimate of arenas—the family, marriage, and sexuality.

## Personal Law, Family Law, and Religious Law

Such things as marriage and kinship rules, inheritance patterns, child custody, and enforced heterosexuality are in some societies tied to a system of law that is variously labeled personal law, family law, or religious law. Sherif (Chapter 6) observes that in Egypt two legal systems, the national or civil legal system and the personal, family, or religious legal system, exist side by side. The personal or family legal system governs aspects of life that are considered family matters and, as such, outside of the jurisdiction of Egyptian or international law.

In the case of religious legal systems, such as Shari'a (Muslim) and Halakha (Jewish), the existence of both a secular, national legal system and a religious legal system is a recognition of the rights of religious communities to govern themselves with regard to matters that are deemed religiously based. Since so many of the structural barriers to women's rights are tied to matters of marriage, children, sexuality, and inheritance, women's rights and the recognized rights of religious communities to practice their religion may come into direct conflict. Radhika Coomaraswamy (1994) is pessimistic about the efficacy of the women's rights model to reform religious laws, especially when these are focused on women's position within the family. Mir-Hosseini (Chapter 9) is more optimistic. She points to the creation, in 1992, of *Zanan*, a new women's journal in Iran, that argues that there is no contradiction between fighting for women's rights and remaining a good Muslim. The magazine's editors and contributors are creating a new way of thinking about women's rights in Iran that Islamizes the notion that women should have choices and equal treatment.

## Action, Agency, and the Rights of Women

To the extent that structural barriers to women's rights exist, it will take more than changes instituted by governments, especially authoritarian governments, to put an end to gender inequality. While the ideals of universal rights are concerns of moral philosophy, their realization in practice is a political matter. These rights, whether conceived of as inherent or as woman-made, have not been established in practice without collective political action. Such has been the case for the rights of men, and what is true for men's rights is also true for women's rights.

Whether their actions are individual or collective, whether they occur in feminist movements, labor unions, political parties, religious movements, anti-colonialist movements, or their own homes, women's activism has always been vital to the promotion of women's rights. Desai's (Chapter 8) account of the many women's organizations in India clearly demonstrates that women do have power when they are able to act collectively, as in the case of the famous Chipko movement in which poor women in northern India saved their forests by literally "hugging the trees." In Argentina advocates confronted formidable structural barriers to women's rights, including a brutal military dictatorship. From her study of two centuries of women's rights struggles in Argentina, Navarro (Chapter 1) concludes that while Argentine activists struggled ceaselessly, they were most successful at historical moments when the forces of democracy, human rights, and the rights of workers were aligned.

## CONCLUSIONS

As I have outlined above, conclusions by each author, while specific to each of the cases and regions represented in this volume, raise significant comparative issues for those of us concerned about women's rights. One of the values of the comparative method is that it leads us to ask questions about ourselves that we might not otherwise think to ask. It broadens our perspective of women's rights and, in the process, complicates the issue. Our goal in *Women's Rights: A Global View* is to make those complications understandable to students, activists, and engaged citizens, and, in so doing, to contribute positively to continuing international dialogues to promote women's rights.

## BIBLIOGRAPHY

Butegwa, Florence. 1997. "Women Taking Action to Advance Their Human Rights: The Case of Africa." In *Women's Rights as Human Rights: Local and Global Perspectives*, ed. Niamh Reilly. Internet document from ICCL Working Conference on Women's Rights as Human Rights, Dublin, March 1997. Internet address: members.tripod.com/~whr1998/documents/icclbutegwa.htm.

Chowdhury, Najma, and Barbara J. Nelson, with Kathryn A. Carver, Nancy J. Johnson, and Paula L. O'Loughlin. 1994. "Redefining Politics: Patterns of Women's Political Engagement from a Global Perspective." In *Women and*

*Politics Worldwide*, ed. Barbara J. Nelson and Najma Chowdhury. New Haven: Yale University Press, 3–24.

Coomaraswamy, Radhika. 1994. "To Bellow Like a Cow: Women, Ethnicity, and the Discourse of Rights." In *Human Rights of Women: National and International Perspectives*, ed. Rebecca J. Cook. Philadelphia: University of Pennsylvania Press, 39–57.

Gruenbaum, Ellen. 1991. "The Islamic Movement, Development, and Health Education: Recent Changes in the Health of Rural Women in Central Sudan." *Social Science & Medicine* 33, no. 6: 637–45.

Gunning, Isabelle R. 1992. "Arrogant Perception, World-Travelling and Multicultural Feminism: The Case of Female Genital Surgeries." *Columbia Human Rights Review* 23, no. 2 (Summer): 189–248.

Human Rights Watch Women's Rights Project. 1995. *The Human Rights Watch Global Report on Women's Human Rights*. New York: Human Rights Watch.

Jaising, Indira. 1995. "Violence Against Women: The Indian Perspective." In *Women's Rights, Human Rights: International Feminist Perspectives*, ed. Julie Peters and Andrea Wolper. New York: Routledge, 51–56.

Marshall, T. H. 1964. *Class, Citizenship and Social Development: Essays by T. H. Marshall*. Introduction by Seymour Martin Lipset. Garden City, NY: Doubleday.

Mayer, Ann Elizabeth. 1996. "Reflections on the Proposed United States Reservations to CEDAW: Should the Constitution Be an Obstacle to Human Rights?" *Hastings Constitutional Law Quarterly* 23: 727–822.

Scott, Joan W. 1988. "Deconstructing Equality-Versus-Difference: or, The Uses of Post-Structuralist Theory for Feminism" *Feminist Studies* 14, no. 1: 33–50.

Stanley, Alessandra. 1999. "Ruling on Tight Jeans and Rape Sets Off Anger in Italy." *New York Times*, February 16. Web address: archives/nytimes.com/archive.

# ABBREVIATIONS

| | |
|---|---|
| ACWF | All China Women's Federation (Fulian) |
| AIWC | All India Women's Conference |
| ATEM | Association for Work and Study of Women |
| CCP | Chinese Communist Party |
| CEDAW | Convention on the Elimination of All Forms of Discrimination Against Women (or Committee on the Elimination of All Forms of Discrimination Against Women) |
| CRLP | Center for Reproductive Law and Policy |
| ERA | Equal Rights Amendment |
| EU | European Union |
| FGM | female genital mutilation |
| FMC | Federation of Cuban Women |
| IDF | Israeli Defense Force |
| IHS | Indian Health Service |
| IMF | International Monetary Fund |
| IWRAW | International Women's Rights Action Watch |
| LAMA | Legal Age of Majority Act |
| MLF | Movimiento de Liberación Femenina (Movement for Women's Liberation) |
| NAWSA | National American Woman Suffrage Association |
| NCNC | National Council of Nigeria and the Cameroons |

| | |
|---|---|
| NGO | Nongovernmental organization |
| NOW | National Organization for Women |
| PSL | Personal Status Law |
| SAPs | structural adjustment policies |
| SEWA | Self Employed Women's Association |
| SEZs | Special Economic Zones |
| SMS | Stree Mukti Sangharsh (Women's Liberation Struggle) |
| UFA | Unión Feminista Argentina; also called ENOUGH |
| UN | United Nations |
| UNHCHR | United Nations High Commissioner for Human Rights |
| UNICEF | United Nations Children's Educational Fund |
| USAID | United States Agency for International Development |
| WAG | Women's Action Group |
| ZANU(PF) | Zimbabwe African National Union (Patriotic Front) |

# 1

# ARGENTINA

## The Long Road to Women's Rights

*Marysa Navarro*

## INTRODUCTION

### Profile of Argentina

Eighty-nine percent of Argentina's 36 million people live in urban areas. Buenos Aires, its capital and major seaport, is itself home to approximately one-third of all Argentines. Per capita, Argentina's economy is the largest in Latin America, although it ranks below Brazil and Mexico in total gross national product (GNP) (World Bank 1999). Eighty-five percent of the population is of European ancestry, most from Spain or Italy. Ninety percent are Roman Catholic in religious affiliation. Since the country gained its independence from Spain in 1816, the Argentine government has shifted among authoritarian, populist leaders like Juan Perón (1946–1955), military dictatorships, and democracy, which it has enjoyed since 1983, when a period of brutal repression by the military ended. Argentina's literacy rate of 96.2 percent and life expectancy of 75 years are indicators of a relatively high standard of living for many Argentines, although 25.5 percent remain in poverty (CIA 1999).

### Overview of Women's Rights Issues

Unceasing in their efforts, women's rights proponents in Argentina have been most successful in achieving their goals during those propitious historical moments when the forces of democracy, human rights, and workers' rights have been in alignment. Progressive legislation for social entitlements such as maternity leave and publicly funded daycare has long been supported by the labor movement. It backed the first Peronist party government, which granted women full political rights in 1947. From 1977 women in the human rights group Madres de Plaza de Mayo risked their lives to protest the disappearance of their children and were a major force in the democratization of Argentina. The restoration of democracy in 1983 unleashed pent-up feminist activity and resulted in a flurry of new initiatives, including ratification of the UN women's convention, a law against sexual harassment, and sex quotas on political party lists. Most resistant to change have been those women's rights concerns, such as parental authority, divorce, and reproductive rights, governed by conservative religious values.

## HISTORY OF WOMEN'S RIGHTS

### The Nineteenth Century

The 1852 constitution declared Argentina a republic whose authorities were elected by propertied male voters. The status of women was not even mentioned, much less debated, in the constitutional convention, so they were implicitly excluded from the political process. The 1870 Civil Code denied women political rights and treated them like male minors and "mentally defective" men. Once women became adults, they acquired certain civil rights, as long as they did not marry. If unmarried or widowed, a woman could sign a contract and even marry without the consent of her father, but she could not serve as a witness or as guardian of a minor. However, a married woman could only sign a contract through her husband. She could not even administer her own property, she could not be a witness, and she could not take a job without his permission. Furthermore, she acquired the nationality of her husband, his last name, and his domicile, and in case of bankruptcy was responsible for his debts. Finally, only her husband was entitled to *patria potestad* (legal parental authority over their children). All this was rationalized by the presumption that when a woman married, she suffered what jurists called a *capitis diminutio*, that is, a diminution of her mental capacity. In another example of nineteenth century obfuscation, in 1888 marriage was declared a civil institution that could be, but was not necessarily, accompanied by a religious ceremony, although when it ended in divorce, neither spouse could remarry.

### *Working-Class and Immigrant Women*

In the 1880s, Argentina experienced expansion of cattle ranching and grain cultivation, the arrival of repeated waves of European immigrants, and heavy capital investment by Great Britain in railroads, banking, and new port facilities, all of which helped to transform it into one of the world's

leading producers of grain, meat, and wool. It also began to produce industrial goods. Factories and sweatshops multiplied, and immigrant men,
women, and children worked up to twelve hours a day in them. Locked,
sometimes literally, in buildings where disease and occupational hazards
were a constant threat, they produced candles, beer, cigarettes, or textiles
and clothing for poor wages, which were even lower for women than for
men. Workers' agitation for safer working conditions and better living conditions got under way as anarchists and socialists founded resistance societies
and trade unions.

Anarchist women formed groups in Rosario and Buenos Aires, including
the Centro Anarquista Femenino, founded by nineteen women, among
them Juana Rouco Buela, María Collazo, Virginia Bolten, and Marta New-
elstein. The Italian Ana Maria Mozzoni published articles in the anarchist
paper *La Questione Sociale*, and in 1895 a group of anarchist women began
publishing a newspaper for women, *La voz de la mujer* (The Voice of the
Woman), which lasted for one year. In their first editorial they declared
themselves to be.

[F]ed up with so much crying and misery; fed up with the endless drudgery of
children (though they are dears); fed up with asking and begging; fed up with being
a toy, the pleasure object of our infamous exploiters or vile husbands, we have decided to raise our voices in the concert of society and demand, yes demand, our share
of pleasure in life's banquet. . . . We decide to join our comrades against our common
enemy, but since we do not want to be dependent on anyone, we raise a shred of
the red flag. (November 1895)

Women participated in the sometimes heated discussions about their role in
the workplace and the trade union movement, their nature, their subordination, the evils of bourgeois marriage, and the liberating force of free love,
from a clearly anarcho-feminist perspective that was not always shared by
their fellow male anarchists.

The socialists, who founded their party in 1896, supported measures that
forbade work "when it endangers motherhood and attacks morality" (Spalding 1970, 226), and in their first program (1907), they affirmed women's
right to vote and the principle of equal pay for equal work for women and
men. The party opened its ranks to women and gave them some prominence
in its organizations. Counted among them was a group of committed activists, feminists and socialists, including Gabriela Laperriere de Coni, Carolina Muzilli, the sisters Xenia and Fenia Chertkoff, Cecilia S. de Baldovino,
and Alicia Moreau de Justo. They wrote for *La Vanguardia*, the party newspaper, organized women workers, became inspectors for the newly created
Department of Labor (1907), and reported on the working conditions
of women and children. They also founded groups like the Centro

Socialista Femenino (1902) to support women's strikes and to sponsor lectures and educational program for women (Navarro 1985).

## The Twentieth Century

### Protecting Women

In the first decade of the twentieth century, as strikes multiplied and workers' violence increased, Argentina's landowning aristocracy confronted what became "the social question," a debate on issues ranging from the problems posed by the presence of large numbers of foreigners in the country, including numerous prostitutes of European origin, to the need to develop public health policies, implement measures to control social agitators, especially the anarchists, and ameliorate the impact of industrial work on working-class women and children. While a consensus among the elite supported repressive anti-anarchist measures, it also favored labor legislation, especially for women and children.

In 1924, Law 11.317 was enacted, replacing the first law on women's and children's labor from 1907. It remained basically unchanged until 1974 and has been only slightly modified since then. The 1924 law reaffirmed Sunday as a day of rest and the eight-hour workday for men. It also forbade the employment of children under twelve, night work for minors and women, any work performed in unhealthy conditions, and the "putting-out system" for minors and women (a system in which workers were paid to do manufacturing work in the home, usually on a piece-rate wage). It established a six-hour workday for children and an eight-hour workday for women or a forty-eight hour week. It demanded that women and children carry a workbook (wherein an employer recorded where an employee had worked, for how long, and why he/she was dismissed), excluded pregnancy as a reason for firing, gave women a maternity leave of six weeks before and six weeks after delivery, with the right to return to the same job, and required establishments employing a specific number of women to provide a daycare center for babies under two years of age. This is an aspect of the law with which employers did not generally comply and which the state has been reluctant to enforce.

The laws protecting women were classified together with those affecting children because both were seen as weak creatures who needed the protection of the state. Also, regardless of their ideological and religious differences, from socialists to Catholics, all legislators saw a profound contradiction between women being employed and their being mothers and wives. The views they expressed in parliamentary debates were echoed in newspapers, scholarly works, professional publications, and school textbooks.

The daily life of women, whatever their social class, contradicted the prevalent views about womanhood, especially those regarding their physical weakness and limited intelligence. However, these views fit the accepted definition of a subordinated womanhood established in the 1870 juridical framework, which treated adult married women as children. Furthermore, women's limited education reinforced their lack of preparation to live in a rapidly changing world. For most of the nineteenth century, social conventions excluded them from higher education—Argentina's first woman doctor was Cecilia Grierson, who graduated in 1889, only to discover that it was illegal for her to practice her profession.

### The First Feminists

Ten years later, Grierson traveled to London to attend the second meeting of the International Council of Women, which elected her vice president. She returned to Argentina a committed suffragist. Despite her efforts, the National Council of Women, founded in 1900, did not become a suffragist organization. Created by and for women, it nevertheless represented a new kind of philanthropic organization in Argentina. It sought to educate women so as to improve their working and living conditions, offering them, among other things, languages and first aid courses.

Grierson and Rawson de Dellepiane, like Petrona Eyle, the president of the Liga Argentina contra la trata de Blancas (Argentine League Against White Slavery), were also founders in 1902 of the Association of University Women, which included, among others, Julieta Lanteri Renshaw and Sara Justo. They were the first generation of middle-class university graduates who went on to criticize their subordination openly. Alicia Moreau de Justo would recall many years later that this first generation, of which she was a part, had "the audacity to break the silence surrounding these issues [women's civil and political rights, the situation of legitimate and illegitimate children, alcoholism, prostitution, and gambling] when many men did not dare to discuss them publicly" (Moreau de Justo 1945, 163). In 1910 the association organized the First International Feminine Congress. It was held in Buenos Aires, and the topics discussed were education, women's legal status, and suffrage. Carolina Muzilli and Rawson de Dellepiane presented papers calling for the reform of the Civil Code.

In the early twentieth century, Argentina's first feminist wave was a small movement that encompassed different perspectives. While all were concerned with the plight of poor women and the exploitation they suffered in the workplace and the home, and all agreed with the need to improve women's education, not all believed that suffrage or civil rights were necessary measures for women's welfare. There were socialist activists like Carolina Muzilli and Gabriela L. de Coni who addressed women's issues within a framework closely defined by the party, centering their efforts on the emancipation of the working class, which they believed would bring about the emancipation of women.

On the other hand, there were socialist women, like Alicia Moreau de Justo, Sara Justo, and others who, very early on, believed in the need to achieve women's civil and political rights. In 1906, together with Lanteri Renshaw and Rawson de Dellepiane, they founded the Centro Feminista (Feminist Center). By the following decade, the Centro had vanished, but it was replaced by other suffragist organizations. Moreau de Justo founded the Unión Feminista Nacional (National Feminist Union) in 1918, Rawson de Dellepiane created the Asociación pro Derechos de la Mujer (Association for Women's Rights) in 1919, and Lanteri Renshaw organized the Partido Feminista Nacional (National Feminist Party), also in 1919. Despite their efforts, and the support they received, they failed to accomplish their objectives. On the question of suffrage, their failure was particularly painful. In 1912 a new electoral law was adopted by Congress, known as *la ley de voto universal* (the universal vote law). It was universal for men only; women were once again excluded, and the possibility of giving them the right to vote was not even discussed. While two provinces granted women the right to vote in municipal elections in the following decade, Argentine women would have to wait until 1951 to participate in national elections.

### Married Women's Civil Rights

The resolution of the civil rights question took place earlier, perhaps influenced by the international context. In the early twentieth century, the subject of women's inequality became a recurrent topic at the meetings of American states, and in 1923 they agreed to study the possibility of eliminating the legal and constitutional constraints affecting women. Five years later, the Sixth International Conference of American States approved the formation of a commission to report on the legal status of women throughout the continent.

The Argentine Civil Code was reformed in 1926. The new law changed the legal status of married women. They were permitted to have a profession, be gainfully employed and keep their earnings, sign contracts without the permission of their husbands, and administer their properties. Although the new law did not alter the *patria potestad* (legal authority over children), it granted women the exercise of that right in case of separation.

### The Infamous Decade: 1930–1943

As the 1930s began, Argentina entered a period of political instability marked by the repeated intervention of the military in the political process. Known as the "Infamous Decade," the years between 1930 and 1943 were a time of intense political corruption. Yet women persisted in wanting to be part of the political process and, in fact, redoubled their efforts. However, women's suffrage was thwarted by a conservative majority in the Senate.

Furthermore, the suffragists were unable to devise a common strategy to strengthen their own position. Weakened by the death of Grierson, Lanteri Renshaw, and many of the first leaders, the suffragist camp was divided with the emergence of the Asociación Argentina para el Sufragio (Argentine Suffrage Association). Founded in 1930 by Carmela Horne de Burmeister, its leaders were avowedly Catholic. They favored suffrage only for literate women born in Argentina, and they opposed divorce, which the feminists, socialists or not, supported. Ideological divisions were further deepened by events in Europe, first the Spanish Civil War and then World War II. The struggle against fascism dominated political discourse, and the question of women's suffrage began to lose urgency. Alicia Moreau de Justo, the reluctant leader of what was left of the movement, became primarily engaged in the struggle against fascism not only in Europe, but also at home. She, along with many old-time feminists and suffragists, opposed Coronel Juan Domingo Perón's candidacy for the presidency on the grounds that his stated support for women's suffrage was just a cover for his demagogic and fascist designs.

### Peronism: 1945–1955

Perón was elected president in a clean electoral process held in February 1946 that brought about the demise of most existing political parties, including the Conservative Party and the Socialist Party. In his first address to Congress he reiterated his support for women's suffrage. The Chamber of Deputies (the lower house of Congress) took up the question of women's suffrage in September 1947. The tone of the debates was very different than it had been in the thirties. Legislators emphasized the positive contributions of women, their participation in the labor force, and their presence in all important historical events. Law 13.010, granting Argentine women the same political rights as men, but excluding them from military service, was unanimously adopted. Although achieving women's suffrage ended the struggle begun by Grierson, Moreau de Justo, and their fellow feminists at the beginning of the century, women's civil rights were far from complete. A married woman still did not have legal authority over her children; she was compelled to take her husband's name, and if she refused, he could divorce her; and finally, a married woman's address was established by the husband, and if he went somewhere else, she was compelled to follow him.

### Evita

According to Peronist mythology, the struggle for women's political rights in Argentina began with Eva (Evita) Perón, the young wife of the president. Peronists generally fail to mention the role of the suffragists and make her entirely responsible for Law 13.010. In her autobiography, Evita stated that one of the first things she had to do when she entered politics was to resolve the old issue of women's political rights. She did not mention the role of the suffragists, but declared her contempt for the feminists, whom she described as women who resented not being born men (Perón 1973, 195).

While Evita played a very minor role in the struggle for women's suffrage, she did play a crucial role in the massive entrance of women into politics. On July 26, 1949, she gathered 1,000 women in a theater and founded the Partido Peronista Femenino (PPF) (also called the Rama Femenina), the women's section of the newly reorganized Peronist Party. In the 1951 elections, Evita delivered the women's vote, 63.9 percent for her husband. Furthermore, Argentines voted for a total of twenty-nine women candidates: six senators and twenty-three deputies, an unusually high number, even by today's standards. In the provinces, fifty-eight Peronist women were elected deputies and nineteen senators.

In 1950, at the height of her power, she was Evita, the charismatic *abanderada de los descamisados* (standard-bearer of the shirtless ones) or, as she preferred to be called, "the bridge of love between Perón and the descamisados." She was Eva Perón, Argentina's First Lady, the only woman member of the Superior Council of the Peronist Party, and president of the PPF. She also headed the Fundación Eva Perón (Eva Perón Foundation), which extended social benefits, such as hospitals, schools, and halfway houses, to the poor. Her death from cancer in 1952 deprived her husband of his most effective spokesperson.

Juan Perón was deposed by a military coup in 1955 and went into exile. For most of the following two decades, Argentina was ruled by the armed forces, which were intent on erasing all signs of Perón's rule. Perón's party was excluded from national elections, its leaders were jailed, the Eva Perón Foundation was dismantled, the use of Peronist symbols or emblems was punished by imprisonment, and even the embalmed body of Eva Perón was abducted and buried in a secret place.

## WOMEN'S RIGHTS TODAY

While women in the United States and Europe were discovering their own oppression and launching the second wave of feminism, in Argentina young men and women were engaged in increasingly violent opposition politics with two immediate objectives: ending the latest set of military dictators and bringing Perón back to Argentina. They were influenced by developments in the Catholic Church, particularly the emergence of the Movement of Third World Priests, who found their pastoral mission among the poorest sectors of society, traditionally Peronist. They were also influenced by the Left, fixed on guerrilla warfare and a total engagement with "the revolution." Women participated in the different guerrilla organizations, especially Montoneros. When the government decided to initiate conversations with Perón, at the time remarried and living in Madrid, by returning Evita's body to him, the guerrillas could smell their triumph and increased their operations.

## The Reemergence of Feminism

In 1970, as violence increased, a group of women connected to political parties met to express their opposition to the situation and the growing violation of human rights. Their manifesto was largely ignored. This was the context in which feminism reemerged in Argentina. Accepting the idea that the personal is political, a small group of women (among them Maria Luisa Bemberg, Leonor Calvera, and Alicia D'Amico) began to meet in 1970 in a women's consciousness-raising group (one of the earliest in Latin America and also one of the very few) and, in contrast with their foremothers, went on to discover gender oppression. When Unión Feminista Argentina (UFA; also called ENOUGH) decided to do something public, they printed a pamphlet for Mother's Day entitled "Mother: Slave or Queen, but Never a Person."

Although Nueva Mujer (New Woman), another women's group, which also emerged in 1970, had a short life, it published two popular books, *Las mujeres dicen basta* and *La mitología de la femeneidad* (Women Say Enough and The Mythology of Femininity). The final women's group from this period was the Movimiento de Liberación Femenina, or MLF (Movement for Women's Liberation), founded in 1972 by María Elena Oddone. More publicly oriented than UFA, it set up shop in one of the busiest streets in Buenos Aires, published pamphlets, sponsored talks, and for two years published a small magazine, *Persona*.

The activities of these new feminist groups, known as *colectivos*, unfolded at a time when the normal resistance to them was accentuated by an increasingly militaristic discourse from the state, from the left, and from the Peronist opposition. Military repression was answered by militarist reactions, all expressed in a violent and sectarian language, dominated by the campaign for Perón's return. In this context, the possibility of an alternative vision, much less a pacifist one centered on the private, personal, sexual realm, was difficult to accept.

Feminists were dismissed as repressed, petty bourgeois, reactionary anti-Peronists who had sold out to Yankee imperialism or were foreign-minded. The problems they posed were ridiculed; they were accused of raising false issues, appropriate for capitalist countries, but out of place in a country fighting for its sovereignty and the return of its historical leader. Anyway, they proclaimed, Evita had already liberated Argentine women and had said everything that needed to be said about women.

Perón returned in 1973 and was elected president for a third term. In March 1974, pursuing a pro-natalist policy, he put an end to all family planning units in public hospitals, and forbade the promotion and sale of birth control devices. The measure brought about several protests from feminists. UFA and the MLA got together and issued a pamphlet, which they distributed throughout Buenos Aires, stating their opposition to nonvoluntary pregnancies and to compulsory sterilization, and their support for a "conscious motherhood." Two new organizations emerged in 1974. One of them, Centro de Estudios Socialies de la Mujer Argentina, or CESMA (Center for the Social Study of Argentine Women), was significant because it was a group created within a left-wing party structure, the Frente de Izquierda Popular, or FIP (Popular Left Front), and opened a debate in Argentina that would later emerge in most Latin American countries. This was the problem of the *doble militancia*—the double commitment to a party and to feminism.

In 1975, as the Mexico City meeting of the International Women's Year approached, a few feminist groups, including the recently formed Agrupación de Mujeres Socialistas (Group of Socialist Women), got together into the Frente de Lucha por la Mujer (Front of Struggle for Women) to elaborate a common platform. The document they wrote, addressed to all Argentine women, included the following goals: daycare; equality of opportunity in education, training, and work; repeal of the decree that forbade the sale and use of birth control devices; legal and free abortion; salaries for homemakers; creation of an institution to oversee the implementation of the legislation against white slavery; incorporation of articles protecting motherhood in the benefit system of the Contract Law; *patria potestad* shared by the mother and father; an end to discrimination against unwed mothers and their children; and repeal of the law that compels the wife to accept the domicile established by the husband (Cano 1982, 91).

Unfortunately, Isabel Perón, who became president after her husband's death in 1974, showed an unusual insensitivity to the issues raised by feminists. Contrary to what happened in other Latin American countries, in Argentina, the only country then presided over by a woman, feminists were totally excluded from the process leading to Mexico City. To make matters worse, although Congress finally took up the issue of the *patria potestad* and approved a law granting authority over children to both the mother and the father, as the feminists requested, Isabel Perón vetoed it.

## Military Repression: 1976–1983

All feminist groups came to a standstill after March 23, 1976, when another group of the military deposed Isabel Perón and established a brutal dictatorship. The first of three juntas, composed of the commanders-in-chief of the army, the navy, and the air force, declared a state of siege, dissolved Congress and all provincial and municipal governments, and dismissed all the members of the Supreme Court and provincial courts. They also took over all unions and professional associations, dissolved all political parties, declared strikes illegal, and made any kind of political activity punishable by a jail term. The junta also established the death penalty for whoever disobeyed its orders and put in place censorship measures that included forbidding newspapers to publish any news about organizations declared illegal, or about the discovery of dead bodies or the disappearance of persons unless the sources were official.

The stated goals of the junta were to end the actions of guerrilla groups and corruption, to reactivate the economy, and to bring back "the values of Christian morals." To achieve its objectives, the junta developed a clandestine system of repression, abducting young and elderly, men and women, priests, nuns, adolescents, and babies, locking them in hidden concentration camps, torturing them mercilessly, killing some, and keeping others in prison. While the disappearance of 8,960 individuals was documented, the actual figure may be as high as 30,000.

### The Mothers and Grandmothers of Plaza de Mayo

Amid the silence, fear, and inactivity imposed by the juntas, only human rights organizations initially dared raise their voices, undaunted by the awesome power of the military. One of them was Asamblea Permanente por los Derechos Humanos (Permanent Assembly for Human Rights), founded by among others, Alicia Moreau de Justo, then in her nineties, but still willing to fight against injustice. Two others became justly famous: Madres de Plaza de Mayo (Mothers of Plaza de Mayo) and Abuelas de Plaza de Mayo (Grandmothers of Plaza de Mayo), all women's groups composed of mothers whose children and grandchildren had disappeared.

The main reason for the massive number of women involved in human rights organizations, and especially in Madres and Abuelas, is the many young people among the disappeared. Almost 72 percent of the disappeared were between the ages of sixteen and thirty-five. While many of the men and women connected with human rights organizations became involved in them for political or moral reasons or because of a concern for human rights violations, Madres and Abuelas were created by women who were mothers and grandmothers. In early 1977, they decided to do what no other human rights group was doing. They went into one of the most public, political, and powerful spaces of Buenos Aires, Plaza de Mayo, and they began to walk, every Thursday afternoon, asking a simple question: Where are our children? Stubbornly and fearlessly, they persisted in their stance, despite the disappearance of their first leader, and held on to the plaza for most of the dictatorship. Their uncompromising attitude, their determination, and their courage had an impact on the disintegration of the juntas. In the world of politics where just about everything and everyone is negotiable, they decided that the lives of their children and grandchildren were not.

### Human Rights and Women's Rights

The participation of women in human rights organizations was also part of a growing *movimiento de mujeres* (women's movement). Women mobilized for different reasons, including bread and butter issues, peace, feminism, and opposition to military service. Feminist groups resurfaced, or new ones were created. By 1981 María Elena Oddone was publishing *Persona* again, and she founded a new group, Organización Feminista Argentina, or OFA (Argentine Feminist Organization). Also in 1981, Derechos Iguales para la Mujer, or DIMA (Equal Rights for Women), was created to reform the Civil Code, especially the question of the *patria potestad*. A feminist bookstore opened, though it lasted for only three years. ATEM 25 de Noviembre (Association for Work and Study of Women) began its activities during the Malvinas/Falklands War. It added November 25 to its name to show its commitment to Latin American feminism and the importance of the issue of violence against women for its members. That was the date chosen at the first meeting of Latin American and Caribbean feminists in 1981 as the International Day Against Social, Sexual and Political Violence.

## Democracy and Women's Rights

With the collapse of military power and the restoration of democracy in 1983, things improved for women because the public policy models favored by the new government had a strong gender component. Furthermore, a group of feminists began to collaborate with various sectors of the women's movement to work out a common agenda. Their immediate objective—to celebrate the First International Women's Day in democracy on March 8, 1984—was an enormous success, with a special homage to Moreau de Justo, who, at ninety-eight, sat in the first row, smiling happily.

After arduous negotiations, the Multisectorial de Mujeres (Women from Multiple Sectors) came up with the following agenda:

1. Ratification of the Convention on the Elimination of All Forms of Discrimination Against Women (CEDAW);
2. Equal legal status for all sons and daughters;
3. Reform of *patria potestad*;
4. Implementation of the law guaranteeing equal pay for equal work;
5. Complete the daycare centers law [completion of an earlier law];
6. Reform of the law on retirement of homemakers;
7. Creation of a government institution for women with the rank of ministry.

At long last, Argentine feminists were able to elaborate a model strategy that strengthened their demands and used a propitious moment in history to their advantage. On May 1985, CEDAW was ratified; the *patria potestad* was finally changed and parental responsibility was shared; all legitimate and illegitimate children were declared legally equal; the sale of birth control devices was decriminalized; and a new divorce law permitting remarriage was adopted. The adult woman is now fully capable, regardless of her marital status; she may choose whether or not to add her surname to her husband's preceded by the preposition "de."

The Multisectorial de Mujeres was a clever initiative that involved women from ten different political parties, women's groups, and feminist groups. In 1988 they were joined by lesbian groups and the following year by some women belonging to CHA (Comunidad Homosexual Argentina [Argentina Homosexual Community]). Accepting the differences among them, it sought to advance a set of objectives that all could share, work together to achieve, and benefit from.

The return of democracy was crucial to the growth of the feminist movement. Democracy was also important for the acceptance of some feminist ideas by the press, the political parties, and the broader women's movement. Even the labor movement opened up to women, and women labor activists were involved in the Multisectorial de Mujeres or attended the yearly conferences dealing with feminist issues sponsored by ATEM.

The major changes during the presidency of Carlos Saul Menem, who succeeded Raúl Alfonsín in 1989, were the creation of an advisory Gabinete de Mujeres (Women's Cabinet) composed of eight women in charge of implementing policies of equal opportunity in all governmental activities, and the signing of a decree that made sexual harassment a punishable crime. In 1991 a bill introduced by the radical Senator Margarita Malharro de Torres became *la ley de cupos* (quota law). It compelled all political parties to give 30 percent of their slates to women candidates and to include them in eligible positions. By 1993 there were a total of thirty-four women in Congress—still fewer than in 1955, but three called themselves feminists. Finally, all the changes adopted since the early 1980s were incorporated in a new constitution approved in 1994.

## THE FUTURE OF WOMEN'S RIGHTS

While Argentines today live in a far more democratic society than they did in 1993, there is still resistance to women's political participation, and as the 1999 elections demonstrated, the numbers of women legislators achieved during the Peronist era continue to be unreachable. Opposition from the Catholic Church to the kinds of changes favored by second wave feminists and other groups on issues of sexuality has clearly surfaced. Abortion is still penalized, except when the mother's health or life is in danger or when the pregnancy is the result of the rape of an insane woman. The campaign to decriminalize abortion has begun and it is gaining support, but it may be another long road for Argentine women to achieve their fundamental reproductive rights.

## BIBLIOGRAPHY

Cano, Inés. 1982. "El movimiento feminista argentino en la década del '70.' " *Todo es Historia*, no. 183 (August), 84–93.

CIA. 1999. *The World Factbook*. http://www.odci.gov/cia/publications/factbook/ ar.html. Retrieved December 27, 1999.

Moreau de Justo, Alicia. 1945. *La mujer en la democracia*. Buenos Aires: El Ateneo.

Navarro, Marysa. 1985. "Hidden, Silent and Anonymous: Women Workers in the Argentine Trade Union Movement." In *The World of Trade Unionism: Comparative Historical Essays*, ed. Norbert C. Soldon. Westport, CT: Greenwood Press, 165–98.

Perón, Eva. 1973. *La razón de mi vida*. Buenos Aires: Editorial Relevo.

Spalding, Hobart A. 1970. *La clase trabajadora argentina*. Buenos Aires: Editorial Galerna.

World Bank. 1999. *World Development Indicators*. Washington, DC: The World Bank.

# 2

# BOLIVIA

## Women's Rights, the International Women's Convention, and State Compliance

*Gratzia Villarroel Smeall*

## INTRODUCTION

### Profile of Bolivia

Bolivia is a multiethnic, landlocked nation located in the heart of South America. With a population of 7,896,300, Bolivia is the country with the largest percentage of indigenous people in Latin America (over 60 percent). While Bolivia has a rich and diverse cultural heritage that dates back to the pre-Columbian civilization of Tiahuanacu, most indigenous peoples currently live in poverty. Spanish, Quechua, and Aymara are considered the official languages. However, Spanish has traditionally been the language of education and business. Bolivia's history is fraught with political instability, military coups, and turmoil. However, since 1982 the country has entered a difficult but promising process of democratization.

In 1985 the International Monetary Fund (IMF) encouraged the Bolivian government to implement an ambitious economic structural adjustment program. The program led to the privatization and dissolution of the mining companies, which left 35,000 miners and their families, who were working as independent contractors, unemployed. Progressive labor legislation was eliminated, the trade unions were disbanded, and state-run social institutions were shut down. Thousands of families were forced to relocate to the larger cities.

### A Case Study

In a booklet produced by the Coordinadora de la Mujer, a clearinghouse for Bolivian women's organizations, we learn the story of Matilda, one of the many recent immigrants from the countryside. She is a typical young indigenous woman living in the poor suburbs of the city. Her day starts at 4:00 A.M. when she gets up to get potatoes to sell in the marketplace. At 5:00 A.M. she stands in a long line to get fresh bread for her family, then spends several hours washing clothes in the river to make a few extra coins that she uses to buy food and some school supplies for her children. After a long morning she returns home to prepare lunch (the largest daily meal for Bolivian families).

Basilio, her husband, is depressed and unemployed due to the dire economic conditions in the country. When Matilda serves him lunch he criticizes her cooking. When she complains about her long, hard-working days, he insults her and beats her until she lies bleeding on the floor. When Matilda is able to get up, she visits a friend's house to tell her about her sad life. Her friend encourages her to stop crying and to start doing something for herself. She invites Matilda to attend a meeting with other women who also suffered from domestic abuse so that she can learn about her rights, as outlined by the Bolivian Penal Code and the International Women's Convention. Matilda learns about the structural cycle of violence that includes her family, her community, and her government and finally sees a ray of hope in her life (Alzerreca 1986).

### Overview of Women's Rights Issues

In recent years, many indigenous women like Matilda have migrated to the cities with the hope of employment and a better standard of living. However, once they arrive in the urban areas, peasant women often discover that their low level of education combined with traditional discriminatory practices against indigenous peoples are great barriers to an improved lifestyle. While Bolivian women from all social classes and ethnic groups suffer from discriminatory laws and customs, indigenous women are still the most oppressed.

One of the most important steps leading to improving the status of all Bolivian women was Bolivia's decision to participate in the United Nations' Convention on the Elimination of All Forms of Discrimination Against Women (CEDAW). It made it possible for the international community to monitor Bolivia's commitment to improving the status of women through the country's periodic reports to the CEDAW and through the independent reports of international women's organizations established in Bolivia. Implementing international human rights instruments is a slow process where successful outcomes are neither clearly visible nor easily measurable. However, the Bolivian government's attention to women's issues throughout the decade of the 1990s is an encouraging development for Bolivian women.

## HISTORY OF WOMEN'S RIGHTS IN BOLIVIA

Until the new Civil and Family Codes were formulated in 1976, laws affecting Bolivian women were organized under the Civil Code of 1830, which stated that by law women had to obey their husbands, had to follow their husbands wherever they chose to reside, and had no legal protection if their husbands applied "moderate domestic punishment" when marital problems required it (Smeall 1994, 325). In the early twentieth century Bolivian law slowly started to change, primarily in response to the political pressure of upper-class Bolivian women who, inspired by Bolivian feminist writer Adela Zamudio, began organizing themselves. In 1939 the General Labor Act provided women with clear and specific protective laws in the area of labor relations. The 1949 constitutional reform recognized men and women as equal citizens regardless of their education, occupation, and income (CEDAW 1991). The right to vote was given to women in 1952 during the Bolivian Social Revolution, and in 1967 the Political Constitution of Bolivia proclaimed equality before the law of all men and women (Iñiguez de Salinas and Linares Perez 1997). The Political Constitution also states that men and women have the right to circulate freely, and the Civil Code of 1976 granted all Bolivian citizens personal liberty and modernized a series of laws related to the Family Code in favor of women.

## WOMEN'S RIGHTS TODAY

### The Impact of CEDAW on Bolivian Women's Rights

On December 18, 1979, the United Nations General Assembly adopted the Convention on the Elimination of All Forms of Discrimination Against Women. Bolivia signed the Convention on May 30, 1980, during the administration of Lydia Gueiler Tejada, the first Bolivian woman president. The treaty was ratified by the Bolivian legislature on September 8, 1989. No reservations were made on the treaty, and Bolivia thereby agreed to comply with all its articles and provisions. CEDAW focuses on three important areas that greatly affect women's lives: their civil rights and legal status in all areas of activity; human reproduction with an emphasis on maternity, employment, family law, and health education; and the impact of cultural factors including traditions, stereotypes, customs, and norms that perpetuate the discrimination of women in all areas of society.

### Bolivia's Report to the Committee on the Elimination of All Forms of Discrimination Against Women

In 1991 Bolivia submitted its first report to the Committee on the Elimination of All Forms of Discrimination Against Women. The eighty-page document reported that Bolivia had established several programs at the legislative and executive level to address issues of concern to women. These included the Commission on Women's Affairs of the Chamber of Deputies, the Department of Social and Labor Promotion, the Office for the Social Promotion of Rural Women, and a program designed to improve infant survival and maternal health. In addition the National Directorate for Social Promotion and Development, under the supervision of the First Lady, was in charge of implementing social policy that affected women and the family (CEDAW 1991).

A 1994 addendum to the report stated that the structural adjustment programs continued to affect the status of women and that rapid rates of urban migration continued to negatively affect the status of rural women who were not trained or adequately prepared to enter the labor markets in the cities. On the positive side, it discussed the introduction of the Women's Program designed to eradicate poverty and promote women's equality by eliminating all forms of discrimination as defined by the Convention (CEDAW 1994).

On October 12, 1993, the Bolivian government went a step further and created the Under Secretary of Gender Issues. This office was established by the Executive Branch directly under the National Secretary of Ethnic, Gender and Generational Issues in the Ministry of Human Development. Its mission was to create conditions and strong institutional structures to promote equal opportunity for all women in the country. This is especially useful and important since many international development programs now consider women to be the central pillars of sustainable development (Iñiguez de Salinas and Linares Pérez 1997). The National Secretariat sought to coordinate policies focused on legal services and violence; education and training; health and sexual and reproductive rights; work and wages; power and citizenship; and communication and culture. It had the capability to declare mandatory resolutions. It worked with the Parliamentary Women's Commission as well as all the political parties that were represented in the Parliament. The National Secretariat set up offices in seven Bolivian provinces and addressed a variety of issues designed to improve the status of women, including rural development, education and popular participation, and appropriate training of government officials working on women's issues (UNHCHR 1995).

## The Committee's Recommendations and Bolivia's Implementation

In their review of Bolivia's report on its implementation of the Women's Convention, the major areas of concern of the Committee on the Elimination of All Forms of Discrimination Against Women were that the Bolivian national programs for women were financed primarily by international subsidies, that the feminization of poverty was caused by structural adjustment policies, and that rural women had numerous disadvantages. The Committee made the following recommendations:

a. That the Government of Bolivia amend article 276 of the Penal Code, which inhibits any sanction against domestic violence if the harm inflicted was mild.

In 1995 the Bolivian government introduced the Law on Domestic Violence, which effectively abolished this article. It also made rape a public crime and broadened the definition of family member abuse. Public agencies stated that reported incidents of abuse had increased markedly as a result of the new law as citizens became more aware of the problem and their ability to end it (Iñiguez de Salinas and Linares Pérez 1997).

b. That the Bolivian government establish quotas for women's high-level participation in public administration especially in political parties.

The Law on Popular Participation established in April 1994 integrated gender equality at all levels of grass-roots organizations and empowered administrations to establish programs for women. The Bolivian government also introduced the Reform and Complementary Law to the Electoral Regime in March 1997. This law required that political parties present a slate with 25 percent of women candidates for senatorial posts. For other political offices a minimum of a third of all candidates had to be women. This was a far-reaching law that guaranteed Bolivian women's political participation at least in the campaigning process (Iñiguez de Salinas and Linares Pérez 1997, 219).

c. That the Bolivian government provide statistics demonstrating the outcomes of various government programs designed to improve the status of Bolivian women including the Popular Participation Plan, the National Plan for the Prevention and for the Eradication of Violence, and educational reform.

d. That the Bolivian government pay closer attention to various aspects of prostitution, which is regarded as a severe case of human rights violations.

e. That the plight of rural women be given greater attention in the next Bolivian periodic report.

The Law on Education Reform of July 1994 promoted free, universal, and mandatory education based on equal opportunity and gender equality. The government gave special attention to bilingual education for young girls, which had a positive impact on the school dropout rate, repeating of classes, and functional illiteracy (Iñiguez de Salinas and Linares Pérez 1997).

f. That the Government make an inventory of the laws that discriminate against women, in order to have them amended.

In October 1995 the government issued a presidential decree providing for equal rights for women and committing the government to end gender-based discrimination.

Overall, the Bolivian government has gradually introduced laws and programs designed to conform to the provisions of CEDAW. While there is still much work to be done, the reporting and evaluation mechanisms included in CEDAW make it possible for governments to address the issue of women's discrimination in an organized way with a clear blueprint of what should be achieved and how, and with a certain time limit in mind. Though many of the programs implemented by the Bolivian government are still too young to yield long-term results, it is a step in the right direction.

While the need to implement the Convention on the Elimination of All Forms of Discrimination Against Women has become increasingly important to the Bolivian government in the 1990s, various studies show that there is still much work to be done. Reports from nongovernmental organizations (NGOs) working in Bolivia provide a more critical perspective than that of the government. We now turn to these concerns.

## Women as Legal Citizens

In 1997 the United Nation's Human Rights Committee concluded that despite the constitutional guarantees of the rights of women in Bolivia, they continued to receive unequal treatment owing in part to traditional attitudes and outdated laws that clearly contradict the provisions of CEDAW (UNHCHR 1997). The Bolivian government also acknowledges that in practical terms the legal structure is not enough to protect women. In some cases, laws that protect women are not widely publicized, so they may not be invoked by lawyers in a court case. In other cases, the law may be known but the people in charge of enforcing it, usually male officials, may not be interested in its implementation. Furthermore, the state and local governments may not have the resources to implement the true spirit of the law. Another major problem with legal representation is the high rates of illiteracy among Bolivian women, especially in the countryside. NGOs report the lack of enforcement mechanisms, especially in the area of labor laws to protect women in the workplace. Women are still subject to sexual harassment and are paid less than men (Ladin 1994).

## Women and Political Participation

Despite recent laws designed to increase women's participation in the political process, such participation is still inadequate. Women currently hold 6.9 percent of the elected congressional positions in Bolivia compared to 11.7 percent in Colombia, 10.8 percent in Peru, and 7.5 percent in Chile (Comision Andina de Juristas 1998). The Bolivian government has acknowledged the manipulation of the female vote by all political parties for their ideological pursuits. It has also denounced the underrepresentation of women in political offices, the lack of female candidates for political positions, and the lack of a female militant attitude (CEDAW 1991). Women who actively participated in bringing down the military dictatorship in the 1970s were disillusioned to find out that their political sacrifice did not translate into political power when the country democratized (Ardaya 1989; Smeall 1994).

As candidates for public office, women face tremendous challenges. Many female candidates have acknowledged that political activity takes a big toll on their families, and it is still rare to see women of childbearing age participating extensively in politics. Even indigenous women, who generally prefer to take a class or ethnic stand instead of a gender stand, have acknowledged the difficulties they face as women in trying to be politically active (Smeall 1990).

## Women in the Labor Force

The Bolivian government and various NGOs report that economic structural adjustment policies have created a climate of unrest and violence in the country. Urban migration is on the rise, especially among indigenous women. Rural women have an increasing role in the labor markets, where the proportion of women has risen from 18.3 percent in 1976 to 38.1 percent in 1992. However, they face very difficult working conditions and tend to concentrate in areas of low productivity and low wages (Talavera and Paz Zamora 1993). The most important occupation for women in the rural areas is agriculture; as they migrate into the cities, they tend to work in commerce. Women's wages still are only 75 percent of what men make. This rate is even lower for professional women, who make 69 percent of men's salaries.

Women's illiteracy rate is 24.8 percent in Bolivia, the lowest in the Andean region, and 20 percent below the Latin American median (United Nations Development Programme [UNDP], as cited in Comision Andina de Juristas 1998). Rural women show the most critical numbers, with illiteracy rates reaching 49.9 percent compared to 23.1 percent for men. Since over 27 percent of Bolivian women do not speak Spanish, their access to education and technical training is very limited, which in turn greatly limits their entry into the labor markets (Talavera and Paz Zamora 1993).

Overall, Bolivian women are more likely to be overworked and underpaid than Bolivian men regardless of their social class. The International Women's Rights Action Watch (IWRAW) states that women from all social classes have very restricted employment opportunities in Bolivia (Ladin 1994). A 1997 Human Rights Committee review also states that Bolivian labor laws do not adequately protect women, especially those engaged in domestic work (UNHCHR 1997). Poor indigenous women are restricted to domestic service and small-scale street vending. Since paid domestic service is considered informal work and is not protected by any labor regulations, indigenous women often work extra hours and days for less than the minimum wage and submit to the whims of their employers. When asked what was the most intense form of abuse that indigenous maids suffered, a young woman answered:

[T]he way they treat us like slaves, as people of an inferior category. Because of that they can mistreat us in so many ways, because of that they can give us scraps of food, or make us sleep under the stairway. [Because of this] the patron and his sons can sexually abuse us. [Because of this] they can exploit us and treat us with disrespect. Because of this we cannot go into their living rooms, except to sweep. [Because of this] we have our separate plate and cup made out of metal, our separate utensils. (Delfina, quoted in Palacios 1988, 65)

Women's salaries in commercial and industrial sectors are less than half of the minimum established by the law, primarily because of the overabundance of female labor. There are also no mechanisms for protecting pregnant women from losing their jobs, as no enforcement mechanisms exist. There are no legal norms concerning sexual harassment of women, yet it is understood that this practice is very common in a society permeated by *machismo* (Ladin 1994).

## Women's Education

Women's education is perhaps the area that requires the greatest attention in Bolivia. Various studies demonstrate that the rate of female school attendance is one of the lowest on the continent. This is especially true for women in the rural areas, where only 64.6 percent of women attend school and usually for only a short period of time (Talavera and Paz Zamora 1993). Bolivian women have a combined school attendance rate of 61 percent compared to 71 percent in Chile, 72 percent in Colombia and 77 percent in Peru (UNDP, as cited in Comision Andina de Juristas 1998).

The Bolivian government's lack of commitment to education is a serious obstacle to improving women's status, particularly in rural areas. Incompatibility of agricultural calendars, inadequate teacher training, and poor programs and educational methods all work against the educational success of indigenous girls. Bolivia has a historically low investment in education. The *1990 World Development Report of the World Bank* ranks Bolivia at the lowest spectrum of the South American education in the percentage of primary and secondary children enrolled in school (Ladin 1994).

The IWRAW report on Bolivia states that the Bolivian government does not acknowledge the seriousness of the problem, particularly with reference to the cultural violence that Indians have been subjected too. Bolivia only began bilingual education in 1992, and it is still restricted to school districts that can afford to institute it. Given the high percentage of indigenous women who do not speak Spanish, governmental efforts are not enough to address the problem (Ladin 1994). According to UNICEF, numerous programs organized by NGOs designed to decrease illiteracy rates among indigenous women in the 1990s have only achieved a 2 percent reduction (UNICEF 1999a).

Many mothers must work to provide for their family. An uneducated family sees little usefulness in educating women, and in poor families girls are obliged, after about third grade, to take charge of household chores and younger siblings (Ladin 1994). Poverty is seen as the most important obstacle to women's education, in the rural areas as well as in the impoverished suburban centers, like El Alto in La Paz. According to a CARE report, adolescent girls bear the brunt of their people's poverty:

Girls are second in line only to their mothers when it comes to household responsibility. The same is not required of boys. In many families, mothers must work to provide for the family by selling small items at the market, or as maids, cooks, or by working other jobs. From a very young age, girls have to take care of the other children, clean the house and cook, while their mothers work. This is part of the culture, redrawn only slightly to fit the changing times. (Bigner 1999, para. 5)

## Reproductive Health

Bolivia has excellent laws that protect pregnant women in the family and in the labor force. However, it is believed that the lack of implementation of these laws is responsible for Bolivia's high maternal mortality rates. According to UNICEF (1999b), Bolivia's maternal mortality rate is one of the highest in Latin America, at 390 per 100,000 births. This rate is higher for indigenous women in the Altiplano of Bolivia, where it reaches 591 per 100,000 births (Murphy-Lawless 1996). Reports demonstrate that abortions and complications connected with pregnancy and childbirth are among the most common reasons for the high number of maternal deaths. While Bolivian population density is low compared to other countries in South America, the fertility rate of 4.7 children among Bolivian women is one of the highest in Latin America (UNICEF 1996). A 1983 study of the Bolivian female population revealed that only 23.6 percent of women use contraception, and of these only 6.1 percent use IUDs or the contraceptive pill. The rest use the rhythm method, which is impractical since women's subordination does not permit them to defer sex in times of high fertility. Over 70 percent of Bolivian women use no contraception at all (Talavera and Paz Zamora 1993). The lack of family planning is due to cultural factors, especially *machismo* and the lack of family planning education.

Abortion is illegal in Bolivia except in cases of rape, incest, or danger to the health of the mother. However, abortions are very extensively performed in Bolivia due to lack of proper information on contraception (CEDAW 1991). A 1985 study by the Bolivian Council for Human Reproduction found that over 25 percent of pregnant women had at one time had an abortion (Ladin 1994). In 1997 the Human Rights Committee criticized Bolivia's laws punishing abortion, because this leads to high levels of maternal mortality from illegal abortion (UNHCHR 1995). According to the *Bolivian Times*, Bolivian women's sexual and reproductive rights are violated every year through unregulated "medical clinics" that perform clandestine abortions:

Marta was 15 when she fell in love with her first boyfriend. She was the same age when she got pregnant by him. With no means to support a baby and basically a child herself, Marta came to La Paz to undergo an abortion. She had been referred to a doctor who practiced the procedure by a friend of a friend. When she arrived at the clandestine clinic near Plaza San Francisco . . . the doctor told her boyfriend to leave and come back in a few hours. Once the "abortion doctor" had Marta alone in the operating room, he raped her. (Capozza 1998, para. 1)

While there has been an increase in high-risk pregnancies, especially among teenage women, only 63 percent of women in the urban areas sought prenatal care consistently in 1992. Those who did not seek maternal care stated that the cost of the service was too high, that they did not trust the health professionals, and that they did not know how prenatal care could help (Talavera and Paz Zamora 1993).

The IWRAW report generally agreed with the Bolivian government's report on health care but criticized the Sanchez de Lozada administration for privatizing health care and relying heavily on NGOs to provide health services to women (Ladin 1994).

### Violence Against Women

With regard to customs and stereotypes that inhibit the equality of women, the 1991 report states that sex-based prejudice and stereotypes affect all aspects of life in Bolivia (CEDAW 1991). It mentions the use of women as instruments of publicity in all the communication media and the impact of the deep-rooted *machismo* that is encountered throughout Latin America. According to the report, the forms of violence most suffered by Bolivian women are physical abuse, and rape. In 1986, of the 1,432 cases of abuse and rape treated at the Clinical Hospital of the City of La Paz, 66 percent were committed against women. Some 77.5 percent of these were caused by husbands or family members and 13 percent were caused by strangers (Talavera and Paz Zamora 1993). Women seldom bring any of these cases to court due to cultural norms and lack of self-esteem or empowerment among women. Many Bolivian women still believe that they owe complete obedience to their husbands.

The IWRAW report states that until 1973 it was the legitimate right of a man to beat his wife or children in the exercise of his paternal authority. Since 1973, the law states that violence is a cause for divorce or separation. However, the law also prohibits spouses and close relatives from initiating legal action against one another except in cases where the injury causes incapacitation for more than thirty days (Ladin 1994). It is very difficult for any doctor to declare incapacitation for even more than five days. Furthermore, these legal norms, combined with solidarity between men and the authorities and the absence of women's shelters, perpetuate domestic violence.

[Women] come beaten [to see me]. These men beat them savagely. They have horrible black and blue marks. They look like tomatoes partly green, partly red. Their legs, their hands, their ribs [all swollen] they come like that. . . . When they talk about their husbands they say: "I hope that he won't leave me." Do they have so much love for their husbands? There are women that have been horribly beaten . . . but they [go back and] serve their husbands with greater love. (Quoted in Alzerreca 1986, 4).

The International Women's Rights Action Watch (IWRAW) report also emphasized that sexual violence is not limited by age, social class, or ethnic origins, despite the common claim that it is a negligible phenomenon, limited to marginalized groups. In the area of sexual violence, the legal standards for proving rape are unreasonably high. Laws characterize sexual violence as a crime against community morality, not the individual. Since it is a crime of private action, the burden of proof falls on the victim, as do lawyers' fees and the responsibility for bringing the accused to court. Articles 308 and 312 of the Penal Code contain the concept of "honest women," but not the concept of honest men, therefore it is quite common for a rapist to call into question the reputation of his victim, and prostitutes cannot be adequately protected by the courts (Ladin 1994).

According to the U.S. State Department report (1998) on Bolivia's human rights, violence against women is pervasive. Of domestic violence complaints studied in 1992–1993, 5 percent involved physical mistreatment and 48 percent involved psychological abuse. The Bolivian government estimates that there are 100,000 incidents of violence annually and that 95 percent of these go unpunished. The Congressional Committee on Women reported that 3.5 cases of rape or statutory rape were reported each day in the first half of 1995, and it estimated that twice that many were not reported (U.S. Department of State 1998).

### Rural Women

The fact that indigenous women are those most affected by discrimination in Bolivia is very revealing since, as mentioned above, Bolivia is the Latin American country with the highest percentage of indigenous population. While indigenous women work along with their husbands in all areas of productive agriculture, their work is not recognized by society as a productive activity. Bolivian society also has developed values and prejudices that relegate indigenous women to an inferior status and deny them any opportunity to test their ability in formal economic circles. Rural women suffer from lack of educational opportunities, lack of technical training, rigidly defined gender roles, and lack of awareness of their legal rights. While many rural children are denied educational opportunities, young girls are often denied education because they start late (between eight and nine years of age) and by age thirteen they must leave school to help with chores at home or to start working (Ladin 1994; CEDAW 1991).

According to the IWRAW report, the closing of the mines in 1985, privatization, and structural adjustment measures have led to massive urban migration where rural women end up seeking productive work doing menial jobs. The major concern is the lack of attention to rural women in development projects. Even the new wave of grass-roots NGOs continue to plan rural projects by focusing primarily on men (Ladin 1994).

## THE FUTURE OF WOMEN'S RIGHTS

The Convention on the Elimination of All Forms of Discrimination Against Women in Bolivia is an obvious example of the impact that globalization is having on how nation-states address domestic problems. The increasing influence of international legal documents, international donors, and international NGOs has made it difficult for the Bolivian government to ignore the status of women in the country. At the same time, the high levels of funding coming from international sources, as compared to those provided by the Bolivian national budget, call into question the future viability of these programs. Furthermore, the structural adjustment policies, that are often required by the IMF and other international donors have the contradictory effect of increasing the feminization of poverty, especially among rural women. International interdependence is indeed a mixed blessing for women.

In addition, the implementation of international legal documents that promote human rights is a slow and difficult process that countries and international organizations can only improve by constant and determined attention to the the equality of women. Since the process may take many years and is often carried out by different administrations with different goals and different objectives, it is important that the Committee on the Elimination of All Forms of Discrimination Against Women provide continuity through regular meetings, reporting sessions, and conferences.

Lastly, governments and international organizations alike must be able to address the pervasive impact of cultural norms and traditions that inhibit the true implementation of the legal document, even when its provisions have been institutionalized by the government. In this sense the focus on grass-roots organizations and women's empowerment is a positive step for achieving the true meaning of CEDAW, especially as it refers to indigenous women in Bolivia.

## BIBLIOGRAPHY

Alzerreca, Enriqueta. 1986. ¿Acaso Mientras Más Me Pega Más Lo Quiero? (Is It Really True that the More He Hits Me the More I Love Him?). La Paz: Coordinadora de Mujeres.

Ardaya, Gloria. 1989. Política Sin Rostro: Mujeres en Bolivia. Caracas: Editorial Nueva Sociedad.

Bigner, Andrea. 1999. Virtual Trip to Bolivia. CARE International, May, 19 paragraphs. http://www.care.org/virtual_trip/bolivia/day5.html.

Capozza, Korey. 1998. "Clandestine Abortions Kill Women." Bolivian Times, May, 17 paragraphs. http://latinwide.com/boltimes/edit-edit-18/tapa.htm. Retrieved August 20, 1999.

CEDAW. 1991. Convention on the Elimination of All Forms of Discrimination Against Women. CEDAW/C/Bol/1 (July 9).

———. 1994. Convencion sobre la Eliminacion de Todas las Formas de Discriminacion contra la Mujer. CEDAW/C/BOL/1/Add.1 (April 11).

Comision Andina de Juristas. 1998. Mujeres en la Región Andina. http://www.cajpe.org.pe/muj_. Retrieved June 22, 1999.

Iñiguez de Salinas, Elizabeth, and Anselma Linares Pérez. 1997. Guía Jurídica para la Mujer y La Familia. La Paz: Subsecretaría de Asuntos de Genero.

Ladin, Sharon. 1994. IWRAW to CEDAW Country Reports. International Women's Rights Action Watch (IWRAW). Minneapolis: Humphrey Institute of Public Affairs, 5–11.

Mejia, Lucila, et al. 1984. Las Hijas De Bartolina Sisa. La Paz: HISBOL.

Murphy-Lawless, Jo. 1996. Childbirth in Bolivia: Supporting Appropriate Strategies for Women in Birth. Trinity College Dublin Centre for Women's Studies. http://www2.tcd.ie/Women_Studies/page11.html. Retrieved August 20, 1999.

Palacios, Beatriz. 1988. "Empleadas y Esclavas." Cuarto Intermedio 7: 60–68.

Smeall, Gratzia V. 1990. "Catholic and Andean Influences on Bolivian Women's Political Participation." Ph.D. dissertation, University of South Carolina.

———. 1994. "Women, Adamocracy, and the Bolivian Social Revolution" In Women and Revolution in Africa, Asia and the New World, ed. Mary Ann Tetrault. Columbia: University of South Carolina Press, 319–42.

Talavera, Rosa, and Rosario Paz Zamora. 1993. "Situación de la Mujer: Algunos Indicadores." In CEDAW, CEDAW/C/Bol/1/Add.1, 1994.

UNHCHR. 1995. *Concluding Observations of the Committee on the Elimination of Discrimination Against Women: Bolivia.* A/50/38, paras. 42–104.

———. 1997. *Concluding Observations of the Human Rights Committee: Bolivia.* CCPR/C/70/Add.74 (Concluding Observations/Comments).

UNICEF. 1996. *The Progress of Nations.* UNICEF Report. http://www.unicef.org/pon96/about.htm. Retrieved August 20, 1999.

———. 1999a. *Alfabetización de mujeres indígenas in UNICEF-Bolivia.* http://www.unicef.org.bo/alfabetizacion.html. Retrieved August 20, 1999.

———. 1999b. Information Statistics—Bolivia. http://www.unicef.org/stats/. Retrieved December 16, 1999.

U.S. Department of State. 1998. Bolivia Country Report on Human Rights Practices for 1997. Released by the Bureau of Democracy, Human Rights and Labor, January 30, 1998.

# 3

# CHINA

## First the Problem of Rights and Law

*Sharon K. Hom*

## INTRODUCTION

### Profile of China

China's 1.24 billion people are still mostly rural, although urban dwellers have increased from 20 percent of the population in 1980 to 33 percent in 1998 (World Bank 2000). In 1949 the communist state was established by the Chinese Communist Party (CCP) under the leadership of its chairman, Mao Zedong. The state managed agricultural and industrial production under centralized planning with the goals of increasing production and equalizing the distribution of goods and services. Beginning in 1978, new economic policies were instituted to promote economic growth through what is now called a "socialist market economy." Household ventures in agriculture and some small-scale capitalist businesses have been established but with state-run enterprises remaining in key industries. China's "one-child policy," also designed to spur economic development and a higher living standard, contributed to a drop in total fertility from 2.5 in 1980 to 1.9 in 1997 (World Bank 2000).

According to official reports, employment of women was at 70 percent in 1994, and Chinese women's economic activity rate is among the highest in the world (United Nations 1995). However, economic restructuring of the state-owned enterprises in the last decade with its massive elimination of jobs, the more than 120 million people moving back and forth between the cities and the countryside, abuses in the implementation of the population control policies, and the persistence of gender-based violence, trafficking in women and girls, and gender discrimination all present ongoing legal and policy challenges for protecting the rights and interests of Chinese women (Human Rights in China et al. 1998).

### A Case Study: "Snow in Midsummer"

In a famous Chinese Yuan dynasty drama written over six centuries ago, *Injustice to Tou O (Tou O yuan)* (also translated as Snow in Midsummer), Kuan Han-ching portrays the injustice inflicted on a young woman who is the ideal of a chaste and filial Chinese woman (Shih 1972; Cheung 1980). At the age of seven, Tou O is sold by her father, who then leaves to seek his fortune at the imperial court. At seventeen Tou O is married, but is widowed shortly afterwards. Because she refuses to remarry as an expression of her faithfulness to her dead husband ("One horse cannot wear two saddles"), she is falsely accused by the scorned man of a murder she did not commit. After enduring torture, she confesses to the murder and is sentenced to death. At her execution, she declares that her innocence will be vindicated by three events: instead of flowing to the ground, her blood will color the white silk banner flying overhead; a heavy snow will fall in midsummer; and a three year drought will follow. All three come to pass. Afterwards, an official appears at the village to investigate and correct possible abuses of power on the part of local officials. Tou O's ghost appeals to this official, who turns out to be her father. Her case is reopened, Tou O is cleared posthumously, and the real villain is punished.

The return of Tou O's father is both a symbol of male patriarchal power and of a male-dominated tradition that informed the whole ordering of society and a woman's proper place in it. However, Tou O appealed to cosmic justice, not the justice of man on earth. She relied upon her belief that the proper order of the universe would not allow such an injustice to go uncorrected. As a woman in the traditional feudal social structure, Tou O's life was defined by her duty to follow the three obediences: her father and older brothers when young, her husband when married, and her sons when widowed; and the four virtues: to know her place and act accordingly within the ethical codes; to be reticent in words; to be clean of person and habit; and not to shirk her household duties. A model of virtue, she believed the existing order would vindicate her innocence precisely because she did not violate any social norms. Yet, the existing order would have denied any claims to justice if she did not abide by its rules. Although Tou O is portrayed as a courageous and virtuous victim, the social power cards were stacked against her from birth. She could only receive justice after death through the haunting of the guilty.

## Overview of Women's Rights Issues

In referring to Chinese women's rights, there is an ideological danger of falling into the reductionist trap (Spelman 1988) by treating "Chinese women" as a single analytical category. In light of the impact of differences in age, geography, membership in over fifty-five ethnic groups, economic status, and class on shaping the diverse, concrete lived experiences of Chinese women, generalizations need to be qualified. However, the term "Chinese women" as a cross-category of analysis (Hom 1994) is still useful as it underscores the commonality of the gendered position of Chinese women and supports the integration of gender issues into overall Chinese human rights and law reform strategies.

China today can proudly point to the formal law on the books that sets forth gender equality and a full panoply of protections for the "legitimate rights and interests" of women. Yet, the daily lived realities of the majority of Chinese women continue to be marked by economic and political inequality, violence, poverty, and illiteracy. In addition to this gap between formal legal protections and their implementation, challenges to women's "rights" in China are related to several factors: (1) the persistence of the law as a tool of CCP policy and its subordination to the changing lines of CCP policy; (2) the authoritarianism of CCP ideology; and (3) the male-dominated power structure's assumptions and values that permeate the legislative reform efforts and the legal discourse (Hom 1992a).

## HISTORY OF WOMEN'S RIGHTS

Tragically, Tou O's life was not simply a literary invention, but a powerful reflection of the inferior status of women under the feudal order. In traditional China, women's lives were determined by arranged marriages, marked by marital abuse and violence, and deformed by social practices such as footbinding and the sale of child brides, and their status was defined as property, as slave labor, and as producers of sons. As early as the first century A.D., Chinese women were expected to conform to an ideal defined within a cosmological view of the oppositional duality of yin/yang and male/female. The *Nu Jie* (Precepts for Women) states that women should be obedient, unassuming, yielding, timid, respectful, and reticent (Croll 1980, 13). The literature exploring the ideological, political, social, and structural factors in Chinese society that contribute to and perpetuate the persistence of gender-based inequality is extensive (see, e.g., Andors 1983; Buxbaum 1980; Croll 1980; Hom 1992a, 1992b; Johnson 1983; Y. Li, 1992; Watson and Ebrey 1991).

In addition to the economic constraints of a poor agrarian country, the literature consistently points to the misogyny and authoritarianism of traditional Confucian ideology and its primary institution of social control, the family, as key factors responsible for the centuries of suffering and oppression of Chinese women. According to the traditional Confucian view of the proper social order, people should have internalized the "rules" of proper behavior and the ruler should govern by virtuous example rather than by an imposed rule of law (V. Li 1978, 13). The Legalists advocated the rule of law (*fazhi*) to rule the state. However, both the Confucianists and the Legalists believed that law was "merely the will of rulers and a means to implement their will" (Liang 1986, 81).

This tradition of Chinese law clearly reflects a role for law as social control. In a society where men (although with different class advantages) are privileged by birth, education, and cultural values, and women are devalued and silenced, law is not only a method of social control available to the emperor and the bureaucratic elite over the majority of the common people, but is also a method of social control by men over women. Law in traditional China accomplishes this not by direct intervention in the family and daily social life but through rigid moral and social norms and by according the patriarchs great power and discretion. In the sphere of power over life and death accorded to the family patriarch, unfaithful or disobedient wives or children could be killed without invoking criminal sanctions. Cursing one's parents was a capital offense that might mitigate a potential charge of homicide for the parent who killed the offending child (Jimmerson 1990, 58–60).

When feudal China began to crumble in the last half of the nineteenth century from the pressures of internal corruption and the impact of Western influences and imperialism, the voices and participation of women were crucial in the political and military struggles to modernize and build a new China. Beginning with the May Fourth Movement in 1917, Chinese women and progressive men condemned the bankrupt social system and institutions of feudal China and demanded the recognition of rights for women: equal participation in politics and government, the abolition of arranged marriages, and equal rights with men in employment and educational opportunities. The May Fourth Movement refers to a mass protest initiated by Chinese students, who were later joined by striking workers protesting the secret treaty among Japan, Britain, France, and Italy granting concessions to Japan in northeast China. Some results of the May Fourth Movement were the introduction of educational reforms by the government in an effort to placate the students and the beginnings of an active women's suffrage movement.

Throughout contemporary Chinese history, although Chinese women rhetorically "hold up half the sky," one constant phenomenon has been the subordination and marginalization of a competing women's agenda to some articulated "broader" agenda defined by a male-dominated leadership. For example, in the power struggles and the agendas of the national struggles against foreign aggression and Western imperialism, against the Japanese invasion of China in 1937 and later the civil war between the Kuomingdong (KMT) and the CCP, "women's issues" had to take a subordinate position in the priorities and strategies (Croll 1980, 117–152). The role of Chinese women in contemporary China continues to be shaped by shifting Party lines as part of a broader national/Party agenda. Whether joining in the industrialization of the country, or ensuring the future of "socialist spiritual civilization" as mothers, or returning to the home in the face of a surplus labor problem (Gao 1994; X. Li 1994), Chinese women are viewed as tools for China's modernization and reform. Thus, the questions of what are the "interests" of women and who gets to define them are still constrained within the rigid, entrenched worldviews of the predominantly male CCP leadership.

## WOMEN'S RIGHTS TODAY

Until the mid-1980s the official version of modern Chinese history re-flected pride in the great progress made in the abolition of the feudal ves-tiges of the old China and in the introduction of women into the political and productive spheres. In the mid-1980s a "feminist outcry" echoed in numerous mass media stories and in official rhetoric and pronouncements: "Chinese women may have come a long way, but they still do not own half the sky." Research efforts by Western feminist scholars suggested that there was an emergence of a new feminist consciousness in the mid-eighties that fueled demands for change, equality, and justice in the workplace, in access to higher education, and in the family sphere (Honig and Hershatter 1988, 308–333).

One official response in contemporary China has been to look to formal law and the development of a legal system to address existing inequalities, to create legal protections for women, and to guarantee women equal and fair access to political participation and economic opportunity. In China's efforts to reform and develop its legal system, not only is it borrowing from foreign examples, it is also struggling with legal concepts and culture that have a history of several thousand years. It is also negotiating its position in the international human rights debates.

### International Human Rights Universalism/Relativism Debates

The Western understanding of universal human rights generally empha-sizes a vision of civil and political rights shaped by a liberal Western tradition. The challenge of East Asian states, including China, to this understanding of human rights derives from a history of colonialism and a suspicion that assertions of Western universal human rights are pretexts for new interven-tions in the domestic affairs of other countries. Thus, "what appears, from the Western perspective, to be a noble campaign for universal rights, is interpreted from an Asian perspective, as cultural imperialism" (Freeman 1995, 14).

The charge of cultural imperialism against the notion of universal women's/human rights is also made by states with "high performance" economies that have engineered the "economic miracle" of rising gross national product. However, at the same time that the Asian "economic miracle" was heralded by Asian governments and Western observers, other voices such as nongovernmental organizations, dissident religious, labor, and other community voices pointed out that beneath the "miracles," there are human costs such as child labor, unsafe working conditions, poor living standards, low wages and underpayment, gender-based sexual harassment, violence, abuse, and discrimination. Against a more inclusive understanding of the ideals of human rights as encompassing social and economic rights, as well as civil and political rights, the claims of Asian nation-states to represent the best interests of their citizens are suspect and incomplete. Thus, their statist invocation of "Asian" culture or a "different" standard as legitimation for a culturally relativist human rights claim is problematic (Hom 1996).

China's relativist position also views any effort to criticize its human rights record as an interference in Chinese sovereignty and domestic affairs. China maintains that women's/human rights must be implemented and interpreted by each sovereign state through its own domestic legislation. However, as a member of the international community, China has signed a number of international human rights documents—including treaties on the prevention of slavery, genocide, torture, racial discrimination, and violations of human rights by terrorist organizations—and acknowledged its international obligations. China is also is an early signatory (1980) of the Convention on the Elimination of All Forms of Discrimination Against Women (CEDAW), and it ratified the Convention on Rights of the Child in 1990. Furthermore, China was the host for the 1995 Fourth World Conference on Women. The Platform of Action adopted by the 1995 conference calls upon governments to take strategic action in the following critical areas of concern: poverty, education, health care, violence against women, economic structures and policies, decision-making at all levels, human rights, media stereotypes and access, management of natural resources and safeguarding of the environment, and the rights of the girl child. Therefore, the development of rights or laws for the protection of women and girl children is not exclusively a domestic Chinese issue.

## The Limits of Law Reforms

Official Chinese assessments of their laws protecting women and girls point to the decrease in infant and maternal mortality rates, the legal abolition of arranged marriages, concubinage, and other feudal vestiges of women's oppression, and the increase in literacy and improvement in health care for women as evidence of the improvement in the status of Chinese women (see, e.g., State Council of the PRC 1994; Report to the Committee on the Elimination of Discrimination Against Women 1997). The extensive legislation that has been promulgated to protect the legal interests and rights of Chinese women collectively set forth principles of equality between men and women in the areas of political, cultural, educational, and economic rights, marriage rights of the person, and family rights. These include the 1982 constitutional provisions that guarantee the equal rights of women with men in all spheres of life, and that the state "protects the rights and interests of women, applies the principles of equal pay for equal work to men and women alike, and trains and selects cadres from among women" (Article 48). In addition to the 1980 Marriage Law, criminal law, and con-stitutional provisions, in 1992 China promulgated the Law for the Protec-tion of Women's Rights and Interests, which was intended to coordinate and guarantee the rights already set forth in existing laws and regulations.

However, the promulgation of formal "protections" can also have nega-tive consequences for women. For example, the State Council promulgated labor regulations (effective September 1, 1988) intended to promote greater gender equality at work; to make special provision for the protection of women in the workplace during menstrual periods and during pregnancy and breastfeeding, if the pregnancy does not violate family planning regu-lations; and to provide administrative punishments for those in the Labor Department and other relevant organizations who fail in their duty to im-plement the new regulations. However, given the ongoing debate about the proper "nature" of women's role in the family and the productive sphere, purportedly protective legislation may in fact act as a disincentive for em-ployers to hire women in the first place (Woo 1994).

In addition, despite public education, grass-roots and women's advocacy groups, and legal initiatives, gender-based violations of women's rights per-sist. Chinese legal scholars and human rights groups point to the persistence of gender-based inequalities and violence in the face of social realities and practices such as trafficking in women and girl children, domestic violence, rape, and discrimination in the economic sector (Human Rights in China et al. 1998; Human Rights in China 1995; Hom 1995; Jordan 1998; Woo 1994). Official government policies, such as the one-child policy, have also contributed to the persistence of female infanticide and abandonment of girl infants (Hom 1992b; Jimmerson 1990; X. Li 1996). The fact that the over-whelming majority of the babies and children in the orphanages in China are female underscores this social devaluation of female girl children.

Furthermore, despite economic changes for Chinese women in the post-Mao reform era resulting in movement of large numbers of women into the productive sector, economic reforms have not necessarily resulted in improvements in the overall position of Chinese women in the economic or social hierarchy. There is increasing domestic dissatisfaction and unrest resulting from problems that economic reforms have engendered or exacerbated, including inflation, unemployment, the visible reemergence of prostitution and trafficking in women and children, the pervasive rising materialism and focus on money (Chu and Ju 1993, 103, 279–282), serious environmental degradation and health hazards (Smil 1993), and the impact of uneven development between the coastal and interior areas and between urban and rural areas. In the rural areas, economic changes have been characterized by differences in distribution of men and women in jobs created by industrialization, the concentration of women in labor-intensive, low-skilled, low-wage jobs, and unequal pay for equal work for women. Although women's incomes in some areas have increased, there are large disparities between women's incomes, and a gap between most women's and men's incomes (Gao 1994, 90–91).

The difficulties of assessing the gender implications and impact of these reforms are partially due to the focus and methodology of much of economic policy research, the diversity of Chinese women's situations and experiences, and the enormous regional differences in terms of demographics, economic status, and policy implementation (Gao 1994, 90). In addition to poverty, rural women and girls face additional problems resulting from high illiteracy and school dropout rates, domestic violence, and the persistence of patrilocal residence and patrilineal inheritance traditions that result in the valuation of boys more than girls (*zhongnan qingnu*).

These continued gender-based abuses also suggest that the assessments of social change by Western observers in the late sixties and seventies were premature and not borne out by current conditions for women. The lives of women in the rural areas, in factories, and in urban workplaces are in sharp contrast to the "reality" asserted by official proclamations that Chinese women are now finally "masters of the People's Republic of China." Thus, despite the promulgation of extensive legislation that sets forth these formal equality norms, the reality for most Chinese women remains a gap between stated legal and policy goals and implementation (Gao 1994; Hom 1992a, 1992b, 1995; Jordan 1998; Woo 1994). The persistence of these social practices and attitudes underscores the necessity of cultural values and structural transformation and change in addition to legal reforms.

## The Role of Chinese NGOs with Chinese Characteristics

The role of the All China Women's Federation (ACWF or Fulian) within China and in the international arena, particularly in light of its visible key role in the Chinese planning for the 1995 World Conference on Women in Beijing, reflects the problematic and important role of Chinese NGOs in any social reform strategies.

Under the legal framework established by the 1989 Regulations for the Registration and Management of Social Groups, all associations, scholarly groups, federations, research associations, foundations, and promotional groups must register and be operationally linked to a governmental administrative unit (*guakao danwei*). In efforts to develop alliances across different political and cultural systems, we need to understand the context, obstacles, and opportunities facing Chinese NGOs or human rights/women's advocates attempting organizational strategies situated within a politically authoritarian regime, especially when interacting in an international arena (Hom 1993).

The predecessor of the Fulian, the All-China Democratic Women's Federation, was formed in 1949 to support, unify, and offer direction to the thousands of women's associations throughout the country and to help millions of women learn economic self-reliance. By 1956, in comparison to the 11 million members of the CCP, the Women's Federation had 76 million members (French 1985, 243). As the mass organization arm of the Party that acts to implement Party policies and to inform Party decision-making on the needs and interests of women, the ACWF occupies a difficult position. For example, in the implementation of the one-child policy, for example, the ACWF served as the propaganda arm, the "service" counseling arm, and advocates for women in cases of domestic abuse and violence.

One of the current challenges facing the ACWF is the articulation and development of a role for itself as an "independent" women's NGO despite its Party affiliation. In this process, the ACWF is negotiating the perceptions of international NGOs, the diverse perspectives and roles of provincial and local fulians and the theoretical assessments emerging from the growing number of Chinese women's studies centers, and its own relationship to the various organs of state power. At the same time, it is increasingly clear to outside observers that the ACWF does not speak with a monolithic voice for "Chinese women," nor is it free from internal criticism and debates (X. Li 1994; Hom 1993).

During the preparatory process leading up to the official Fourth World Conference on Women and parallel NGO Forum, Chinese women found themselves in exciting and difficult positions. Within the context of existing Chinese political, legal, and cultural constraints, Chinese women had to negotiate the tensions and opportunities of international human rights exchanges. For some of them, this was the first time they had heard the expression "women's rights are human rights" or the term "NGO." It was also the first opportunity for many Chinese women to network with women and groups from all over the world. Yet, their silences during the conference and the forum, as well as their voices and their reflections, provide important lessons for the possibility and difficulties of building networks and human rights strategies that draw on international approaches. One Chinese journalist noted:

Consciously or unconsciously, they [Chinese women] put themselves into the role of official spokespeople, enthusiastically explaining the "great progress made by women of our country" and arguing with "certain foreigners with ill-intentions." China lacks an understanding of human rights; it is even more lacking in comprehension of feminism. Today, we should not only struggle with the authorities to achieve the human rights and women's rights that we need, but also with the men and women who are permeated by several thousand years of feudal culture and decades of Party culture. (Chuanrenyuan 1995)

She concludes with the observation that more women in China now dare to openly call themselves "feminists."

As Chinese women cross literal or symbolic national borders with greater frequency, the official efforts to enclose them within nationalistic discourses have been only partially successful, despite the public acceptance by women of spokesperson roles during the conference. As reflections by Chinese women underscore, no matter what the present obstacles, the opening up of discursive spaces during this recent period and the seizing of opportunities presented by women to engage in activist research, to use the newly established women's centers to build a supportive place for investigation of social problems, to create networks within and outside of China, along with the rich memories of new friends and exposure to new ideas and approaches (Ford Foundation 1995), will have an ongoing impact that will be difficult to measure in the limited time frames of the present.

## THE FUTURE OF WOMEN'S RIGHTS

To the extent that a radical reenvisioning of social change is required, one that goes beyond formal equality guarantees of legislation or official rhetoric and slogans, any reordering necessarily requires a change in the predominantly male hierarchy of power or an end to patriarchal socialism, or its current formulation as market socialism. To a regime that values order and stability above all else, and that claims the moral supremacy and legitimacy of the whole over the individual, the reenvisioning of a social order without patriarchy and hierarchy may be an idealistic and ultimately unrealizable proposition. But the pervasiveness and impact of cultural assumptions shaping powerful ruling ideologies take on a reified legitimacy if left unchallenged in theory and in practice.

In the Special Economic Zones (SEZs), large numbers of young women from the rural areas flow into the cities to work in the factories, concentrated in light industries like textiles, electronics, toys, and plastics. These *dagong-meis* (working little sisters) constitute the majority of the work force in the SEZs and as much as 90 percent of the work force in some factories (Woo 1994, 287). The plight of these working little sisters includes facing sexual harassment in the workplace, low pay, poor and dangerous working conditions, long hours, and poor, crowded housing conditions. Yet, these working little sisters in China are not silent either about what they perceive as the injustices of their situation or the fact that the fruits of their bitter, hard labor accrue to the boss. They ask, why not become a boss one day, complain "I'm not a ball to be kicked around," and assert their hopes that one day they will be able to successfully escape the net they find themselves in (*Shanghai Jingjiyanjiu,* January 1994). In the end, the Chinese feminist voices raised in anger and frustration at the injustice of the existing hierarchy may not, like Tou O, be content to appeal to and rely on cosmic justice or to wait for the bitter vindication after death in the haunting of the guilty. Nor should they. What is at stake is the realization of a more inclusive social justice necessary for the survival and sustainable development of the whole society.

From the perspective of the majority of Chinese women today, particularly rural and poor women, Chinese women continue to suffer from persistent discrimination in the workplace and physical violence and abuse at home, or endure lives overburdened with the dual demands of family and work in the country's productive sphere. Clearly, the "revolution" for and "liberation" of Chinese women are still far from complete (Andors 1983; Wolf 1985). Ultimately, it will be the outrage of the *dagongmeis* (working little sisters), the visions of Chinese women and girls for a more just social order, and the political negotiations of domestic Chinese women's groups and human rights activists that will ensure that human rights and women's rights are lived realities. International human rights NGOs and activists can contribute to this difficult process by being open to the development of new alliances and multiple simultaneous strategies (Hom 1993), strategies that resist the seduction of the geopolitical power games of governmental bodies, and that stake out an independent substantive human rights agenda that avoids cultural imperialism and privileging nativism claims.

One lesson that I think international human rights debates and practice underscore is that avoidance of the hard tasks of making value choices in the name of inclusiveness or cultural relativism runs the risk of masking a moral bankruptcy. In the face of the shameful record of violence, inequality, and inequity of this century not only for Chinese women, but also for the majority of the world's people, human rights and women's rights remain an unrealized vision and a social justice challenge for the next millennium.

## BIBLIOGRAPHY

Andors, Phyllis. 1983. *The Unfinished Liberation of Chinese Women: 1949–1980.* Bloomington: Indiana University Press.
Buxbaum, David C., ed. 1980. *Chinese Family Law and Social Change in Historical Perspective.* Seattle: University of Washington Press.
Cheung, Ping-cheung. 1980. "Tou O yuan as Tragedy." In *China and the West:*

*Comparative Literature Studies*, ed. William Tay, Ying-hsiung Chou, and Heh-hsiang Yuan. Hong Kong: Chinese University Press, 251–75.

Chinese Academy of Social Sciences. 1989. *Information China*. Vol. 2. New York: Pergamon Press.

Chuanrenyuan. 1995. Overshadowing Feminism: Thoughts on the Beijing Women's Conference. *China Rights Furum* (Winter): 16–18.

Chu, G. C., and Y. Ju. 1993. *The Great Wall in Ruins: Communication and Cultural Change in China*. Albany: SUNY Press.

Croll, Elisabeth. 1980. *Feminism and Socialism in China*. New York: Schocken Books.

Ford Foundation. 1995. Reflections & Resources: Stories of Women Involved in International Preparatory Activities for the 1995 NGO Forum on Women (in Chinese and English). Beijing: Ford Foundation.

Freeman, Michael. 1995. "Human Rights: Asia and the West." In *Human Rights and International Relations in the Asia-Pacific Region*, ed. James T. H. Tang. London: Pinter.

French, Marilyn. 1985. *Beyond Power: On Women, Men, and Morals*. New York: Summit Books.

Gao, Xiaoxian. 1994. "China's Modernization and Changes in the Social Status of Rural Women." In *Engendering China: Women, Culture, and the State*, ed. C. Gilmartin, G. Hershatter, L. Rofel, and T. White. Cambridge, MA: Harvard University Press, 80–97.

Hom, Sharon K. 1992a. "Law, Ideology, and Patriarchy in the People's Republic of China: Feminist Observations of an Ethnic Spectator." *International Review of Comparative Public Policy* 4: 173–91.

———. 1992b. "Female Infanticide in China: The Specter of Human Rights and Thoughts Towards (An)other Vision." *Columbia Human Rights Law Review* 23: 249–314.

———. 1993. "Listening for Diversity: Broaden Debate Among Rights Groups in the Round-up to 1995." *China Rights Forum* (Winter): 12–15.

———. 1994. "Engendering Chinese Legal Studies: Gate-Keeping, Master Discourses, and Other Challenges." *Signs: Journal of Women in Culture and Society* 19, no. 4: 1020–47.

———. 1995. "Economic Reform and Social and Economic Rights in China: Strategy Brainstorming Across Cultures." In *From Basic Needs to Basic Rights: Women's Claims to Human Rights*, ed. Margaret A. Schuler. Washington, DC: Institute for Women, Law, and Development.

———. 1996. "Commentary: Re-positioning Human Rights Discourse on 'Asian' Perspectives." *Buffalo Journal of International Law* 3, no. 1: 251–76.

———, ed. 1999a. *Chinese Women Traversing Diaspora: Essays, Memoirs, and Poetry.* New York: Garland.

———. 1999b. "Lexicon Dreams and Chinese Rock and Roll: Thoughts on Culture, Language, and Translation as Strategies of Resistance and Reconstruction." *University of Miami Law Review* 53: 1501–15.

———. Forthcoming. "Cross-Discipline Trafficking: What's Justice Got to Do with It?" In *Orientations: Mapping Studies in the Asian Diaspora*, ed. Kandice Chuh and Karen Shimakawa. Durham: Duke University Press.

Hom, Sharon K., and Xin Chunying, eds. 1995. *English-Chinese Lexicon of Women and Law.* Beijing: UNESCO and China Translation and Publishing Corp.

Honig, Emily, and Gail Hershatter. 1988. *Personal Voices: Chinese Women in the 1980's.* Stanford: Stanford University Press.

Human Rights in China. 1995. *Caught Between Tradition and the State: Violations of the Human Rights of Chinese Women.* New York: Human Rights in China.

Human Rights in China, Asia Monitor Resource Centre, China Labor Bulletin, and Hong Kong Christian Industrial Commerce. 1998. *Report on Implementation of CEDAW in the People's Republic of China: A Report with Recommendations and Questions for the Chinese Government Representatives.*

Jimmerson, J. 1990. "Female Infanticide in China: An Examination of Cultural and Legal Norms." *UCLA Pacific Basin Law Journal* 8: 47–79.

Johnson, K. A. 1983. *Women, the Family and Peasant Revolution in China.* Chicago: University of Chicago Press.

Jordan, Ann D. 1998. "Human Rights, Violence Against Women, and Economic Development: The People's Republic of China Experience." *Columbia Journal of Gender and Law* 5: 216–72.

Li, Victor 1978. *Law Without Lawyers: A Comparative View of Law in China and the United States.* Boulder: Westview Press.

Li, Xiaojiang. 1994. "Economic Reform and the Awakening of Chinese Women's Consciousness." In *Engendering China: Women, Culture, and the State,* ed. C. Gilmartin, G. Hershatter, L. Rofel, and T. White. Cambridge, MA: Harvard University Press, 360–82.

Li, Xiaorong. 1995. " 'Asian Values' and the Universality of Human Rights." *China Rights Forum* (September): 32–36.

———. 1996. "License to Coerce: Violence Against Women, State Responsibility, and Legal Failures in China's Family-Planning Program." *Yale Journal of Law and Feminism* 8: 145–91.

Li, Yu-ning, ed. 1992. *Chinese Women Through Chinese Eyes.* Armonk, NY: M. E. Sharpe.

Liang, Zhiping. 1986. "Explicating 'Law': A Comparative Perspective of Chinese and Western Culture," trans. Fa Bian, Zhongguo Shehui Kexue, April. *Journal of Chinese Law* 3 (Summer): 55–91.

National Committee on U.S.-China Relations, Inc. 1994. *The Rise of Nongovernmental Organizations in China: Implications for Americans.* National Committee China Policy Series, No. 8. New York: National Committee on U.S.-China Relations, Inc., May.

Report to the Committee on the Elimination of Discrimination Against Women. 1997. Third and Fourth Periodic Report of States Parties, China, CEDAW/c/CHN/3–4, June 10. Beijing: Chinese Government.

*Shanghai Jingjiyanjiu* (Shanghai Economic Research) (January 1994): 49.

Shih, Chung-wen, trans. 1972. *Injustice to Tou O ("Tou O yuan"): A Study and Translation.* Cambridge: Cambridge University Press.

Smil, V. 1993. *China's Environmental Crisis: An Inquiry into the Limits of National Development.* Armonk, NY: M. E. Sharpe.

Spelman, Elizabeth V. 1988. *Inessential Woman: Problems of Exclusion in Feminist Thought.* Boston: Beacon Press.

State Council of the PRC. 1994. *The Situation of Chinese Women*. Beijing: State Council of the PRC.

Tao, Chen. 1993. "Zhongguofunujiefangyundung zhauchienlema?" (Is the Chinese Women's Movement Moving Forward?) *Tansuoyuzhengming* 6 (November 11): 23–27.

Tao, Jianmin. 1993. "Shehuijinbu yu Funujiefang" (Social Progress and Women's Liberation). *Tansuoyuzhengming* 6 (November 11): 28–32.

United Nations. 1995. "The World's Women 1995." New York: United Nations.

Watson, Ruby, and Patricia Ebrey, eds. 1991. *Marriage and Inequality in Chinese Society*. Berkeley: University of California Press.

Wolf, M. 1985. *Revolution Postponed: Women in Contemporary China*. Stanford: Stanford University Press.

Woo, Margaret. 1993. "Courts, Justice and Human Rights." *China Briefing, 1992*, New York: Westview Press, 81–102.

———. 1994. "Chinese Women Workers: The Delicate Balance Between Protection and Equality." In *Engendering China: Women, Culture, and the State*, ed. C. Gilmartin, G. Hershatter, L. Rofel, and T. White. Cambridge, MA: Harvard University Press, 279–95.

World Bank. 2000. "Entering the 21st Century." World Development Report 1999/ 2000. Oxford: Oxford University Press.

# 4

# CUBA

## The Search for Women's Rights in Private and Public Life

*Araceli Alonso*

## INTRODUCTION

### Profile of Cuba

Cuba is the largest island of the West Indies, with a population of 10,999,041 in 1997, and an average annual rate of natural increase of 0.57 percent. The infant mortality rate is 8.9 per 1000, and life expectancy was 74.75 years in 1997 (Oficina Nacional de Estadística 1998). The literacy rate is 94 percent. The ethnicity/race of the country has been estimated to be 51 percent mulatto, 37 percent white, 11 percent black, and 1 percent Chinese (CIR 1997). Elections have been held every five years since 1976 for the National Assembly, which in turn elects the thirty-one-member Council of States. The President and Secretary of the Council of the States and of the government is Fidel Castro Ruz, also the First Secretary of the Communist Party, the only political party of Cuba. Cuba's major industrial products are sugar and tobacco. The main trading partners of Cuba today are China, Canada, Mexico, Spain, and Russia (CIR 1997).

### A Case Study

Marina is an intellectual from Havana. She is the author of seven books and the mother of two girls, ages thirteen and seventeen. In a personal interview in 1999, Marina commented on women's rights in Cuba:

It is true that the Revolution made education and medical attention more available for all Cuban women regardless of income and/or color. But it is also true that black and mulatto women are still in the lowest status of society. It is also true that the Revolution opened up new working opportunities for qualified women, but you do not see women in power positions. The power is still in the hands of men, and the political power is in the hands of a single man.

The revolutionary government made laws to protect the integrity of women and domestic service was abolished, but women then became the maids of the Revolution, "the power of women at the service of the Revolution" we used to say back in the 1960s.

Don't get confused about the slogan "equal pay for equal work." It sounds nice, but in Cuba it only meant that women and men have been underpaid no matter what kind of hard and sophisticated job they had to do.

The official discourse says that the Revolution gave women dignity, but the reality is that it took away one of the fundamental human rights—freedom. I, as a woman, as a human being, want to be free; free to write, free to talk, free to make decisions for me and for my family, free to choose the house I want to live in, free to work where I want and to study what I like, free to leave the country, and also free to come back.

### Overview of Women's Rights Issues

Despite contradictions, there is no question that socialism has made a difference in the circumstances of Cuban women, particularly for those who were most oppressed under capitalism—black women, agricultural laborers, and landless peasants. After seizing power in 1959, the Castro government moved quickly to make good the revolution's promise to provide all citizens with the basic necessities of affordable food, housing, and medical care. In addition, the new leadership put in place programs and policies such as free and equal access to education and employment, vocational training, and daycare that meant unprecedented opportunities for many women. As a result, many Cuban women enjoyed intellectual, and in some cases economic, advantages never dreamed of by their mothers and grandmothers.

## HISTORY OF WOMEN'S RIGHTS

Under the Spanish civil code of 1889, married women were treated as legal nonpersons; husbands acquired nearly total control over their wives' property and earnings, and divorce was not permitted (Stoner 1991). Nineteenth century Cuba venerated an image of womanhood modeled on the Virgin Mary. The feminine ideal was to be chaste, self-effacing, and devoted; in sacrificing their needs and comfort to the well-being of their families, madres heróicas (heroic mothers) reproduced the culture's values and provided the nation with model citizens. Implicit in this notion was a clear-cut separation between the public and private domain: women's existences were expected to center on the home, leaving the public arena to the interests and activities of men (Smith and Padula 1996). Only women from the lowest stations engaged in paid labor, most commonly in the forms of sewing, laundry, or factory piecework done in the home. In addition, acute poverty often drove young girls and women from the countryside to the capital, where the chief alternatives were domestic service and prostitution (Randall 1974).

In the early years of the twentieth century, it became more acceptable for middle-class women to be educated, even at the college level, and to take jobs as teachers, secretaries, and office workers. Meanwhile, inspired by revolutionary events in Mexico and Russia, a progressive faction of the legislature began to call for expanded rights for women (Smith and Padula 1996). Divorce was legalized in 1918 despite strident objections from conservatives that an orderly household required male control, and that divorce would only encourage promiscuity and end in the destruction of the family. Stoner (1991) reminds us that it was widely accepted for Cuban men to take mistresses and preside over extramarital households, and that, from the point of view of men in the upper classes, there was little to be gained by the disruption of the state-sanctioned system of family and inheritance. For many women, however, socially isolated and economically dependent, the price of national stability was too often entrapment in abusive and violent marriages (Smith and Padula 1996). Although the new law passed and made it possible for wives to sue their husbands, divorce was still not socially accepted.

## The Development of Women's Organizations

As women's economic and educational horizons broadened, they began to organize social clubs and literary societies and to concern themselves with moral reforms for poor relief. These interests often drew them into more active political engagement. An example is the Havana's Club Femenino (Women's Club), a benevolent society begun in 1917 to support the arts and cultural events and to assist the less fortunate. This effort included a project to educate poor women about maternal and infant health. However, as these middle- and upper-class women became acquainted with the lives and problems of the poor, they also learned about the injustices that kept women in poverty and ignorance, and perhaps more important, discovered that they had issues in common with them. In 1923 the Club Femenino brought together thirty-one women's organizations for Cuba's first National Women's Congress (Smith and Padula 1996). The delegates discussed a range of issues, including the rights of illegitimate children, protections for single mothers, adultery, prostitution, and equal pay for equal work. Contending that it was the proper obligation of mothers to force the government to respond to the needs of the family, they concluded that women's suffrage was vital to the welfare of the nation.

The chief historical significance of the Women's Congress was its insistence on a social role for government (Stoner 1991). Taken as a whole, the objectives of the Congress represented an expansion, rather than a rejection, of women's traditional roles. Relative affluence afforded middle-class women the resources of time and energy to involve themselves in political activism, but it also determined the direction and scope of their energies. This activism created a line of separation between the struggle for women's rights and the struggle for more sweeping social reforms, preventing the movement from becoming truly radical in nature (Randall 1974).

More radical groups also began to appear in Cuba in 1923, and the Cuban Communist Party (Partido Comunista de Cuba [PCC]), founded in 1925, soon attracted many politically conscious young women with its far-reaching goals of social transformation. Socialist feminists such as Ofelia Domínguez Navarro, Mirta Aguirre, and Mariblanca Sabás Alomá subjected Cuban feminist concepts to a more radical class analysis than ever before (Randall 1974). They also managed to get several class-related issues placed on the agenda at the Second National Congress of Cuban Women in 1925.

Due to a rapidly growing industrial sector, there was an enormous expansion in the number of women workers in the early 1920s, particularly in textile manufacturing, where they represented a cheap, expendable source of labor. Even so, women tended to be welcome in the work force only as long as they were single and unlikely to become pregnant (Stoner 1991). In 1925 President Gerardo Machado responded to women's complaints of unfair hiring and employment practices by issuing a decree that fixed female quotas in certain jobs and required that working mothers be allowed to breast-feed their infants at work. Nevertheless, Machado reneged on his 1924 campaign promise to give women the vote, and in 1929 when hunger and deprivation spread across the island during the Great Depression, women activists added their voices to calls for the overthrow of the Machado regime.

Machado was ousted in 1933 and succeeded by an interim government led by a former professor of medicine, Ramón Grau San Martín. A year later, in 1934, Grau San Martín not only extended the vote to women but also signed the first working women's maternity law, which entitled pregnant women to a twelve-week maternity leave. Moreover, factories with more than fifty women workers were required to provide daycare centers for children under age two (Smith and Padula 1996). Unfortunately, the provisions of the maternity law were not extended to domestic servants or agricultural workers, and the response of many manufacturers was a flagrant lack of compliance, some refusing to hire women, especially married women (Capote 1973).

Leftist groups were not slow to identify themselves with women's concerns, and as these events unfolded, the Communist Party moved to solidify its support among women. As a result, the first International Women's Day was celebrated on March 8, 1931, and in 1934 the National Women's Union was organized. The organizers went on to figure prominently in the consolidation of Cuban socialism over the next three decades.

## The Batista Era

In 1940 Colonel Fulgencia Batista was elected president, and oversaw the drafting of a new constitution that included a number of strikingly advanced provisions relating to the status of women. Specifically, Article 16 reaffirmed the right of women to retain Cuban citizenship regardless of marriage; Article 20 prohibited discrimination on the basis of sex; Article 43 entitled women to full control of their private property and salary; Article 62 introduced the principle of equal pay for equal work; Article 97 upheld universal suffrage; and Article 68 reasserted the rights of working women to paid maternity leave, with the added provision that single and married women should be treated equally in respect to hiring. In addition, the 1940 constitution broke new ground by extending the rights of inheritance to illegitimate children (Stoner 1991; Columbié 1990).

Thus, in the liberal republic of the pre-revolutionary 1950s, Cuban women could claim essential equality with men in the eyes of the law. However, women still constituted only 13.7 percent of the total labor force in 1953, and earned far less than men for doing the same work (Casal 1980; Martínez Guyanes 1974; Larguia and Dumoulin 1986; Randall 1974). The obstacles to receiving a higher education barred the great majority of women from careers in the professions. For poor and rural women, who seldom received any schooling at all, there had been little real improvement. Although some domestics were treated as members of the family (Smith and Padula 1996), many more were subjected to economic and sexual exploitation for which there was no legal recourse. In addition, black women continued to endure legal discrimination on the basis of race, and were not allowed to study in some schools (Rubiera Castillo 1997) or even work in front-office jobs (Smith and Padula 1996).

The consequences of the Batista dictatorship and its alliance with the United States were extreme social inequality and widespread unemployment. Out of a population of 5.5 million, 400,000 families resided in shantytowns, and 90 percent of rural children were infected with parasites. There were almost no medical clinics, hospitals, or schools to serve the poor. There was one physician for approximately every thousand inhabitants; and 65 percent of the physicians were based in Havana, with the rest located in other major cities and towns.

### The Revolution Experience in Women's Roles

Women were full participants in the 1956–1959 insurrection against Batista (Randall 1974; Casal 1980; Smith and Padula 1996). When the new government came into power, its leaders openly acknowledged the revolution's debt to women. At the first General National Assembly, held on December 2, 1960, a formal declaration was read before more than a million Cubans gathered in the Plaza de la Revolution, recognizing the contributions of women in Cuban struggles throughout its history and condemning all forms of gender inequality and exploitation. This unique document, known as the Primera Declaración de la Habana, committed the new government to the procurement of full social, civil, and political equality for both sexes (Holt-Seeland 1981). In the heady atmosphere of revolutionary enthusiasm, the traditional notions of woman as mother and homemaker seemed at last about to give way to a new assertiveness and unprecedented participation in social and political life.

The new leadership recognized that it was not enough to give women legal rights without the practical means to exercise them. Moreover, they understood that women could not resolve their problems alone; it was necessary for the state to ensure the conditions that would enable women to pursue full equality. As the first step toward achieving these ends, all of the existing women's groups were combined into a single organization, the Federación de Mujeres Cubanas (Federation of Cuban Women [FMC]) under the direction of Vilma Espín. Its purpose was to facilitate the transition of Cuban women into the agricultural, industrial, and service sector economies of the new society. Through educational programs and consciousness-raising activities, the FMC retrained women whose only experience had been in domestic service. Rehabilitation programs were also developed to assist those who had made their living as prostitutes (Espín 1991).

One of the FMC's first tasks was to establish a system of childcare. Other than a handful of infant care facilities maintained by private charities, there were virtually no daycare centers in Cuba prior to the revolution (Randall 1981). Within a year of its founding, one thousand former domestic servants had been trained as daycare workers, and a cooking school, begun at the same time, provided cooks for the *círculos infantiles* (daycare centers) (Espín 1991). To alleviate some of the time pressures on working women, the FMC also helped to set in place a scheme known as "Plan Jaba," which gave working women priority in the markets and *bodegas* (government stores), allowing them to go to the front of the long lines in which people now waited to purchase most goods and products (Espín 1991). Women joined the federation in large numbers, almost 400,000 in its first two years between 1960 and 1962. By the time the fifth FMC Congress was held in August 1990, its membership comprised over 80 percent of all Cuban women between fourteen and sixty-five years of age, nearly 3 million women, making it the largest women's organization in the history of Latin America (Smith and Padula 1996).

State support for working women was accompanied by a steady increase in the percentage of women employed, from 13.7 percent in 1953 to 40 percent in 1993 (Martínez Guyanes 1974; Larguia and Dumoulin 1986; Casal 1980). The period between 1975 and 1985 saw the highest incorporation of women into the labor force. In 1975 the rate was 24 percent; in 1983 it was 37.5 percent; and by 1993, an estimated 40.6 percent of the potential female labor force was employed outside the home (Aguilar et al. 1998, 12).

The 1970s also saw important formal renewals of the commitment to improve the status of women, including, in 1975, both the Cuban Communist Party's Thesis on the Full Equality of Women and the enactment of a piece of landmark legislation, the Family Code, that gave spouses equal rights and responsibilities in the household. It also required that children be instructed in the revolutionary principle that men and women were to participate equally in all aspects of society and share the same responsibilities (*Código de la Familia* 1975). In addition, the First Socialist Constitution of 1976 included two specific mentions of gender: Chapter V, Article 41, which stated that discrimination based on race, skin color, sex, and national origin was proscribed by law; and Article 43, which granted equal rights for men and women economically, socially, politically, and within the family.

## WOMEN'S RIGHTS TODAY

By 1980, Cuban women had made certain gains under Castro's administration. They no longer had to face giving birth without medical attention or fear that they would not be able to provide their children with the minimum necessities of food, clothing, and basic medical and dental care. Access to contraception and abortion, the elimination of domestic servitude and prostitution, universal education, and state policies that encouraged women's employment combined to bring women greater economic independence and more diverse professional opportunities than ever before.

### The Division of Labor

Unfortunately, these gains were purchased at a price. There was still little change in the division of domestic labor; women were still expected to perform all of the duties of homemaking even after a full day at a wage-earning job. The demands that the "second shift" placed on women made it difficult or impossible for them to attend the evening classes, meetings, and work sessions which were the means to climb to positions of authority in the

Communist Party. Additionally, men complained about their wives' and daughters' participation in the multitude of reform projects—such as the 1961 literacy campaign that sent thousands of volunteers to remote areas of the country to teach reading—which began to feature prominently in Cuban life under socialism (Randall 1981).

Because of their dual role, women were often employed for fewer hours than men and were much more often absent from work. Thus, although women were widely represented in the professions and there was equal pay for equal work, they could rarely occupy higher ranking positions. Consequently, there continued to be significant disparity between men's and women's earnings. As an example of that, Nuñez Sarmiento (1991), in her study on women's employment in Cuba, found that women at a brick factory earned 54 cents for every peso (100 cents) earned by men due primarily to female absences from daily work.

For now, it appears, the Family Code's injunction that household chores should be shared equally by all members of the family continues to be more honored in the breach than in the observance. The Fifth Congress of the FMC reported in 1990 that inequality in domestic work continues to be an ongoing problem (see Instituto de Cooperación Internacional with the collaboration of the FMC 1992; Popowsky Casañ and Castañeda Marrero 1996).

In 1985 the FMC argued that the option to take unpaid family leave, granted to women by the 1974 maternity law, ought to be extended to men, and that families, not the state, should decide which spouse should be excused from work. Though this measure ultimately passed, few men have taken advantage of it, and women continue to assume the primary duties of caring for children (Smith and Padula 1996). Further, Espín (1986) claims that managers still try to reduce the disruptions and inconvenience of maternity leaves by keeping women in low-level positions or firing them when they become pregnant.

Smith and Padula (1996) contend that the widespread use of women volunteers begun during the revolutionary effort has evolved into a routine form of exploitation in the post-revolutionary era. In 1986, for example, Espín complained that the FMC organized a crew of women volunteers to build a bakery on the understanding that when it opened the women would be hired as full-time paid workers. The women completed the bakery, but men were hired to staff it, not the women who had built it. The Cuban sociologist Marta Nuñez Sarmiento (1991) has reported similar examples of women being exploited as contract laborers in agriculture.

## Concepts of Femininity and Masculinity

Neither sex appears to have abandoned the inherited notions of masculinity and femininity that characterized the pre-revolutionary gender relations (Quintero et al. 1998). Lutjens (1994) observes that Cuban women have never found any contradiction between their desire to look and feel feminine and their emancipation on military front lines or in the workplace. She cites Greer's (1985) references to the "pearlised nail polish and lipstick worn by women who have been trained to kill," and the "heroines of work, who cut cane, go down the mines and drive huge cranes, [and] are depilated, deodorized and scented" (370). While feminine dress and behavior are not necessarily incompatible with equality, the persistence of traditional behaviors helps to perpetuate outmoded gender divisions by reproducing the old images of womanhood and underlying attitudes that were integral to the old order.

## Reproductive Rights

Cuba's policies concerning reproductive rights have also invited criticism (Smith and Padula 1996). After the imposition of strict separation between church and state, legal hindrances to the practice of birth control fell away. However, the new government was slow to make contraceptive devices available to women. Additionally, sterilization was authorized only for women who had three or more living children or for whom pregnancy might prove life-threatening. The reason given was the prohibitive cost of providing these services, but the fact that women seeking sterilization were required to obtain the written consent of their husband—though men did not need their wives' permission to undergo vasectomy—seemed to recall the old order's attitude toward female autonomy (Rodríguez Dominguez 1985).

The lack of preventive measures of birth control resulted in an alarming increase in the frequency of surgical abortions; and although during the first decades Castro's regime actively opposed abortion, by 1974, 40 percent of all pregnancies ended in abortion (Alvarez Vázquez 1985). Ultimately, in the 1970s, Cuba did begin to import contraceptives such as the IUD and the birth control pill, which were distributed free of charge in the national health clinics. However, the decision of which method to use was made by the care providers; women themselves received no information about the side effects and potential health risks. Not until the late 1980s did the Cuban Society for the Development of the Family issue a pamphlet describing the advantages and disadvantages of the various contraceptive methods; but this, too, was silent on the health risks associated with the IUD, which Cuban gynecologists continued to recommend as the preferred method for teenagers (Smith and Padula 1996; Krause 1987).

## Domestic Violence

The official position is that socialism generates dignity, equality, and respect among its citizens. On this basis, Cuba denies the existence of domestic abuse and rape (Alvarez Suárez et al. 1998) and therefore the need to legislate against domestic abuse and to provide shelters for battered women. Unfortunately, as the Cuban researcher Ileana Artiles de León points out, "No country, regardless of culture, religion, or economy, is exempt from violent acts against women" (1997, 33), and such abuses do indeed occur in Cuba.

### Women, Late Socialism, and Survival

The loss of markets with the collapse of the socialist bloc, the U.S. trade embargo, and natural disasters have devastated the Cuban economy, with dire consequences for women. In the context of economic dislocation and domestic hardship, the national objective has shifted from one of "socialist rejuvenation" to a struggle for existence. The essential social programs providing health care, education, and daycare still manage to function in very hard conditions. Shortages of basic necessities make everyday life very difficult and frustrating for most Cubans, especially for working mothers who still have full responsibility for the home after a long day of working outside. Electricity blackouts routinely sweep the cities, and bicycles have replaced automobiles, because gasoline is almost impossible to obtain. Hospital patients must supply their own sheets and even lightbulbs from home, and medicines of every sort are in short supply (Pichs 1992; Lutjens 1994). Food rationing has become so restrictive that, as Randall (1995) says, people very often go to bed at night with a glass of sugar water to dull their hunger.

Extreme shortages have meant that women spend an even greater portion of their day waiting in lines to buy food and other necessities. Key ingredients such as tomato sauce (essential to Cuban cuisine) and cooking oil are scarce and often impossible to obtain, as they are only available for purchase with dollars. Women are increasingly preoccupied with strategies to feed their families (Campuzano 1996; Rodríguez Calderón 1992). As a consequence, women, in particular working mothers, have had to develop new strategies to provide their household with higher incomes.

After their "official" jobs as nurses, doctors, engineers, teachers, and so on, women are now working "unofficially" as hairdressers, tailors, and laundresses for others. Some women have decided to leave their jobs and have began working as street vendors or doing any kind of job related to the tourist industry. Unavoidably, women have less time for community involvement, and even the FMC has expressed concern with their decreasing participation in public affairs (Lutjens 1994; Espín 1991).

Despite its current difficulties, Cuba continues to stand by its official commitment to women. The Family Code remains in force as the formal statement of socialist equality in private life, and the newly ratified (1992) constitution not only upholds the earlier laws barring discrimination based on skin color, sex, and national origin, but goes even further, adding to the list "religious belief and any other affront to human dignity." More recently, however, state-sponsored projects to revive tourism have resulted in such dubious undertakings as the March 1991 issue of *Playboy* magazine and the 1998 issue of *Sol y Son* magazine, showing images of Cuban women that resembled the display of exotic women dancers of the Tropicana nightclub projected by the old order in pandering to foreign travelers. Inevitably, too, the relaxation of the *periodo especial* (a name given by Castro to the Cuban crisis after the breakdown of the Soviet Union) has also opened the door to a flourishing black market in foreign goods and dollars, and drawn hundreds of women into prostitution (Smith and Padula 1996).

## THE FUTURE OF WOMEN'S RIGHTS

In overseeing the political formation of Cuban women, the Federation of Cuban Women ought to have been women's most formidable advocate. However, the priorities of the FMC were economic development, national survival, and above all the defense of the revolution (FMC 1992). Ultimately, the FMC and Cuban women in general have participated very little in drafting the policies that have governed their lives and the lives of their children and families. Moreover, as Smith and Padula bluntly observe, "Sharing power with women was not a government priority" (1996, 55). Indeed, Lutjens (1994) argues that the FMC has continually exhibited a traditionally selfless, feminine character. Its tasks and interests were defined by a male elite, and in its enthusiasm for the development of the new society, it has evolved into an effective arm of social control for the Castro regime. The aim of the FMC was to mobilize and monitor an important sector of the Cuban society, "the firm and powerful mass made up of our women," and to control and unite women in order to "build a conscious force on behalf of the revolution" (Espín 1975, 94).

When women were able to participate in the public domain of policy-making, their needs and opinions were taken seriously. Ironically, many of their particular needs arose from their roles as mothers in the private sphere, which remained out of view to male policy-makers. In the 1970s, however, policy-makers attempted to address this gulf by reallocating childbearing responsibilities to state-run daycare centers or *círculos infantiles,* and through an equal partnership between mothers and fathers as stated in the Family Code. As already demonstrated in this chapter, these prescriptions were only a partial solution. Perhaps this is not surprising given that the concerns of women have taken second place in a nationalist program whose priority has been class relations and the needs of the state.

Although the Cuban Family Code continues to be the formal statement of socialist equality in private life, and families are at present a crucial focus of current policies and FMC efforts, the gendered practices of private and public life have not been eliminated by Cuba's socialist strategy for women. Cuban women are still wives, mothers, and grandmothers constrained by domestic life and by the new identities they developed in socialist public life.

The revolution has not, as expected, made gender inequity a thing of the past. Deeply engrained cultural values of *machismo* have been hard to eradicate in private life and public life. Furthermore, state policies have always prioritized women's roles as mothers and homemakers. Socialist Cuban women have had to fulfill their obligations of citizenship, retaining primary responsibility at home even as they assumed a greater role in the nation's economic production (Smith and Padula 1996; Campuzano 1996). The strain of multiple roles as homemakers and laborers has kept women from full participation in public life and left them exhausted and overworked.

Political equality and a fair legal system are obviously essential to establishing the frameworks within which gender change can take place; they also help protect women from the most egregious forms of discrimination. However, the history of women's rights in Cuba shows that these factors are not sufficient to effect the shifts in social consciousness and practices that are needed for true parity.

Discrepancies between the communist political ideology and social reality, along with the economic crisis that afflicts the island, have made deep changes in the lifestyle and values of the Cuban population, especially in the younger generations. Women are concerned about the future of their daughters and granddaughters. In Marina's own words, younger girls have seen their mothers and grandmothers "exhausted, fragmented, overworked, depressed, and frustrated," so they want a different life for themselves. The FMC claims that women won't come back to the home and abandon either their jobs or their rights. This assumption might be true for the present generation of working women, but not for the future generations that wish for a better standard of living without being as "tortured" as their mothers have been. Many younger women have forgotten the struggle for social equity and visualize a comfortable future in the home. As capitalism permeates daily life in Cuba, the challenges to retain the accomplishments of the revolution while addressing unresolved gender conflicts will become more acute.

## BIBLIOGRAPHY

Aguilar, Carolina et al. 1998. "Las mujeres y los medios masivos de comunicación en tiempos de globalización y neoliberalismo." In *Encuentro Internacional de Solidaridad entre Mujeres*. Havana: FMC, 27–31.

Alvarez Suárez, Mayda, Carolina Aguilar, et al. 1994. *Mujer y poder: Las cubanas en el Poder Popular*. Havana: FMC.

Alvarez Suárez, Mayda, Rebeca Cutié, et al. 1998. "Discriminación y violencia contra la mujer." In *Encuentro Internacional de Solidaridad entre Mujeres*. Havana: FMC, 12–23.

Alvarez Vázquez, Luisa. 1985. *La fecundidad en Cuba*. Havana: Editorial Ciencias Sociales.

Arés Muzio, Patricia. 1996. "Género, pareja y familia en Cuba. Conservación de una identidad cultural o creación de nuevos valores." *Revista Cubana de Psicología* 13 (1): 3–7.

Artiles de León, Ileana. 1997. "Violencia: un problema social y de salud." *Sexología y Sociedad* 2, no. 8 (December): 30–35.

Campuzano, Luisa. 1996. "Ser cubanas y no morir en el intento." *Temas: Cultura, Ideologia, Sociedad* 5: 4–10.

Capote, María Elena. 1973. "Por ellas y para ellas." *Mujeres* (May): 52–55.

Casal, Lourdes. 1980. "Revolution and *Conciencia*: Women in Cuba." In *Women, War, and Revolution*, ed. Carol Berkin and Clara M. Lovett. London: Holmes and Meier, 183–206.

Center for International Research (CIR). 1997. Bureau of the Census, Washington, DC.

*Código de la Familia*. 1975. Havana: Orbe.

Columbié, Tamara. 1990. *Legislación y mujer*. Havana: FMC.

*Constitución de la República de Cuba, 1976*. 1985. Havana: Editorial de Ciencias Sociales.

Departamento de Orientación Revolucionaria del Comité Central del Partido Comunista de Cuba, ed. 1976. *Tesis y resolución: Sobre el Pleno Ejercicio de la Igualdad de la Mujer*. Havana: PCC.

Domínguez, Jorge. 1995. "Cuba en un nuevo camino." In *Cuba en crisis*, ed. Rodriguez Beruff et al. Puerto Rico: Editorial de la Universidad de Puerto Rico, 23–43.

Espín, Vilma. 1975. "Deborah." *Revista de la Universidad de Oriente* (March): 57–96.

———. 1986. "La batalla por el ejercicio pleno de la igualdad de la mujer: Acción de los comunistas." *Cuba Socialista* 2 (March–April): 27–68.

———. 1991. *Cuban Women Confront the Future*. New York: Ocean Press.

Federación de Mujeres Cubanas (FMC). 1990. *Proyecto the Informe Central: V Congreso FMC*. Havana, March 5–8.

———. 1992. "Carta de la FMC a Fidel." *Granma* (January 3): 1.

Flors, Elsy. 1993. "Actualidad financiera." *Cuba Internacional* 31: 7–8.

Greer, Germaine. 1985. "Politics—Cuba." In *Women: A World Report*. New York: Oxford University Press, 271–91.

Holt-Seeland, Inger. 1981. *Women of Cuba*. Westport, CT: Lawrence Hill.

Instituto de Cooperación Internacional; Agencia Española de Cooperación Internacional. 1992. *Aproximación a las mujeres cubanas*. Havana: FMC.

Krause, Monika, ed. 1987. *Compilación de artículos sobre educación sexual para el médico de la familia*. Havana: Grupo Nacional de Trabajo sobre Educación Sexual.

Larguia, Isabel, and John Dumoulin. 1986. "Women's Equality and the Cuban Revolution." In *Women and Change in Latin America*, ed. June Nash and Helen Safa. South Hadley, MA: Bergin and Garvey, 344–68.

Lutjens, Sheryl L. 1994. "Remaking the Public Sphere: Women and Revolution in Cuba." In *Women and Revolution in Africa, Asia, and the New World*, ed. Mary Ann Tétreault. Columbia: University of South Carolina Press, 366–94.

Martínez Guyanes, María A. 1974. "La situación de la mujer en Cuba en 1953."
    *Santiago* 15 (June/September): 195–226.
Nuñez Sarmiento, Marta. 1991. *Mujeres en empleos no tradicionales.* Havana: Edi-
    torial de Ciencias Sociales.
Oficina Nacional de Estadística. 1998. *Anuario Estadístico de Cuba.* Havana: ONS.
Pichs, Ramón. 1992. "Problemas y opciones del sector energético en Cuba." *Boletín
    de Información Sobre Economía Cubana* 1 (May): 9–19.
Popowsky Casañ, Perla, and Ana Violeta Castañeda Marrero. 1996. *Mujer, salud y
    desarrollo desde una perspectiva de género.* Havana: FMC.
Quintero, Nerida, Norma Vasallo, et al. 1998. "Participación política y acceso a la
    toma de decisiones." In *Encuentro Internacional de Solidaridad entre Mujeres.*
    Havana: FMC
Randall, Margaret. 1974. *Cuban Women Now.* Toronto: The Women's Press.
———. 1981. *Women in Cuba: Twenty Years Later.* New York: Smyrna Press.
———. 1995. *Our Voices Our Lives: Stories of Women from Central America and
    the Caribbean.* Monroe, ME: Common Courage Press.
———. 1996. "Cuban Women and the U.S. Blockade." *Sojourner: The Women's
    Forum* (November): 10–11.
Rodríguez Calderón, Mirta. 1992. "Sin tiempo para el desaliento." *Bohemia* 74
    (March 6): 38–42.
Rodríguez Dominguez, Pedro. 1985. *Temas de salud sobre la mujer.* Havana: Edi-
    torial Científico-técnica.
Rubiera Castillo, Daisy. 1997. *Reyita, sencillamente.* Havana: Instituto Cubano del
    Libro.
Smith, Lois M., and Alfred Padula. 1996. *Sex and Revolution: Women in Socialist
    Cuba.* New York: Oxford University Press.
Stoner, Kathryn Lynn. 1991. *From the House to the Streets: The Cuban Woman's
    Movement for Legal Reform, 1898–1940.* Durham, NC: Duke University Press.

# 5

# DENMARK

## Women's Rights and Women's Welfare

*Lynn Walter*

## INTRODUCTION

### Profile of Denmark

Denmark is a small country (43,100 square kilometers) with a population of 5,215,718 in 1995 (*Denmark in Figures* 1995). Life expectancy is high, 78.0 years for women and 72.9 years for men in 1995 (Ligestillingsrådet Statistik 1999), and the birthrate of 1.8 is low (Holst 1995). It is a parliamentary democracy with a constitutional monarch, Queen Margrethe II. In 1973 Denmark joined the European Union. While its market economy is one of the strongest in Europe, it is known more for its large public sector, which supports such social welfare programs as old age pensions, unemployment compensation, public health care and education, family allowances, daycare centers, and paid parental leave.

### A Case Study

In her interview for an official government publication on the lives of Danish women, Annette Lund-Hansen discusses her deliberations on whether to take advantage of a recent expansion of parental leave and extend her maternity leave for her third child from twenty-four weeks to fifty-two weeks. After the birth of her first two children, Annette took her twenty-four weeks of maternity leave and then returned to her job as a nurse, placing the children in publicly supported childcare centers. She has the family support to combine having children and being employed in a skilled occupation, which places her at an advantage compared to single mothers. Annette is pleased with her circumstances, but is concerned about the shortage of childcare places for her newborn Amalie when she does return to work and about how her co-workers at the hospital will manage if she decides to extend her leave (Ottensten 1995). Perhaps she will return to work part-time, as so many Danish women do. Her choices are not easy ones, but they are ones that her grandmother would likely not have had. Since the development of an economic system in which people work for wages outside of the farm and home, Danish women have actively worked to create a society in which having fulfilling jobs is consistent with having healthy families.

## Overview of Women's Rights Issues

The modern political age in Denmark began with the adoption, on June 5, 1849, of a constitution that reduced the powers of the monarchy and recognized the voting rights of most adult men (Eckhardt 1995, 40). It was an important step toward parliamentary democracy, universal citizenship rights, and the egalitarian values that shape the contemporary state of Denmark. Along the way, women too gained the right to vote, as well as to get an education and to pursue a career, and an entitlement to more of the nation's wealth and welfare through such provisions as publicly funded parental leave and childcare. However, the existence of conflicting interests between the entrenched, powerful classes and those who have claimed a larger share for themselves has meant that the goals of expanding rights and of achieving a more egalitarian distribution of resources have not gone unchallenged. Danish women know this well, because they, along with the farmers and workers, have struggled for nearly two centuries toward equality.

This study of "the woman question" in modern Denmark follows four historical themes—married versus unmarried women's rights, the concerns of women with children, middle-class versus working-class women's issues, and the idea of entitlements. Historically, the issue of a woman's marital status appears as a woman's right to *choose* either the independence of unmarried life or the patriarchal traditions of married life. The concerns of mothers are also linked to gendered conceptions of family in such questions as who decides how many children to have, who will care for them, and who will support them. These concerns have been especially critical for working-class and single mothers, who need to support themselves and their families. Their need for paid work expresses the class as well as gender interests that intertwine to weave the history of the woman question in Denmark. Of all the differences among women, class difference is the one most situated in the institutions and values of Danish society. Class consciousness led to the idea that everyone is *entitled* to social security in the form of a decent standard of living, education, and health care; and the characterization of modern Denmark as a social welfare state is based on the vital role that its government plays in providing for the security of its citizens. The history of the woman question in Denmark is one in which women have come to claim certain of the entitlements of the social welfare state as their own.

## HISTORY OF WOMEN'S RIGHTS

### The Nineteenth Century

The first public stirrings of the woman question came in 1850 when nineteen-year-old Mathilde Fibiger published her book, *Tolv Brev* (Twelve Letters), about her life as a governess and her longing for something more. Writing under the name Clara Rafael, Fibiger lamented that women's intellect and ideas were not taken as seriously as those of the men of her class (Bendix 1976, 132).

For the first time in my life I am sorry that I was not born a man. How narrow and empty are our lives compared to theirs! Is it right that half of humanity should be excluded from intellectual pursuits? Or has our Lord really made us of lesser stuff than men (as one of the most interesting gentlemen in these parts declared in utter seriousness) so that we must be content to automatically carry out the trivial work that is our lot in life? Has our spirit not strength, our heart not passions? Oh yes, but our true life has not awakened, our spirit is imprisoned, and prejudice stands guard at her cell. (Rafael 1976, 23–24)

### *Middle-Class Women's Issues*

Her words ignited a public debate on education for women, one of the central goals of the middle-class women's rights advocates of Fibiger's day. Equal access to education represented the right to seek enlightenment in the world of ideas and to apply professional training to careers outside the home. Access to education and careers was correlated with the right to be treated as an independent person, one who retained control over her own property and income and who represented herself before the law. Many of these rights were attained in the second half of the nineteenth century. In 1859 came women's right to a primary education and in 1875 their right to be admitted to universities (Eckhardt 1995, 41). The Majority Act of 1857 gave unmarried women the right to represent themselves before the law, which meant that they could sign contracts in their own name and control their own economic affairs. Also in 1857 inheritance laws were equalized, and unmarried women were given the right to open their own businesses (Busch 1965, 33–34). The idea that married women should have the right to legal and economic independence was more threatening to traditional ideals of family life. For that reason, married women were not granted control over their own wages until the 1880s; and the Majority Act of 1857 did not apply to married women until 1899 (Busch 1965, 49–45; Eckhardt 1995, 41).

A woman's marital status was a key factor shaping cultural attitudes toward her rights. The cultural ideals of family life in the nineteenth century bid married women confine themselves to caring for their home, husband, and children while their husbands earned a living and controlled the family's resources. Facing harsher economic realities than the middle class did, married working-class women more often worked outside the home and worried about how to care for their children while they did so.

In 1871, when Fredrik and Mathilde Bajer founded the Danish Women's Society (Dansk Kvindesamfund), the first women's rights organization in Denmark, middle-class conceptions of the proper family form were so strong that even they did not challenge them directly. Instead, the Danish Women's Society worked to improve women's status within marriage. Husbands and wives were to have "complementary" roles in the family, roles that were presumably of equal worth but not identical (Rosenbeck 1987, 317). On the other hand, the society maintained that women should be permitted to gain economic independence in order to be able to *choose* whether to have a career or a family and, effectively, whether to marry or not. Thus, they promoted equal access to education and careers for those middle-class women who chose not to marry and the improvement of the status of homemaking and childcare for those who did.

### Working-Class Women's Issues

Like marital status, socioeconomic class shaped cultural attitudes toward women's rights and the strategies used to realize them. Working-class women perceived their most critical problems as low pay, long working days, poor working conditions, unemployment, and, at times, resistance from working-class men and their unions. Olivia Nielsen, one of the first female labor union leaders, and other women activists among the working class directed their struggle toward improving women's lives through increasing their share of the nation's economic resources and through making it easier for women to have a job and children at the same time. In 1885 they formed the General Union of Women Workers (Kvindeligt Arbjederforbund) to represent unskilled women workers and to demand better working conditions and pay for their union sisters (Olsen 1984, 230–31; Rosenbeck 1987, 312).

Social reformers expressed their concern that working-class women were being physically harmed by their employment. To address this problem, parties across the political spectrum called for protective labor legislation in the forms of a ban on women working at night and support for maternity leave. In her analysis of the history of protective labor legislation, Ravn (1995a, 221–22) notes that both middle-class women's organizations and some of the female labor unions were united in their opposition to the proposed ban on night shift work for women.

On the other hand, both middle- and working-class women's organizations supported maternity leave, arguing that there was something special about being a mother, as opposed to being a father, that should be acknowledged with a maternity leave policy in the workplace. In 1901 women who worked in industry achieved a four-week maternity leave, but the proposed night shift ban was never implemented in Denmark. Ravn (1995b, 50) identifies these cases as exemplifying how women's rights advocates framed some issues, such as maternity leave, in terms of the differences between men and women, while on other issues, such as the prohibition against night work, they adopted an equality perspective.

## 1900–1930: Women's Rights

### Political Rights

During the debates over protective labor legislation and the efforts by women and men to gain equal access for women to education and careers, women had no political rights. Whatever gains they made had to be ratified by the men of the governing class. Nevertheless, it was not until 1894 that the Danish Women's Society openly raised the question of women's right to vote. At that time the Copenhagen chapter openly broke ranks with the national organization, which still considered the suffrage demand to be too radical.

One reason for the relatively late adoption of political rights as a women's issue was that the political rights of men were not firmly established in the Danish constitution. The political rules and power structure of the upper house of parliament were stacked in favor of the king and the conservative Right party, which had the constitutional power to veto legislation, even as a minority. At that time the Right's opposition to women's suffrage was bound up with their resistance to the growing power and influence of farmers and workers relative to their shrinking base in the remnants of royal and aristocratic privilege and in the most prosperous of the propertied classes. They maintained that political rights should be based on property and property taxation and saw their veto power as a counterweight to the passions and supposedly misguided policies of the popular classes. However, by 1901 the Left party, the political party of the Danish farmers, had a large enough majority to force the conservatives and the king to enact true parliamentary democracy in Denmark.

With the power of the conservative minority clearly weakening, women's rights advocates saw an opportunity to win their political rights and focused their work more intensely on achieving women's suffrage. In 1899 several women's groups developed an umbrella organization, the Danish Women's Union Suffrage Committee (Danske Kvindeforeningers Valgretsudvalg), whose sole purpose was to promote women's suffrage; among the groups joining were both middle-class suffrage organizations and working-class women's trade unions (Dahlgård 1980, 132).

The suffragettes put forth three arguments in favor of women's right to vote (Eckhardt 1995, 41). First, they asserted that women's suffrage was just, because women were half of the adult population in a democratic country. Second, they maintained, women had the right to vote because they had special female competencies, based on their role in the family, which would be of use to the whole society. Their final line of reasoning was that women's interests could best be represented by women, especially in areas where the interests of women and men were in conflict. The main anti-suffrage argument was that giving women the vote would undermine the roles of men and women in society, whose separate and complementary gendered spheres were of benefit, they argued, to the family and the larger society (Eckhardt 1995, 41).

When the men in parliament eventually supported women's suffrage, it came in the form of a plank in the new 1915 constitution. On June 5, when King Christian X signed the new constitution recognizing women's right to vote and hold office, an estimated 20,000 women joined a demonstration to celebrate the historic event, carrying the banner of the Danish Women's Society at the head. The suffragettes who organized the event did so not in order to thank the parliament for rights, which they considered their just due, but rather to demonstrate how much Danish women valued the rights of citizenship (Dahlgård 1980, 139). From that point on, the Danish Women's Society has been associated with the use of a parliamentary strategy to further women's rights and interests, including access to all occupations and equal pay.

### Economic Rights

Women attained certain important economic rights by the end of the nineteenth century, but women's right of access to all occupations and equal pay for equal work were yet to be achieved. In 1882 women in Copenhagen earned 58 percent of unskilled male wages and 45 percent of skilled male wages, and in 1890 about one-third of women over fifteen years of age worked for pay (Dahlgård 1980, 92, 105). These issues took different forms depending upon whether the women were employed in the public or private sector of the economy. The wages and working conditions of public sector employees were directly under governmental authority, whereas the private sector employment issues were considered to be the sole domain of labor contracts between the employees, through their labor union representatives, and the employers, through their trade associations.

Not surprisingly, therefore, women's legal right to equal pay and access to any occupation was attained in the public sector first. The 1919 Public Employees Act required equal pay for equal work for all civil servants, and in 1921 an equal treatment law gave women the right to seek any public sector job, except in the priesthood and the military (Borchorst and Siim 1984, 74). One controversial aspect of the equal pay provision of the 1919 Public Employees Act was a breadwinner allowance. All employees had the right of equal pay for equal work, but those who were breadwinners also received a cost-of-living supplement. Breadwinners were defined as all married men and unmarried women and men who headed households or who had children under eighteen years of age. This particular form of unequal treatment of married women existed until 1958 (Dahlgård 1980, 149).

The breadwinner allowance is another indication of the differences in attitudes toward married and unmarried women. However, new marriage laws enacted in 1922 and 1925 declared that men and women were equally responsible for supporting each other and their children. The Matrimonial Property Act of 1925 legally ended the assumption that the husband was the head of the family and replaced it with the ideal of spousal equality (Pedersen 1971, 333). The Danish Women's Society actively supported these changes, because they believed them to be consistent with their goal of raising the status of married women's roles in the home (Borchorst and Siim 1984, 73).

## 1930–1960: Women's Welfare

Public debate over married women's employment continued throughout the 1930s. By this time, however, both middle- and working-class women's organizations had become convinced of the importance of the right of married women to be employed. Acknowledging the discrimination against married women's employment, the chairwoman of the Danish Women's Society remarked with irony that the government should advertise for female clerks by asking that the job seekers "should be unmarried and live with their parents" (Rosenbeck 1987, 226). Resistance to married women's employment was still found among male workers and in the Social Democratic Party. The Social Democratic Party was in power during the 1930s, representing the interests of working-class families in alliance with the labor movement (Borchorst and Siim 1984, 80). Markussen (1980) states that throughout the 1930s the Social Democratic Party actively promoted a conservative family ideal in which women stayed home to care for their families and men were the breadwinners. The party and the unions saw their role as providing secure employment at a "family wage" for working-class men and supporting working-class families when the economy failed to do so. These ideals led the social democrats to support publicly funded daycare centers for children who needed them because their mothers had to work outside the home, but not for mothers who did not need to work (Borchorst and Siim 1984, 80). Their position did not really change until the economic boom period of the 1960s made married women's labor an economic necessity.

The Social Democratic Party built the social welfare state in Denmark. Its fundamental platform was that, when necessary, government should provide a decent living standard and security. If workers became unemployed or unable to work, government should be there to help maintain families through such programs as unemployment compensation, health care, and disability and old age pensions. The formation of social democratic programs was tied to a shift from the evaluation of individual cases of neediness to the conception of social welfare as an entitlement or right of citizenship (Siim 1990, 85). In establishing social welfare as a universal entitlement, social democrats and their allies in the labor movement set the stage for dramatic changes in the 1960s in governmental programs for employed mothers.

According to Rosenbeck (1987, 226), in the 1920s and 1930s the woman question was replaced with "the mother question." The mother question had several facets: whether women had the right to control their own fertility, whether mothers should be employed, and how to encourage mothers to bear and rear children. Thit Jensen and Jonathan Leunback were the two major figures associated with the "voluntary motherhood" campaign to inform people about contraception and encourage them to use it to limit their family size. The Working Women's Educational Association (Arbejderkvindernes Oplysningsforening) was formed by Marie Nielsen of the General Union of Women Workers to provide working-class women with birth control information (Dahlgård 1980, 178). The Danish Women's Society, however, was reluctant to support birth control for fear that such support would hurt their campaign for equality (Rosenbeck 1987, 218). Women in the Social Democratic Party wanted reproductive rights, including abortion rights, but the party as a whole was more ambivalent. Two governmental commissions, one on pregnancy and the other on population, were established in the 1930s. In 1937, with the recommendation of the pregnancy commission, abortion became legally available to protect the life and health of the mother, and in cases of rape and incest and fetal genetic defects. The population commission report proposed that sexual information, which had also been proposed by the pregnancy commission, be tied to education about family life and children in Mother's Assistance institutions where unwed mothers could go for help.

## WOMEN'S RIGHTS TODAY

### Social Welfare Policies

From the German occupation of Denmark in 1940 through the 1950s was a period of relative inactivity for women's rights advocates and of more conservative ideals of gender and family life. Nevertheless, by the 1960s, when the issue of married women's employment once again came to the fore, public opinion had shifted in favor of married women's right to be employed. In part, this attitudinal change was driven by the labor shortage that resulted from the economic boom period of the 1960s and the need to tap labor reserves. It was also promoted by middle- and working-class women's organizations.

### Daycare

Bringing more young married women into the labor force meant addressing the problem of caring for preschool children while their mothers were at work. The most important solutions were the expansion of government-sponsored childcare and improvement in parental leave policies. These two programs became the backbone of the Danish social welfare system's response to the practical right of married women with children to be employed and to have a family. From then on, the idea that women should have to choose either family or employment was no longer part of the broad cultural consensus. Women did respond to developments in the social welfare state that enhanced their ability to combine paid work and family, and their labor force participation rate rose from 43.5 percent in 1960 to 75.5 percent in 1997 (OECD 1988, 35; Nordic Council of Ministers 1998, 124).

Denmark has encouraged married women with children to enter the labor force and to think that public daycare is good for their children. In 1997, 51.5 percent of children under the age of three were in daycare, as were 84.7 percent of children three to six years of age (Nordic Council of Ministers 1998, 62). Correspondingly, in 1990 almost 80 percent of women with preschoolers were employed. A 1985 survey determined that 60 percent of preschoolers (birth to age 6) were in public daycare, 23 percent in private, informal daycare, and 17 percent in the care of a parent during the day (Leira 1992, 56–57). In 1987, municipalities covered over 80 percent of daycare costs, with parents contributing 18 percent (Leira 1992, 51).

### Paid Parental Leave

Publicly funded childcare is the first leg of a three-legged stool supporting the employment of women with children. Paid parental leave with guaranteed return to an equal employment status is the second. Although maternity leave is a long-established employment right in Denmark, that option has recently been expanded. Maternity leave is now fourteen weeks plus four weeks pregnancy leave that must be taken before the birth. Paternity leave is two weeks. Either parent may take the additional ten weeks of parental leave. Pay varies by labor contracts, locality, and private versus public sector employment, but is guaranteed up to a maximum maintenance allowance. Since 1994, either parent may also take a paid childcare leave of thirteen weeks for each child under age nine, or twenty-six weeks if it is taken while the child is under one year of age. With the agreement of the employer, childcare leave may be extended up to fifty-two weeks (Regeringens Børneudvalg 1996). Unlike public childcare programs, parental leave provisions officially recognize and financially support mothers', and fathers', desire to stay home with their infant children in their first months of life. Like public childcare, this provision too is seen as in the interest of happy, healthy children, more a child's right than a mother's entitlement.

### Equality in the Labor Force

The third leg of support for mothers' employment is women's equality in the labor force. Because working conditions and wages are considered bargaining issues rather than political issues, Denmark was relatively late in adopting equality laws covering employment in the private sector (Nielsen and Thorbeck 1976, 187). In 1976 it adopted the European Economic Community directive on equal pay for equal work. The Equal Treatment Act was passed in 1978 to prohibit sex discrimination in hiring, promotion, firing, and training (Eckhardt 1995, 47). In 1992 women's wages in manufacturing jobs were 85 percent of men's wages (Nordic Council of Ministers 1995, 240) and their salaries 70 percent of men's in full-time white collar jobs (Ligestillingsrådet 1994, 45).

Differences in wages are largely an artifact of a very sex-segregated labor market. Women are overrepresented in lower paying service jobs and in public sector jobs. Over two-thirds of men work in the private sector, while over two-thirds of women work in the public sector (Siim 1993, 38). In the 1980s and 1990s, jobs and wages in the public sector declined relative to those of the private sector, stalling the progress of women as employees of the social welfare state. The sex-segregated labor force is related, in part, to cultural ideals about women being better than men at doing care work, like childcare, nursing, and social work.

### Cultural Views and Policies

In the 1970s a new women's movement arose that challenged this cultural conception of women. The young, middle-class women who joined the movement noted that neither equal rights nor governmental supports for employed mothers had overcome a critical underlying cultural assumption—that women were responsible for personal service and childcare in the family and in the workplace. While recognizing that women in many parts of the world envied the status of Danish women, especially for Denmark's excellent childcare and parental leave policies (Polakow 1997), they pointed out that businesses, unions, political parties, and the European Union were all male-dominated institutions. This fact belied the stated cultural norm of women's equality. One of the means they used to address cultural change was consciousness-raising. Uncovering the ways their own attitudes reinforced women's inequality unleashed their power to improve women's position in the family and in public life (Walter 1990).

The new women's movement proposed strategies that required institutional changes, including sex quotas on election lists, affirmative action in employment practices, a six-hour workday, and changes in cultural practices regarding family relations, sexuality, and reproduction. Some of their calls have been heeded. For example, the Socialist People's Party and the Social Democratic Party have instituted sex quotas on their election lists (Borchorst and Siim 1984, 194). Laws enacted in 1985 and 1990 mandate that women and men be nominated in equal numbers for all public commissions and boards. Another legislative act in 1989 instituted a weak form of affirmative action, which allowed for special dispensations from provisions requiring the equal treatment of men and women when these dispensations are needed to address the problem of the ways that women's practical (as opposed to legal) inequality impedes the achievement of their equality in employment, training, and so on (Ligestillingsrådet 1994, 68–70).

The lesbian and gay movements initiated action that led to statutes passed in 1987 and 1989 prohibiting discrimination on the basis of sexual orientation in access to public services and giving registered same-sex couples all the legal rights of registered opposite-sex couples (Koch-Nielsen 1996, 15). Since 1973 abortions have been legally available upon request during the first twelve weeks of pregnancy and by permission of a committee of experts afterwards. All expenses of abortion, pregnancy, and birth as well as contraceptive information are free through the national health care system.

In this democratic country with comparatively liberal ideals about sexuality and women's equality, laws and programs like these have widespread public acceptance, but such was not always the case. It has taken Danish women's own political activism and the establishment of powerful social democratic institutions promoting egalitarian values and social welfare to make the social and political changes that support women's equality in contemporary Denmark.

## THE FUTURE OF WOMEN'S RIGHTS

Still left to be done is to integrate the sex-segregated labor force and to continue to reduce the hierarchy of power that it reinforces. However, certain structural changes may make this more difficult. For example, more intense competition from an increasingly global economy threatens to lead to cuts in social welfare services and employment for women. The loss of some political sovereignty to the European Union may make national political solutions less effective. Will these potential threats lead to a setback in women's position in society, or have two centuries of struggle over the woman question so changed the culture that there can be no turning back from the level equality and entitlements that women have come to expect and to rely upon? There is some cause for optimism (Walter 1999).

First, Denmark has achieved a level of political representation of women that makes political institutions more receptive to addressing women's interests (Siim 1993). In 1998 elections, women comprised 37 percent of parliament (Ligestillingsrådet Statistik 1998), up from 17 percent in 1971 (Raum 1995, 34). In 1997 women's representation on local councils was 27 percent; their representation on public boards, committees, and councils was at 39 percent in 1996 (Ligestillingsrådet Statistik 1998). Since the 1980s women have been more likely to vote left of men and to voice more support for the public sector (Togeby 1994). One can also point to the recent expansion of parental leave as an indication of continued support for the social welfare state. The core national values of class and gender equality are more grounded in the structures of law, labor, and government. Lastly, advocacy was built into the structures of society with the establishment in 1975 of the Equality Council to help enforce and promote equal opportunities between men and women in society. All these point to continuing public support for women's rights and entitlements. Whether public support will be enough depends upon implementing new strategies to address new problems.

## BIBLIOGRAPHY

Bendix, Eva 1976. Efterskrift (Afterword to) *Tolv Brev*, by Clara Rafael, Lindhardt og Ringhof.

Borchorst, Anette, and Birte Siim. 1984. *Kvinder i velfærdsstaten, mellem moderskab og lønarbejde gennem 100 år*. Serien om Kvindeforskning nr. 16. Aalborg, Denmark: Aalborg Universitetsforlag.

Busch, Birgit. 1965. "Den danske kvindesags historie indtil opnåelsen af den politiske valgret." In *Kvinderne og valgretten*, ed. Ellen Strange Petersen. Copenhagen: J. H. Schultz Forlag, 9–116.

Dahlgård, Inga. 1980. *Women in Denmark, Yesterday and Today*. Copenhagen: Det Danske Selskab.

*Denmark in Figures*. 1995. Copenhagen: Royal Danish Ministry of Foreign Affairs.

Eckhardt, Vera. 1995. "Demokrati og indflydelse-et kvinderetsligt perspektiv." In *Kvinder, demokrati og indflydelse*, SAMKVIND, Skriftserie 19: 40–52.

Hernes, Helga Maria. 1988. "The Welfare State Citizenship of Scandinavian Women." In *The Political Interests of Gender*, ed. Kathleen Jones and Anna Jónasdóttir. London: Sage, 187–213.

Holst, Hanne-Vibeke, ed. 1995. *Women in Denmark*. Copenhagen: Department of Information of the Royal Danish Ministry of Foreign Affairs in connection with the United Nations Fourth World Conference on Women.

Koch-Nielsen, Inger. 1996. *Family Obligations in Denmark*. Copenhagen: Danish National Institute of Social Research.

Leira, Arnlaug. 1992. *Welfare States and Working Mothers*. Cambridge: Cambridge University Press.

Ligestillingsrådet. 1994. *Årsberetning* (Annual Report). Copenhagen: Ligestillingsrådet.

Ligestillingsrådet Statistik. 1998. Tables 10.5 and 10.10 at www.lige.dk/publikati/ statistik/10–5.htm and /10–10.htm, November 16, 1998.

———. 1999. Table 2.1 at www.lige.dk/publikati/statistik/statistik_main/key_ statistics.htm, October 10, 1999.

Markussen, Randi. 1980. "Socialdemokratiets kvindeopfattelse og politik fra 1960–1973." *Den jyske historiker* 18: 13–168.

Nielsen, Ruth, and Jytte Thorbeck. 1976. *Ligestillingslovgivning*. Copenhagen: Juristforbundets Forlag.

Nordic Council of Ministers. 1995, 1998. *Nordic Statistical Yearbook*. Copenhagen: Nordic Council of Ministers.

OECD (Organization of Economic Co-operation and Development). 1988. *Economic Outlook: Historical Statistics 1960–85*. Paris: OECD.

Olsen, Anne. 1984. "Kvindeligt Arbejderforbund-mellem kvindekrav og partikrav." In *Kvindfolk, en danmarks historie fra 1600 til 1980* (Womenfolk, A Danish History from 1600 to 1980), ed. Anne Margrete Berg, Lis Frost, and Anne Olsen. Copenhagen: Gyldendal, 227–42.

Ottensten, Lizette. 1995. "Back to the Fireplace." In *Women in Denmark*, ed. Hanne-Vibeke Holst. Copenhagen: Department of Information of the Royal Danish Ministry of Foreign Affairs in connection with the United Nations Fourth World Conference on Women, 8–9.

Pedersen, Inger Margrete. 1971. "Recent Trends in Danish Family Law." *International and Comparative Law Quarterly* 20: 332–41.

Polakow, Valerie. 1997. "Family Policy, Welfare, and Single Motherhood in the United States and Denmark: A Cross-National Analysis of Discourse and Practice." *Early Education and Development* 8, no. 3: 245–64.

Rafael, Clara. 1976. *Tolv Brev*. Lindhardt og Ringhof.

Raum, Nina Cecilie. 1995. "The Political Representation of Women: A Bird's Eye View." In *Women in Nordic Politics: Closing the Gap*, ed. Lauri Karvonen and Per Selle. Aldershot, England: Dartmouth, 25–35.

Ravn, Anna-Birte. 1995a. " 'Lagging Far Behind All Civilized Nations': The Debate over Protective Labor Legislation for Women in Denmark, 1899–1913." In *Protecting Women: Labor Legislation in Europe, the United States, and Australia, 1880–1920*, ed. Ulla Wikander, Alice Kessler-Harris, and Jane Lewis. Urbana: University of Illinois Press, 210–34.

———. 1995b. "Equality Versus Difference and Gender Versus Class in Danish Women's History." *NORA, Nordic Journal of Women's Studies* 3, no. 1: 45–54.

Regeringens Børneudvalg. 1996. *Tid til børn—tid til arbejde: En pjece om muligheder for bedre sammenhæng mellem arbejdsliv og familieliv* (Time for Children—Time for Work: A Piece about the Possibilities for Better Relations Between Work Life and Family Life). Copenhagen: Regeringens Udvalg.

Rosenbeck, Bente. 1987. *Kvindekøn, Den moderne kvindeligheds historie 1880–1980* (The Female Sex: The Modern History of Femininity, 1880–1980). Copenhagen: Gyldendal.

Siim, Birte. 1990. "Women and the Welfare State: Between Private and Public Dependence. A Comparative Approach to Care Work in Denmark and Britain." In *Gender and Caring: Work and Welfare in Britain and Scandinavia*, ed. Clare Ungerson. New York: Harvester Wheatsheaf, 80–109.

———. 1993. "The Gendered Scandinavian Welfare States: The Interplay Between Women's Roles as Mothers, Workers and Citizens in Denmark." In *Women and Social Policies in Europe: Work, Family and the State*, ed. Jane Lewis. Aldershot, England: Edward Elgar, 25–48.

Togeby, Lise. 1994. "Political Implications of Increasing Numbers of Women in the Labor Force." *Comparative Political Studies* 27, no. 2: 211–40.

Walter, Lynn. 1990. "The Embodiment of Ugliness and the Logic of Love: The Danish Redstocking Movement." *Feminist Review* 36 (Autumn): 103–26.

———. 1999. "The Future of Social Welfare in Denmark." In *Speaking Out: Women, Poverty, and Public Policy*, ed. Anne Statham and Katherine A. Rhoades. Madison: University of Wisconsin, System Women's Studies Consortium, 119–28.

# 6

# EGYPT

## Multiple Perspectives on Women's Rights

*Bahira Sherif*

## INTRODUCTION

### Profile of Egypt

Egypt's Nile River and its fertile valley, where most Egyptians live, stretches 550 miles from the eastern Mediterranean Sea south into the Sudan. Three percent of the land is arable, and 2 percent is devoted to permanent crops. Two percent of the land is irrigated. Forty-five percent of Egypt's 66,050,004 people (1999 estimate) live in cities, many in poverty and slums. Ethnically, 99 percent of Egyptians are of Eastern Hamitic stock or Bedouin (Berber). Ninety-four percent of Egyptians are Muslim, mostly Sunni, with the remaining 6 percent being Coptic Christian and other religions. Arabic is the official language, although French and English are widely understood by the educated classes. Five years of education are compulsory between ages six and thirteen. Literacy was estimated at 50 percent in 1995. Egypt is a republic with a legal system based on English common law, Islamic law, and Napoleonic codes.

### A Case Study

Leila, a 35-year-old veiled Muslim woman, is married and has two daughters, aged twelve and ten. She lives in a suburb of Cairo and works at a government job in the center of the city. Leila's day begins at 5:30 when she takes the girls to her mother's, who then takes them to school, while she starts her one-and-a-half-hour commute to work. Home again by 4:30, Leila picks up her daughters and shops at the local vegetable market, the butcher's, and the grocer's for ingredients for dinner. Her husband Hussein, a clerk for a travel agency, comes home; and, while Leila prepares dinner, he helps their daughters with their homework. After dinner, Hussein pays his daily visit to his mother as Leila finishes the household chores and puts the children to bed. Her day ends around 11 P.M.

Although both Hussein and Leila are working, they are having a very hard time making ends meet. Even so, Hussein is extremely displeased that his wife is working outside of the home, because he feels that their home does not look as good as his maternal home and that his friends disrespect him for not being the sole provider. Thus, he is considering a job in the United Emirates where he could earn more money. Meanwhile, Leila and Hussein constantly argue about the distribution of household duties and the extent of her financial contributions to the household.

## OVERVIEW OF WOMEN'S RIGHTS ISSUES

Beginning in the late nineteenth century, Egyptian male reformers and nationalist modernizers took up the question of women's status and role in society. A struggle began between those who promoted women's emancipation because they perceived it to be crucial to the development of the society and the nation, and those who claimed that it was an alien Western concept, detrimental to the health of the society. This debate continues in the current struggle between Islamist and modernist factions, with the role of women remaining central to the discussion.

Muslim Egyptian women's rights must be assessed in the context of contemporary postcolonial political, economic, and ideological struggles. These rights must also be examined from the perspectives of the women themselves, who locate themselves, their situations, and their aspirations quite differently from what Western feminists or Western scholarship often assume. Further, it must be noted that Egyptian Muslim women do not constitute a homogeneous category. Great inequalities persist among Egyptian women, based on class affiliation and rural-urban differences.

## HISTORY OF WOMEN'S RIGHTS

Beginning in the late nineteenth and early twentieth centuries, the modernist school in Egypt sought to meet the challenges of the West and modernization by building a new civilization. This was to be accomplished by abandoning adherence to the traditional formulations of the established schools of law, in favor of a new interpretation of the Koran and the Shari'a (Islamic law), based on the principles of Islam. The movement is associated with Shaykh Muhammad 'Abduh (1849–1905), who advocated educational and legal improvements, the emancipation of women, economic development, and governmental reorganization in order to allow Egypt to face the technological and economic changes taking place in the Western world (Botman 1999, 30).

The most prominent proponent of women's emancipation was his associate, Qasim Amin (1863–1908), whose book, *Tahrir al-mar'a* (The Liberation of Women; 1899), brought the issue of the status of women to the forefront and provoked Egypt's first major journalistic debate on the issue of women. Amin advocated major reforms in education and divorce procedures for women, as well as arguing against their veiling and seclusion. He predicated these appeals on the idea that women were at the heart of the progress or backwardness of a nation, and that change was part of the natural order in life. Amin declared that "the family is the foundation of the nation. And since woman is the foundation of the family, her progress or backwardness in intellectual level is the first influence on the progress or backwardness of the nation" (1976, 14). Furthermore, he pointed out that if women did not work to meet society's needs but were restricted to reproductive roles, they became a burden on the nation and a cause of its weakness. Amin suggested that if women were educated and allowed to function in public life, they would develop their minds and be able to contribute to the progress of the nation.

Although Amin is credited with setting the stage for the public reforms and debates concerning women's issues, female feminist discourses in Egypt began much earlier than previously thought (Baron 1994, 6) and preceded the male discourse. However, women's debates in the harems and their writings were hidden from widespread view, while Amin's works were known publicly (Badran and Cooke 1990, xxvi). Thus, his writings are considered the primary revolutionary discourses on women, even though they were not the first.

Egyptian men's pro-feminist stand arose out of contact with European society, where it was apparent that women were usually visible. In contrast, Egyptian women's feminism originated as an upper-class phenomenon between the 1860s and the early 1920s and grew out of women's own learning and observations (Badran and Cooke 1990, xxvi). For example, by the 1890s Eugenie Le Brun Rushdi, a Frenchwoman who had married an upper-class Egyptian and converted to Islam, held a salon that served as a place for upper-class women to meet, debate, and analyze the condition of women in the society. Salons such as these provided a forum for other collective intellectual activities, including women's lectures and political discussions. Evidence of this discourse is found primarily in journals circulated in the harems of that time. Women began to realize that while Islam guaranteed females certain rights, the customs and traditions imposed on them had deprived them of those rights. They discovered that many so-called Islamic practices such as veiling, segregation, and seclusion were not ordained by Islam, as they had been led to believe.

The memoirs of Huda Sha'rawi, one of the most pivotal women of that period, reveal the existence of women's debates on Islam and veiling in a Cairo harem salon of the 1890s (Baron 1994, 5). By 1914 Huda Sha'rawi, with the support of the princesses of the Egyptian royal family, had initiated the Intellectual Association of Egyptian Women. She and other early Egyptian feminists advocated that through the correct understanding and practice of Islam, women could regain basic rights from which they, their families, and the larger society would benefit. This theme would recur in the contemporary situation, particularly with the growing Islamist influence.

While the first feminists grounded their growing consciousness in Islam, by 1919 women were actively involved in the nationalist debate against the British. Led by Huda Sha'rawi, women's public participation in a nationalist march is considered the turning point that brought the Egyptian feminist movement out in the open (Ahmed 1982, 160). Although the issues at stake were nationalist, and in no way feminist, women's very participation empowered them to take a more public stance on issues relating to the condition of women.

In 1923 Huda Sha'rawi formed the Egyptian Feminist Union (EFU). The union's agenda centered on women's political rights, such as voting and qualifying for parliamentary representation, but there were social aspects as well. In 1924 the union and the Women's Wafd Committee presented the Egyptian Parliament with a set of demands for increased educational opportunities for women and girls, voting rights, parliamentary representation, the elimination of polygamy, and restrictions on divorce. Further, in 1924, after attending the International Conference on Women in Rome, Huda Sha'rawi cast off her veil and thus encouraged other middle- and upper-class women to follow her lead. This unveiling represented a rejection of a whole way of life, and the veil became a symbol of exclusion and backwardness.

The Egyptian Feminist Union remained the primary vehicle for women's activities throughout the 1920s and 1930s. At its pinnacle, membership reached 250 women. Members set up schools and health clinics, hosted a Conference for the Defense of Palestine in 1938 in order to show solidarity with Palestinian women, and held the first Pan-Arab Feminist Conference in 1944, which resulted in the establishment of the Arab Feminist Union. By the early 1940s the EFU began to break into factions. While the original founders of the group tended to be upper-class, secular women who spoke French and looked toward the West for inspiration, members who joined later were primarily middle-class women who spoke Arabic and were rooted in local culture (Botman 1999, 41). World War II altered social and political conditions in Egypt, spawning a nationalist resurgence and the emergence of other secular and religiously based women's groups.

After the 1952 Revolution, which overthrew the monarchy, the Egyptian state developed a comprehensive goal to promote social justice and self-reliance for all of its citizens, regardless of gender, ethnic origin, or religion (el-Baz 1997, 148). Women did gain some economic, social, and cultural strength through their increased participation in education and employment. However, the revolutionary government's reluctance to address family law restrained women's equal participation in the public sphere.

## WOMEN'S RIGHTS TODAY

### Women's Legal Rights

A primary focus for all groups concerned with women's rights—whether secular, Muslim, or Islamist—is the Personal Status Law (PSL) or family law, which is derived from the Shari'a. All other Egyptian laws are modeled after French civil law. Reforming the codified family law has become a political issue in the last two decades in all countries, including Egypt, which have retained this part of the Shari'a (Najmabadi 1991; Botman 1999). The provisions of the Qur'an (Koran) are most explicit in the area of family matters and are thus more closely intertwined with the sacred in the law (Anderson 1968, 221). Furthermore, for many, the secularization of the law in other areas has reinforced the need to preserve what religious tone remains. Attempts to reform the PSL are seen as a direct assault on Islam and on Islamic groups.

The Egyptian Personal Status Law regulates, at least in theory, the interactions between men and women in the family. It specifies all laws relating to marriage, divorce, child custody, guardianship, and inheritance, and defines women as legal subordinates to men. Egypt follows the Hanafi school of Shari'a law according to which the husband is in charge of supporting his wife and children financially. In return, he is authorized to restrict his wife's movements, confine her activities, and make decisions on her behalf. For her part, the wife must care for her spouse and children and must obey her husband (Botman 1999, 48). The PSL reflects and defines the patriarchal structure of the society, institutionalizes inequality in the family, and is used by men to validate their domination over women.

The Personal Status Law was proclaimed as law in 1920. It was amended in 1925 and remained constant until 1979, when, amid great controversy, it was amended again, by including the right of the wife to keep the family home after divorce and the right of the first wife to be informed in case of the husband's marriage to another, as well as her right to demand a divorce on that basis. These amendments to the law were popularly termed "Jihan's Law," after the wife of then President Anwar Sadat, and were eventually partially abrogated on procedural grounds in 1985. However, in June of that year, a similar law (Law No. 100) amending the 1925 and 1929 laws was enacted and is now the law in place (Karam 1998, 145).

The new law stipulates that in the case of a polygynous union the first wife retains the right to seek divorce, but it is no longer her automatic right. She must prove that her husband's second marriage is detrimental to her either materially or mentally. Further, the first wife now only has the right to sue for divorce in the first year of the new polygynous marriage. (It should be noted that it is socially unacceptable among the middle and upper classes for men to engage in polygynous unions and, in fact, is not seen as an option. The revisions in the law are important on a symbolic level in terms of giving men certain legal rights over women in the context of the family.) The new provision to the law stipulates that in cases of divorce, after the wife's period of child custody ends, the husband is entitled to the house, at which time she is required to leave. The conditions of alimony were also altered, with the husband being responsible for only one year of support. Further, the husband can now withhold alimony if his wife disobeys him, leaves the house without his consent, or works against his will, or if her work is perceived as jeopardizing family life. The amount of alimony a wife receives is based on the judge's assessment of the man's financial situation. Judges have also been granted the power to enforce new child custody stipulations that return boys to their fathers when they reached the age of ten and girls when they turn twelve (Botman 1999, 86)

The decision to grant a divorce always rests with a male judge, since there is a ban on promoting women to the position of judge. Culturally, it is believed that women should not hold positions which require "male" characteristics such as rationality and lack of emotion. While there have been major attempts by women's groups to provide access for women to judiciary posts, the current political climate advocates a much more domestic role for women, making such a shift unlikely in the near future.

A major debate between secular and Muslim-oriented women's groups concerns the vast gap between laws protecting the rights of women and their actual implementation. Many women, especially those from less privileged backgrounds, lack awareness of their legal rights. Hence, in the last several years concerted efforts have been made to teach women about their legal rights. Such programs aim at assisting women in light of cultural values and belief systems that legitimize men's domination over women's lives and that may prevent women from feeling justified in seeking these rights.

While not under the auspices of the PSL, the nationality law is also problematic because it denies Egyptian women married to foreigners the right to pass their nationalities on to their children while granting this right to men. Further, Egyptian married women are granted passports only through the written approval of their husbands or male guardians. Travel abroad thus requires a husband's consent. A husband can also forbid his wife to work outside of the home if he can prove that her work interferes with her household duties. While legally women can stipulate clauses in their marriage contracts that would amend these rights, few women choose this option because of the cultural stigma attached to such an action.

Apart from the Personal Status Law, which is based on a very conservative interpretation of Islamic law, the Egyptian legal system has several favorable aspects for women. In 1981 Egypt became the first Arab nation to ratify the Convention on the Elimination of All Forms of Discrimination Against Women. At least in theory, Egyptian law grants women equal access to employment and training opportunities. Women, simultaneously, have the right to paid maternity leave and unpaid childcare leave. Companies employing more than 100 female workers must provide nursery facilities. Women are also protected against working in physically or morally hazardous professions, but this form of protection also serves to deny them access to certain professions, such as judicial posts (el-Baz 1997, 156).

Additionally, within the family sphere, the Shari'a protects women's material possessions. All of a woman's possessions, including her jewelry, property, and earnings are legally her own. Should a wife choose to share her possessions with her husband, it is her choice but not her obligation to do so. While in practice it is often difficult to maintain separate material spheres in a marriage, this provision in the law does provide women with a certain amount of financial independence. In contrast, men must by law provide materially for their families and any unmarried females in their extended circles. In today's economic climate, where households are tied into a global economy that increasingly necessitates dual income earners, the strict gender hierarchy in families advocated by the PSL is under constant negotiation.

## Economic Development and the Role of Women

In 1974 the Sadat regime adopted the "Open Door Policy" that encouraged the private sector to increase the productive capacity of the economy. As the government withdrew its commitment to guarantee employment to all college graduates, unemployment increased. The expectation that women would enter the labor force thus became a liability to the state rather than an asset. Justifying ideologies based on sexual division of labor began to appear, supported by the newly emerging Islamic fundamentalist groups, advocating that women's place was in the home (el-Baz 1997, 149). Article Eleven of the 1971 Constitution, which committed the state to help reconcile women's family obligations and their equality to men in the public sphere, was amended with the addition of the phrase "provided that this did not infringe on the rules of the Islamic Shari'a." The new Constitution diverged from the secular language of the 1960s and created opportunities for Islamic groups to oppose women's rights on the grounds that they were in opposition to Islamic principles (Hatem 1992, 241).

Throughout the 1980s, the Open Door Policy became increasingly institutionalized. While this policy has been relatively successful on a macro level, it has had negative consequences for the more vulnerable sectors of society, namely, the poor, and specifically poor women and their children (el-Baz 1997, 149). As key resources such as health care and education have become scarcer, low-income women and children are the least likely to have access to them. Also affected by the economic restructuring are formerly middle-class civil servants and unemployed college graduates. Thus, any discussion of women's rights must make clear that women's priorities vary by class. Poor women must be included in the women's rights dialogue in order to link all women in the society to the structures of opportunity.

## Employment and Women

Although Egyptian women have officially had the right to work outside of the home for the last fifty years, their actual contributions often go un-recognized and are also increasingly the subject of scathing criticism. Al-though many accounts of women's economic activities understate their actual contributions, a more accurate picture of women's employment can be found in the Labour Force Sample Survey (LFSS) of 1988 (el-Baz 1997, 152). According to this survey, women's labor force participation is at 35.4 percent, with rural and urban rates at 32.5 percent and 18.8 percent, re-spectively. Women's economic participation in the government is at 29.5 percent, in other parts of the public sector at 13.1 percent, and in the private sector at 39.3 percent. Women's participation in agriculture is greater than men's, estimated at 53 percent (CAPMAS 1990, cited in el-Baz 1997, 152). Furthermore, women also carry out most household chores, especially in rural areas, and are estimated to work up to sixteen to nineteen hours per day. Despite these figures, women are not recognized as vital participants in the labor force; therefore, they have limited access to government-sponsored training and educational opportunities.

Given the prevalent ideology of men as breadwinners, unemployment is perceived as a male problem, even though it is estimated at 10 percent for men and 25 percent for women. Women are thus encouraged to retire early, and current legislation offers women half-time employment for half salary. Additionally, recruitment efforts in the private sector focus on men, with women often being perceived as an economic liability due to maternity leave. In the period from 1976 to 1986, the proportion of women employed in the private sector sank from 47 percent to 30 percent. By 1993, 15 to 20 percent of all Egyptian households were primarily dependent on women's incomes (el-Baz 1997, 153). Nonetheless, increasingly conservative social attitudes advocate that women's "natural" role is in the home with their children. This conflict between the public discourse about women and the social and economic realities of their lives is reflected in the lack of social services and public policies for women.

## The Educational System and Women's Participation

Although illiteracy has been declining over the last three decades, according to the 1986 census, 62 percent of adult women were illiterate, compared to 38 percent of men; and 76 percent of rural women were illiterate, compared to 45 percent of urban women. Poor and rural parents tend to withdraw their daughters from school as soon as they are old enough to earn extra money or to work around the house. It is estimated that as of 1990, twice as many girls drop out of school as boys (el-Nashif 1994, 1, 3). Cultural norms, particularly among the poor and in rural areas, favor continuing the education of boys over that of girls in times of economic stress. Increases in the cost of education also influence poor parents' decisions concerning schooling for their children, especially for girls. The dominant cultural belief among the poor and village dwellers still is that girls marry and bear children, and therefore do not need the same level of education as boys. In contemporary Egypt, this view does not hold true among the middle and upper classes, where education for young women is seen as a necessity both for self-fulfillment and as future career preparation. These days many middle-class Egyptians also believe that an educated young woman has better marriage chances since her future husband will be interested in the earning potential of his future wife.

## Health Issues and Gender Inequalities

High illiteracy rates, heavy workloads, multiple pregnancies, limited economic resources, and lack of access to good health care exacerbate the health problems of women, especially poor and rural women. Gender-based health risks for girls begin at birth. Because cultural norms emphasize the importance of sons, the birth of a daughter is often a disappointment to parents of all classes. Among the lower and rural classes in particular, girls are often nursed for shorter periods of time, fed inadequately, and face a higher risk of death (UNICEF 1990, 17). Mortality rates for children under one year of age are 28 per 1,000 for girls and 24 per 1,000 for boys ("Beijing National Report" 1995, 39).

The maternal mortality rate is 320 per 100,000. Early marriage and childbearing are risks to women's health as well as to their chances for education and employment. The proportion of adolescent marriages is reported at 15.3 percent, but is potentially much higher given the practice of doctors issuing age assessment certificates to enable families to marry off younger girls (el-Baz 1997, 154).

### Family Planning

Even though Egypt has the longest history of contraceptive initiatives in the Middle East, the quality of family planning services is often poor, and contraceptives are not readily available. Poor and rural women are more reluctant to use artificial birth control methods, which are rumored to be detrimental to women's health. Many unwanted pregnancies end in self-induced abortions, because abortion is prohibited in Egypt except in cases where pregnancy threatens the life of the mother.

Infertility, even though it is barely acknowledged or studied, is also an important problem. In a society where it is imperative for women of all classes to bear children and thus attain social status through motherhood, the inability to bear children leads to serious social consequences. Alternatives to motherhood and domesticity are largely absent, and adoption is not allowed under Islamic law. Thus, for all women biological parenthood is imperative, especially since under Islamic law a man has the right to replace an infertile wife through divorce or a polygynous marriage. While polygyny is not an option that is exercised by upper- and middle-class men, the threat of divorce hovers over childless marriages. Among all classes and educational levels women are typically blamed for reproductive failings, and they also bear the burden of overcoming this condition through a therapeutic quest that is often traumatic and unfruitful (Inhorn 1994, 5). Furthermore, infertile women face the tyranny of social judgment, for they are cast as being less than other women, as depriving their husbands and husbands' families of offspring, and as endangering other people's children through their supposedly uncontrollable envy.

### Female Circumcision

In the West, the most controversial and publicized issue concerning women's health in the Islamic world and Africa is the practice of female circumcision. This practice is extremely widespread in Egypt, especially among the poorer classes and in rural areas. It is considered imperative for girls to be circumcised since cultural norms stigmatize uncircumcised girls and prevent them from marrying. Estimates are that 50 to 80 percent of all Egyptian women are circumcised, but precise figures are not known. A recent study by researchers from Ayn Shams University found that 98 percent of all girls in the Egyptian countryside and poor girls in Cairo had been circumcised (both Muslims and Coptic Christians), while the estimate for upper-class girls in Cairo was approximately 30 percent (Botman 1999, 106).

While female circumcision is often presented as a requirement of Islam, this is a fallacy. To the great embarrassment of the Egyptian government, the issue was raised at the 1994 International Conference on Population and Development in Cairo. Subsequently, a decree was issued to limit the practice to hospitals. The government refrained from completely outlawing the practice due to pressure by Islamic groups who deem female circumcision to be necessary based on a saying of the Prophet Muhammad. Critics, however, point out that the Prophet's own daughters were not circumcised and that circumcision is not practiced in Saudi Arabia, the most conservative Islamic country in the Middle East. In 1997, under pressure from Islamic fundamentalist groups, the government lifted the ban on female circumcision. Despite international efforts to publicize the physical and psychological dangers of circumcision, the practice is gaining legitimacy as Islamists revive the belief that it is religiously mandated. The controversy around female circumcision is indicative of the tension between ingrained cultural values with respect to gender, Islamists' quests for "authenticity," and Western perspectives that advocate universal women's rights to control their bodies.

## THE FUTURE OF WOMEN'S RIGHTS

### The Islamist Movement and Feminism

Experts on Egyptian feminism are often misled by the rhetoric of the new Islamic movement. In reality, the Islamist call for women to retreat from the work force and back into an idealized patriarchal household has been neither totally male inspired nor massively obeyed. Moreover, Islamist messages are part of a larger agenda fueled by severe economic issues and a search for a non-Western identity in a postcolonial context. While the Islamist groups constitute a powerful constituency, there is growing international pressure on the Egyptian government to adhere to United Nations conventions concerning women's rights. Economic dependence on United States Agency for International Development (USAID) and other international donor organizations such as the International Monetary Fund and the World Bank forces the current regime to present itself as complying with the values and ethos of Western-inspired human and women's rights (al-Ali 1997, 181). This has set the stage, in part, for the recent flurry of grassroots pro-feminist activism around such issues as women's political participation, women's equality in the workplace, women's reproductive rights, and violence against women. Issue-oriented networks such as the Women's Media Watch, the Female Genital Mutilation (FGM) Taskforce, and a network of organizations working on a project concerning women and violence have gained momentum over the last several years (al-Ali 1997, 181).

A growing feature of the new Islamic movements, as well as more secular groups, is women's own explorations of their rights under Muslim family law. Islamist women activists are gaining a voice within mainstream Islamist discourse by challenging their male counterparts for misinterpreting Islam. They emphasize Islam's compatibility with UN-stipulated standards of

women's rights and point to continuing pre-Islamic traditions that undermine women's position in society. These movements are increasingly able
to reach various segments of society and to advocate that women take an
active role in understanding the original tenets of Islam, which accord both
women and men rights and obligations in the familial sphere.

## Women as Symbols

In the contemporary context of postcolonial Egypt, women are symbols
of the cultural integrity of dominant ideological beliefs. Culturally, women
of all classes are perceived of as wives and mothers. To earn status women
must marry and reproduce. Legally, their husbands control their ability to
work or travel and hold unilateral rights of divorce. Children belong to the
husband's family and may be lost to the mother in the case of divorce.
Family honor and reputation or, conversely, shame, rest mainly on the public behavior of women, thereby reinforcing a high degree of sex segregation
in the society. Nonetheless, in contemporary Egypt these ideals are often at
odds both with women's actual experiences and with their own aspirations
and desires. Through increased access to education, more women are able
to earn their own income, and thus to wield more formalized power in their
families. Meanwhile, by retaining their traditional informal access to power
through strong same-sex associations, women are increasingly becoming
aware of their legal rights. Thus, their position is strengthening within families, particularly vis-à-vis their husbands.

Women manipulate cultural symbols as forms of resistance to dominant
male-privileged discourses. One example can be found in the highly politicized issue of the urban, educated woman's return to veiling in contemporary Cairo. The *hijab*, the wearing of a head veil and loose-fitting
clothing, has come to signify the sum total of traditional institutions governing women's role in an "orderly" Islamic society. The *hijab* refers primarily to a large piece of cloth that is wrapped to cover the hair. It is worn
differently by different classes of women. Poor and middle-class women tend
to wear a large, often white or beige, polyester cloth that resembles a nun's
wimple. Upper-middle class and wealthy women are likely to wear colorful
silk scarves around their hair wrapped in various fashionable styles with
knots, etc. These scarves are always color-coordinated with the women's
clothes. In most cases the face is completely visible. Only women who associated with Islamist movements and who are extremely conservative also
cover their faces with a black veil. They are also the ones who will wear
black shoes, socks, and gloves. In Egypt, this tends to be a rare sight. In
the ideological struggles surrounding the definition of Islam's nature and
role in the modern world, the *hijab* has acquired the status of a "cultural
symbol." This accounts, in part, for the willingness of some women to adopt

these new forms of Islamic dress, thereby literally cloaking themselves in orthodoxy and modernity.

For married working women, in particular, the new veiling conveys a message to both their husbands and the larger society. It conveys the social message that a woman can hold down a job without abandoning her roles of wife and mother. Veiling becomes a means for women to assert some control over the ambiguous moral situation created by new economic and social pressures. The veil has become an advertisement for religiosity, modesty, and good reputation. Veiling makes it possible for women to negotiate the desired combination of education and income, both within their marriages and in the outer world, without the connotation of immorality which working outside of the home carries. For women, both within their families and in the wider community, wearing the veil makes a statement about what it is to be a "real Muslim woman."

## Conclusions

A feminism that emphasizes the equality of the sexes, equality of opportunity, and the irrelevance of sex in the definition of social roles can only be promoted in a climate where economic and social differences are taken into account. Middle- and upper-class women's power is enhanced through social policies, same-sex organizations, and opportunities for employment outside the home. For poor and rural women, survival is the priority. In order to truly promote women's rights in Egypt, social policies and religious forces must take into account these inequalities in access to knowledge, enforcement of their rights, and economic privileges.

Further, Western women's rights advocates must recognize that the popular Islamic fundamentalist discourse on women derives its legitimacy as much from Islam as from an anti-imperialist ideology that portrays the West as a decadent culture. Such gendered discourses as these must be placed within their social and historical contexts in order to understand women's movements and attitudes toward them.

## BIBLIOGRAPHY

Abdel Kader, S. 1992. *The Situation Analysis of Women in Egypt*. Cairo: Central Agency for Population, Mobilization and Statistics (CAPMAS) and UNICEF.
Ahmed, Leila. 1982. "Feminism and Feminist Movements in the Middle East, a Preliminary Exploration: Turkey, Egypt, Algeria, People's Democratic Republic of Yemen." *Women's Studies International Forum* 5, no. 2: 153–68.
al-Ali, Nadje. 1997. "Feminism and Contemporary Debates in Egypt." In *Organizing Women: Formal and Informal Women's Groups in the Middle East*, ed. Dawn Cahtty and Annika Rabo. Oxford: Berg.

Amin, Qasim. 1976. *Tahrir al-mar'a* (The Liberation of Women). Reprinted in Muhammad 'Imara, *Qasim Amin: Al-lla'mal al-kamila*, vol. 2. Beirut.

Anderson, J.N.D. 1968. "The Eclipse of the Patriarchal Family in Contemporary Islamic Law." In *Family Law in Asia and Africa*, ed. J.N.D. Anderson. London: George Allen and Unwin, 221–34.

Badran, Margot. 1991. "Competing Agenda: Feminists, Islam, and the State in Nineteenth and Twentieth Century Egypt." In *Women, Islam and the State*, ed. Deniz Kandiyoti. Philadelphia: Temple University Press, 201–36.

Badran, Margot, and Miriam Cooke. 1990. Introduction to *Opening the Gates: A Century of Arab Feminist Writing*, ed. Margot Badran and Miriam Cooke. Bloomington: Indiana University Press, xiv–xxxvi.

Baron, Beth. 1994. *The Women's Awakening: Culture, Society and the Press*. New Haven: Yale University Press.

el-Baz, Shahida. 1997. "The Impact of Social and Economic Factors on Women's Group Formation in Egypt." In *Organizing Women: Formal and Informal Women's Groups in the Middle East*, ed. Dawn Cahtty and Annika Rabo. Oxford: Berg.

"Beijing National Report." 1995. Cairo: National Women's Committee, National Council for Childhood and Motherhood.

Botman, Selma. 1999. *Engendering Citizenship in Egypt*. New York: Columbia University Press.

CAPMAS. 1986. "National Census." Cairo.

———. 1990. "Labour Force Sample Survey (LFSS)." Cairo.

CAPMAS and UNICEF. 1991. "Women's Participation in the Labour Force." Cairo.

Hatem, M. 1992. "Economic and Political Liberalization in Egypt and the Demise of State Feminism." *International Journal of Middle East Studies* 24: 241.

Inhorn, Marcia. 1994. *Quest for Conception: Gender, Infertility and Egyptian Medical Tradition*. Philadelphia: University of Pennsylvania Press.

Karam, Azza. 1998. *Women, Islamisms and the State: Contemporary Feminism in Egypt*. New York: St. Martin's Press.

Macleod, Arlene Elowe. 1991. *Accommodating Protest: Working Women and the New Veiling in Cairo*. New Haven: Yale University Press.

Najmabadi, A. 1991. "Hazards of Modernity and Morality: Women, State and Ideology in Contemporary Iran." In *Women, Islam and the State*, ed. Deniz Kandiyoti. London: Macmillan.

el-Nashif, H. 1994. *Basic Education and Female Literacy in Egypt*. Cairo: Third World Forum, Middle East Office.

Talhami, Ghada. 1996. *The Mobilization of Muslim Women in Egypt*. Gainesville: University of Florida Press.

UNICEF. 1990. *Sex Differences in Child Survival and Development*. Evaluation Series No. 6. Aman: Regional Office for the Middle East and North Africa.

———. 1993. *Report on the State of Women and Children in Egypt*. Cairo.

Zuhur, Sherifa. 1992. *Revealing Reveiling: Islamist Gender Ideology in Contemporary Egypt*. Albany: State University of New York Press.

# 7

# THE EUROPEAN UNION

## *Madeleine Shea*

## INTRODUCTION

This analysis of women's rights development in the European Union (EU) focuses on three EU policies that influence the ability of women to balance their roles as workers and as mothers of young children: maternity leave, parental leave, and childcare. These three policies were enacted in the EU in the early to mid-1990s. They are part of a package of EU women's rights policies that includes increasing equality in social security programs, increasing the percentage of women in government leadership roles, banning sexual discrimination in the workplace, and promoting disadvantaged women's entry into the workplace. In order to be productive employees and healthy, caring mothers of preschoolers, women need a different set of workplace supports than other workers. Most women experience pregnancy and the need to care for young dependents. Without public support, in the form of leave time, wage remuneration, and high quality childcare services, they may be forced to leave rewarding jobs and/or to place their own health and that of their young dependents at risk. Both outcomes have negative consequences for women, children, families, and society (Gornick, Meyers, and Ross 1998).

### Profile of the European Union

The European Union is a supranational governing body in Europe. This means that EU laws take precedence over laws made by the governments of its member countries. Some compare the EU to a federal government. It has a democratically elected parliament. It has a unique form of presidency; each member nation serves a six-month term in the EU presidency on a rotating basis. It has a court system, and it has its own bureaucracy. The EU has less power than the federal government of the United States partially because it has more limited power to tax and spend. However, it has more power than other intergovernmental organizations like the United Nations or the Council of Europe.

In the 1950s leaders in France and Germany had a vision about how to prevent another world war. They believed that economic and political interdependence was the answer to preventing irreconcilable conflict. If the prosperity of France depended on the prosperity of Germany, the two countries would be more likely to cooperate than they had earlier in the twentieth century. This vision was another impetus for the birth of the European Union.

Political and economic interdependence is not separate from social interdependence. Social policies are enacted, expanded, and cut back in economic and political contexts. Women across European countries have banded together to make sure that their interests are not forgotten in supranational policy-making.

### Overview of Women's Rights Issues

The EU has a historical and well-institutionalized focus on women's rights. It is an important governing body for women in Europe because it has exerted significant power over its member states' gender equality laws (Hoskyns 1996). When the EU passes a directive (a binding law) extending the rights of women, member states must change their national and local laws to comply with EU law or face sanctions. In addition to this direct power, the European Union has indirect power over the ideas and debates about women's rights in other nonmember countries. This occurs as advocates and elected officials compare the rights of women in their own countries to those of women in the European Union.

In 1999 the EU included fifteen member countries. These nations are diverse not only in the languages spoken but also in their histories regarding women's rights, their economic power, the power of women in national politics, and the place of women in their cultures and their institutional structures. For example, the per capita gross domestic product in EU countries in 1990 ranged from $7,323 in Greece to $19,282 in Luxembourg, and participation of women in national parliaments in the early 1990s ranged from 5.3 percent in Greece to 33 percent in Denmark.

**EU Membership by Date of Accession**

1957 Belgium, France, Germany, Italy, Luxembourg, Netherlands

1973 + Denmark, Ireland, UK

1981 + Greece

1986 + Portugal, Spain

1995 + Austria, Finland, Sweden (Shea 1997)

Despite the differences, these fifteen countries have given up some of their national power to the European Union to achieve common goals. In national deliberations about whether to join the EU or not, women have mobilized and been vocal about their fears, concerns, or hopes about EU membership. For example, Norwegian women, afraid that EU membership would result in the degradation of their hard-earned national women's rights, are credited with Norway's vote not to join the EU. Women in other countries with less-established women's rights, such as the United Kingdom, have seen advantages to EU membership.

## HISTORY OF WOMEN'S RIGHTS

Economic principles drove the early development of women's rights in Europe. In the 1957 Treaty of Rome, a founding treaty of the EU, the French insisted on a provision for equal pay for women and men. Women in France were some of the only women in continental Europe who earned the same wages as men for the same work. France did not feel it could compete in a free market with other states where women were paid less than men for the same work. The other founding members of the EU were not pleased about this provision. The idea of wage equality between women and men came into conflict with deeply held male breadwinner ideals (Duncan 1995). However, these nations knew that a common market in Europe would have to include France to be meaningful, and France would not join without this provision. Women's rights laws diffused throughout Europe stem from this early demand of the French for equal pay for women and men in a common European market.

A confluence of history, politics, and economics in the European Union's forty-year evolution has resulted in the institutionalization of women's rights as one of its most important social arenas. Today, a woman in the EU is entitled not only by her Danish or French citizenship, but also by her European Union citizenship, to fourteen weeks of paid maternity leave with the right to return to the same job. Mothers and fathers of children under the age of eight are entitled by their European Union citizenship to three months of unpaid parental leave. This leave is over and above maternity leave. It allows parents to meet the caring needs of infants and young children without losing their jobs or social benefits. The EU has not passed binding laws about childcare. However, it has promoted high childcare standards that have become a starting point for national childcare debates. These are three of many policies enacted in the EU to promote equality between men and women.

### European Union Maternity Leave, Parental Leave and Childcare Policies

*Maternity Leave* (1992)

14 weeks with full job protection; remuneration equivalent to sick leave benefit; paid time for prenatal exams; prohibits dismissal of workers who apply for leave; maintenance of social security rights; assessment of health and safety risks in workplace with re-assignment when indicated; eligibility—no more than 12 months employment.

*Parental Leave* (1996)

3 months unpaid; non-transferable right; can be taken on part-time or full-time basis until child is eight years old; protection against dismissal; right to return to same or equivalent job; full social security benefits while on leave; no employers are excluded from having to offer this right.

*Childcare* (1992)

Recommendation states that services should: be affordable; combine reliable care with a pedagogical approach; be available in all areas, urban and rural; be accessible to children with special needs and meet their needs; work closely with communities and be responsive to parental needs; be flexible and diverse. There should also be training for childcare workers appropriate to the importance of their work. (Shea 1997)

Women's rights in the EU are focused on the role of women as workers. Maternity leave and parental leave are rights of full-time workers. The EU has few if any laws targeting nonworking or part-time, flexibly employed women. As in the United States, the most disadvantaged women often work in casual, part-time, flexible or unreported jobs. EU laws do nothing to address the rights of migrant workers or these other classes of the work force. Therefore, they do not completely address women's disproportionate risk of poverty and inequality in much of the European continent (Hoskyns 1996).

Women's rights in the European Union have roots in the precedents of the EU itself. The 1957 Treaty of Rome guarantee of equal pay for men and women was the seed for an expanded EU role in gender equality in the workplace. This legitimization, if you will, of women's rights in the EU spawned advisory committees on working women's issues and action programs that kept women's equality in employment on the front burner of legislative politics. The relatively high priority given to gender equality in employment in the EU social policy package is remarkable when compared to national social policy priorities in EU member states. For example, few EU policies target the elderly and retirees, very powerful national constituencies. Some argue that it would be impossible for the EU to build supranational-level consensus in well-entrenched national policy arenas (Leibfried and Pierson 1995). For this reason, it has had to focus on newer policy concerns and opportunities. Policies that facilitate the employment of working mothers fall into this category because in many countries large majorities of women did not demand equality of opportunity in employment until recently.

Women's rights in the European Union also have roots in the precedents and standards raised by international organizations like the United Nations (UN) and the International Labor Organization (ILO). It is striking how EU standards mirror those set by these bodies. There are two explanations for overlapping laws. First, the membership of the UN and ILO includes the European Union and its member nations. Evidence shows that the ILO put pressure on the EU to implement policies that help parents to balance their employment and family roles, including maternity and parental leave policies. Second, women's rights advocates and policy-makers at the supranational level exchange ideas regularly, they go to many of the same meetings and conferences, and they often transfer employment between organizations.

The United Nations, like many intergovernmental organizations, came into being after World War II. Its philosophy, shaped by the devastation of two world wars, is based on the thinking of Thomas Hobbes (1588–1679). In *Leviathan* (1651) Hobbes argues that by nature, individuals are selfishly individualistic and will fight unless a higher body of law and power controls this tendency. As a result, many of the UN's policies targeting women are concerned with violence against women or basic human rights (Meehan 1993). Despite this focus on fundamental human rights as opposed to gender equality, the UN provided a precedent for the European Union's equal opportunity laws in its 1948 Declaration of Human Rights calling for equal pay for women and men. This was quite a radical concept at the time. The only two EU countries with equal pay provisions in national law in the 1940s were France and Italy.

While the International Labor Organization is an agency of the UN, it has a longer history and is important in its own right to the development of EU maternity and parental leave policies. In 1919, twenty-six years before the birth of the United Nations, the ILO drafted the first international standards for maternity leave. These standards called for twelve weeks of paid leave. They were adopted by six EU member states between 1920 and 1952. In 1952 the ILO expanded the provisions of the 1919 maternity leave law. Seven EU nations signed this law. Interestingly, almost all of the countries that signed the ILO standards into national law were predominantly Catholic. Maternity leave was originally focused on protecting women in the workplace. This protection sometimes worked against promoting equal opportunities to work. Strong protectionist policies, such as long paid leave, can be associated with discrimination against hiring women who might become pregnant. Scandinavian states, acknowledged today for some of the world's highest standards for women's rights, did not adopt the ILO maternity leave conventions of 1919 and 1952. Some attribute this to the Scandinavian "universal" approach to promoting welfare, which is in contrast to the employment and family-based approach to welfare in Catholic countries (Wennemo 1994).

## Institutional Structure

The development of leave and childcare policies in the European Union reflects the increasing organizational capacity of the European Union institutions. There are four institutions in the European Union important to the development of EU women's rights: the European Commission, the European Parliament, the Council, and the Court of Justice.

The European Commission, sometimes referred to as the Commission, is the bureaucracy of the European Union. Its staff includes a mix of career and appointed bureaucrats. They reside in Brussels and are charged to provide a "European perspective" rather than a national perspective on lawmaking in Europe. One might compare the Commission to U.S. federal departments all lumped into one institution. However, partially due to the weakness of the European Parliament compared to the U.S. Congress, and partially due to the short term of the EU presidency, the European Commission has more power than a U.S. bureaucracy does.

Most women's rights policies have been drafted in the Equal Opportunities Unit of the European Commission. So while the Commission is credited with advocacy for women, it is important to remember that this advocacy role really happened in a part of the bureaucracy completely focused on the rights of women. During the development of the maternity leave law a Greek woman was in charge of the Equal Opportunities Unit. Greek women did not have high levels of maternity leave coverage at the time. Some women's rights advocates argue that the passion this Greek woman brought to the maternity leave issue was instrumental in its becoming a right for all European women.

The Commission played a major role in women's rights agenda setting and policy-making in the European Union in the 1980s and 1990s. In addition, it actively organized and supported networks of women's rights stakeholders in this time period. Two of several examples are the Network on Childcare and the European Women's Lobby. These networks provided a mechanism for the European Commission to gather information from its member states as well as a means to communicate European-level issues and initiatives back to local and national women's rights groups. The European Commission's active use of these networks to build consensus around its planned legislation was important to the development of the policies studied, not only at the European level, but also at local and national levels.

The European Parliament is made up of democratically elected representatives of EU member countries. Members of Parliament (MEPs) meet in Strasbourg, France, and serve two-and-a-half-year terms. In 1995, 35 percent belonged to the Group of the Party of European Socialists; 28 percent belonged to the Christian Democratic Group; and the remainder was split between eight groups representing liberals, communists, "green" parties, and other smaller or more nationally oriented groups.

The Committee on Women's Rights, a nationally and politically diverse group of MEPs, oversees the development and implementation of equal opportunity laws. It worked closely with the European Commission on the language of the maternity and parental leave laws. Like the full European Parliament, it advocated much more generous leave terms than those actually written by the Commission. Debates in the European Parliament reveal the broad support across party lines for the maternity leave and parental leave legislation. In 1995 the European Parliament announced its intention to persevere in efforts for a law covering not only parental leave but also all problems concerning the reconciliation of family and professional life.

Heads of state from each member country sit on the Council, where strong national perspectives on "European" ideas are debated. Prior to the mid-1980s, when voting rules changed, decision-making power was weighted heavily toward the member governments. Now, while passing binding law in the EU often requires a unanimous vote of member countries, in the case of proposals concerning the health and safety of workers and equality between women and men in respect to labor market opportunities and treatment at work, majority rule applies. Given the differences in size and economic power of member nations, different countries have different voting power.

### The Council (1996)

Representatives of the Governments of the fifteen Member States Permanent Representatives Committee (COREPER)
Legislation: Number of Votes Per Country:

10 France, Germany, Italy, UK

8 Spain

5 Belgium, Greece, Netherlands, Portugal

4 Austria, Sweden

3 Denmark, Finland, Ireland

2 Luxembourg

Qualified Majority: 63 votes out of 87
Blocking Coalition: 25 votes (Shea 1997)

The European Court of Justice is the "Supreme Court" of the European Union. Its role is to interpret and enforce EU laws and treaties. It has made judgments on more than fifty equal opportunity cases. In the 1980s, before the enactment of EU maternity and parental leave laws, leave cases were brought before the Court as claims against EU equal treatment laws. The Court's decisions about equality in maternity leave and parental leave rights at this time did not challenge national laws and precedents. However, these decisions prompted the mobilization of women's groups in member states, particularly Germany, to demand national changes in laws. This resulted in increased support for future legislative change at national and EU levels.

In 1990, in *Dekker v. Stichting Vormingcentrum*, the European Court of Justice made a landmark decision concerning maternity leave (Hoskyns 1996). In this case, the Court ruled that "because only women become pregnant, any kind of detriment in the work situation relating to pregnancy constitutes direct discrimination for which no justification can be argued." Prior to this, some countries, such as the UK, restricted the rights of pregnant women to claim discrimination for unfair practices related to pregnancy. EU law took precedence over national laws, expanding women's rights in Europe.

The subject of night work during pregnancy is another contentious area in the interpretation of equal treatment laws. The ILO and many national governments have long-standing legislation banning night work during the final weeks of pregnancy. These policies originated several decades ago in a climate marked by protectionist attitudes toward women. At that time the conditions of the workplace and the nature of women's jobs were different than they are today. There were proportionately more jobs in manufacturing, with few health and safety protections in the workplace. Banning night work in pregnancy can have negative effects on women as a group when employers base hiring or promotion decisions on their expectations about women's future employment constraints. In a recent case, the European Court threw out the protectionist logic and ruled that a ban on night work for women was discriminatory, even in the case of pregnancy.

European Court of Justice rulings have sometimes been supportive of women's rights to equality in employment, such as when it struck down the ban on women's night work or supported women's rights to take leave in pregnancy. At other times, notably when the Court upheld national governments' rights to restrict men's rights to take maternity leave, the European Court has been restrictive. When only women are allowed to take leave after the birth or adoption of a baby, women's rights in employment are, in practice, restricted. The inconsistency in the Court's decisions reflects the contradiction between laws that support women as equals in the workplace and laws that protect women, especially pregnant women and women who have recently given birth. A shift appears to be occurring in the Court toward an "individualization" of rights in which equality between men and women is considered a fundamental right.

## WOMEN'S RIGHTS TODAY

### Social Views

Social views of women's rights in the European Union vary by country. They also vary by race, class, gender, and economic factors within and between countries. However, differences, once marked, are blurring as ideas, laws, and economic conditions are diffused throughout Europe.

One way to characterize national cultures is by the degree to which they support a male breadwinner ideal versus a gender equality ideal (Duncan 1995). While there are many national twists to these ideal prototypes, it can generally be stated that in the European Union, the Nordic countries, France, and Belgium promote gender equality by subsidizing high quality preschool childcare and by providing generous paid leave opportunities for mothers and fathers of young children. The UK, Ireland, the Netherlands, Germany, and the Mediterranean countries have policy legacies that support men as the main family breadwinners, albeit differently. For example, in some countries men have traditionally been paid more when they marry and assume family responsibilities. In other countries, women were under strong social pressure to discontinue employment after having a baby.

Social views of women's rights in the European Union were also influenced by the massive unemployment experienced across much of Europe in the early 1990s. Traditional ways of reducing unemployment, such as job creation, were not desirable since most members of the European Union were focused on reducing their national debt to qualify for monetary union. For this reason, leaders across Europe were searching for new solutions to reduce unemployment. There was a Europe-wide trend toward part-time retirement of elderly workers prior to statutory retirement ages. New job rotation programs were announced in some countries where workers were encouraged to take leave for education or family purposes. Encouraging workers to temporarily withdraw from the labor market was linked to incentives to provide opportunities for people in need of work. In countries that have generous periods and rates of unemployment remuneration, such as Germany and the Netherlands, the costs of unemployment are not only political, but also financial. Maternity leave and parental leave fit perfectly into this climate. These policies are a relatively low-cost way to encourage workers to take time away from work to care for their children. At the same time these policies do not promote long-term labor force withdrawal of productive workers. Policy advocates in the European Commission and European Parliament argued these points persuasively. Review of the popular press in Europe during the 1990s reinforces the importance of massive unemployment on shaping social views about maternity and parental leave.

Given the male breadwinner ideology prevalent in many EU member nations, it is surprising that there was never any debate at the EU level about another strategy to lower unemployment—encouraging married women's long-term withdrawal from employment. This is Germany's approach, and it would have fallen on sympathetic ears in Italy, Luxembourg, Ireland, and the UK. If parental leave had been designed to be a longer-term right only for women, it may well have been a policy to encourage women's labor market withdrawal. However, it was written as an individual right for women and for men. It is not meant to be an extension of maternity leave but a right that can be taken at any time during a child's early years. Maternity leave also is for a relatively short period compared to national rights in some EU member states, again facilitating women's return to employment. The European Union's institutional focus on women's rights to equality in employment, and the power dynamics between EU institutional actors and women's and business lobbies, explain a strategy that supports women's participation in society through employment. This is a critical divergence from what may have been the natural course for a majority of EU member states.

## Political Views

At national levels in much of Europe, democratic politics is a key explanatory factor for the development of social policies, including women's rights (Esping-Andersen 1990). However, the political environment of the European Union is quite different from that found in nation-states. The link between the interests of the citizens of Europe and outcomes of the EU policy process is more fragmented and nebulous. This is partly because of the low level of understanding Europeans have about EU institutions and processes. Seventy-one percent of Europeans polled in the mid-1990s said they were not well informed about the EU. This lack of knowledge has been confirmed repeatedly in the media. In Britain, the Treaty of Rome gave weight to fears that the EU was a Roman Catholic move for European dominance; and in Denmark there was a scare that the EU was going to allow German police officers to operate on Danish soil.

Party politics takes on a whole new meaning when the link between EU policies and the work of members of the European Parliament or national government leaders is not strong. Just prior to the 1994 European Parliament elections, the majority of Europeans were not even aware how members of the European Parliament were elected. The chain of communication between the general population and the EU institutions is discontinuous, and unlike the situation in many member states, the democratically elected members of Parliament have very limited power. Elected heads of state in the Council have enormous power; but their meetings are held in secret, so the general population does not have information on which to base pressure or participation.

The amalgamation of diverse national interest groups into "Euro-groups" also results in new dynamics that appear to be heavily shaped by the European Commission. The proliferation of EU lobbyists is recent. To facilitate the participation of labor and women's groups, the European Commission encouraged the organization of new Euro-groups, which it funds and to which it gives special access to EU institutions and processes. Some argue that existing interest groups are often ignored because they are less under the control of the Commission. The populations of "women" and "workers" in Europe are as diverse as Europe itself. Representing such diversity in a small number of European umbrella groups is difficult.

Regarding women's rights, there is evidence that stakeholders for and against the expansion of women's rights in Europe (i.e., lobbies, governments, and political parties) came together on an issue-by-issue basis to form issue networks. These networks were loosely tied, but they mutually reinforced each other through indirect ways. Stakeholders who advocated leave and childcare included:

- the Equal Opportunities Unit of the European Commission;
- the Committee for Women's Rights in the European Parliament;
- the European trade union lobby;
- Nordic and French stakeholders in various networks and official capacities;
- the advisory committee on equal opportunities;
- the EU childcare network;
- the European Women's Lobby;
- family lobbies.

In opposition to this issue network was a group including small business and other employer lobbies, a small minority of right-wing parties in the European Parliament, the UK, and other national governments, depending on the debate. The UK, fiercely resistant to any EU role in any social policy, was a vocal and powerful opponent to the maternity and parental leave policies. Interestingly, it opted to be excluded from EU social policies by not signing the social chapter of the Maastricht Treaty. The Maastricht Treaty was an agreement made between members of the European Community in December 1991 that changed the name of the European Community to the European Union. This treaty extended the scope of the European Community to include political cooperation and monetary union. The social chapter of the treaty extended its influence to social policy domains. In refusing to sign the social chapter, the UK lost its power to veto or block new legislation. The UK is the only country that did not sign the social chapter. The effect of not signing meant that citizens of the UK were the only EU citizens not entitled to European social rights legislated under the social chapter. This was not lost on women's rights advocates who became more empowered at local and national levels. Ironically, the increased voice that British women are receiving in national platforms may move Britain closer to convergence with EU policies in the long term.

Some have accused the European Union of being an "elitist" form of government. At many levels this case study supports this assertion. People who work for the European Commission must be fluent in at least two languages. Most speak at least three. The result of this requirement is that many EU bureaucrats have elite educational credentials. The European Women's Lobby is considered to be more representative of the views of white, professional, middle-aged women than poor or minority women. The most powerful business lobby is also accused of representing big business at the expense of small and medium-sized businesses. Despite this imbalance of power, a situation that is not at all unique to the European Union, the provisions of EU maternity leave and parental leave laws and childcare recommendation are more generous than they were in some of the EU member states. For example, prior to the implementation of the EU maternity leave law, women in the UK were not eligible for maternity leave unless they had worked for the same employer full time for two years or part time for five years. The effect of the change in eligibility requirements was to expand the rights to leave for 45 percent of British working women.

At face value, the enactment of maternity and parental leave laws may not seem all that earth-shattering. After all, many EU member states already had their own, in some cases quite generous, parental and maternity leave rights. However, the rolling back of the welfare state dominant in the 1990s in the United States was also happening in Europe. In some countries, sick leave benefits, statutory pensions, and disability insurance were slashed. It is striking that at the same time that the sacred cows of social rights were falling, the social rights of working parents were consolidated and secured.

## THE FUTURE OF WOMEN'S RIGHTS

The European Union is clearly influencing women's rights in Europe. However, its focus is on the rights of full-time working women. Many rights critical to the well-being of all women—universal health care, reproductive health services, housing subsidies, educational opportunities, and fiscal policies, to name a few—are conspicuously absent from EU legislation or its agenda. These vital policies remain the subject of national laws. The EU, with little power to tax and spend and less interest in women's rights than a well-functioning European common market, is likely to continue to focus on regulatory policy and on setting minimum standards important for fair competition.

## BIBLIOGRAPHY

Duncan, Simon. 1995. "Theorizing European Gender Systems." *Journal of European Social Policy* 5, no. 4: 263–84.

Esping-Andersen, Gosta. 1990. *The Three Worlds of Welfare Capitalism*. Princeton: Princeton University Press.

Gornick, Janet, Marcia Meyers, and Katherine Ross. 1998. "Public Policies and the Employment of Mothers: A Cross-National Study." *Social Science Quarterly* 79, no. 1: 35–54.

Hoskyns, Catherine. 1996. *Integrating Gender: Women, Law and Politics in the European Union*. New York: Verso.

Leibfried, Stephan, and Paul Pierson. 1995. *European Social Policy: Between Fragmentation and Integration*. Washington, DC: The Brookings Institution.

Meehan, Elizabeth. 1993. *Citizenship and the European Community*. Newbury Park, CA: Sage Publications.

Shea, Madeleine A. 1997. "Supporting Working Parents: Leave and Childcare Policy Development in the European Union." Dissertation. Ann Arbor, MI: UMI.

Wennemo, Irene. 1994. *Sharing the Costs of Children*. Stockholm: Swedish Institute for Social Research, 25.

# 8

# INDIA

## Women's Movements from Nationalism to Sustainable Development

*Manisha Desai*

## INTRODUCTION

### Profile of India

India is a democratic republic with the second largest population in the world, close to a billion people. It gained independence in 1947 from Great Britain and became a republic in 1950. It is a diverse country with 80 percent of its population belonging to various Hindu religions; 14 percent are Muslims, 3 percent Christians, and 2 percent Buddhists, Sikhs, and Jains combined. Its people speak over a thousand different languages. Hindi and English are the official languages, and the government recognizes fourteen others. India began with a mixed economy in 1947 but has increasingly liberalized since the 1980s. Women account for 25 percent of the paid work force but constitute a much larger percentage of informal workers. The literacy rate is 64 percent for men and 39 percent for women. The school enrollment ratio of girls to boys is 71 to 100 for primary school, 55 to 100 for secondary school, and 37 to 100 at the tertiary level. Women's suffrage was won at independence in 1950.

### A Case Study

In 1995, inspired by the earlier activists and their traditions, village women from the hills and forests of the Uttarkhand region (in the northern part of the state of Uttar Pradesh) renewed efforts to save their forests, most of which are publicly owned, from outside exploiters. In July 1995 word spread in the villages that a lumber corporation had smuggled in loggers to cut down trees in the Rayala jungles in Tehri Garhwal. Village women trekked uphill for fifteen kilometers to confront the contractors. Anticipating trouble, the contractors fled, but not before cutting down several trees and hundreds of saplings. "Shocked at such wanton destruction, women villagers then and there took a vow to protect the trees and in a symbolic gesture tied *Rakshasutras* (safety threads) around 2,500 trees" (Bhai 1999, 26). Since 1995, the Rakshasutra campaign has grown all across the Uttarkhand region. This campaign represents the ideal that the rights of women in India include the right to a secure and sustainable future.

### Overview of Women's Rights Issues

Such militant actions are only a recent variation in a struggle for women's rights in India that is over a hundred years old. The first wave of this struggle lasted roughly from about the late nineteenth century to independence in 1947. The social reform and nationalist movements of the era influenced this wave, the initial focus of which was on improving women's status. It was only toward the end of this wave that women's rights in the political and domestic arena became a focus.

By contrast, the second wave, from the late 1960s to the mid-1980s, was aimed at fulfilling women's economic and social rights. It was part of a larger wave of grass-roots movements for social and economic justice by the urban and rural poor. Women in this wave appropriated the identity of feminists and in the process redefined the language and methods of feminism. Finally, the third wave, an extension of the second, has linked issues of women's rights and feminism to issues of the environment. It emerged in the late 1980s, and its main focus is providing strategies for alternative development.

In all three waves, there were strands that explicitly and implicitly defined and redefined existing and new rights. The extent to which the language of rights became embedded in the movements was shaped, in part, by the international context. For example, the dominance of the human rights discourse in the various UN-sponsored world conferences, in which Indian women participated in great numbers, also influenced the women's movements in India.

## HISTORY OF WOMEN'S RIGHTS

### Social Reform and Women's Rights

The social reform movement of the early and mid-nineteenth century to improve the status of Indian women represents one of the first systematic attempts at solving the "woman question." It focused on issues such as widow remarriage, polygamy, female education, purdah (veiling and other forms of the seclusion of women), property rights, and sati. (Sati is the practice of the immolation of the widow on the funeral pyre of her dead husband. Practiced by some upper caste Hindus, incidences of sati increased during colonial rule, and there have been about fifty cases of it since independence in 1947.) Although primarily aimed at the reform of practices related to Hinduism, later on Muslim leaders also joined the reform movement (Everett 1979; Forbes 1982; Minault 1981).

The reform movement contained several strands. One is the "liberal" strand, of Western-educated upper caste. The Hindu caste system consists of hierarchical, occupation-based strata with brahmins (priest-scholars) at the top, then kshatriyas (warriors), vaishyas (traders), and shudras (peasants) at the bottom. Outside the caste system are the menial workers or the "untouchables." The first three strata are the upper castes, while the bottom two constitute the lower castes. At independence the caste system was legally abolished and affirmative action programs called "reservations" were instituted in education and government employment to address the centuries-long oppression of the lower castes. The upper caste Hindu men sought internal reform to modernize society and to convince the British of their ability to govern themselves. The conservative strand, made up of upper caste Hindu scholars viewed reform as a means of revitalizing and preserving Hindu values and stemming fundamental change (Jayawardena 1986). Neither the Hindu elite nor the Hindu scholars questioned the traditional gender division of labor or articulated issues as women's rights. Only the radical, lower caste strand viewed the existence of the caste system itself as the cause of women's subordination and questioned its very existence (Omvedt 1974).

The two nonradical strands of the movement drew support from the ancient Hindu texts to justify reforms. The reformers argued that the position of Indian women was high during the "golden vedic age," from 1500 to 1000 B.C.E., and that the status of women had deteriorated since then due to outside influences, particularly conquests by various Muslim rulers from Central Asia and internal corruption among the brahmins. The main strategy of the early reformers was introducing legislative change.

The reformers were able to overcome the resistance of orthodox Hindus and the British government through debates with Hindu scholars. After years of such debates, they were able to pressure the government to pass new legislation. Thus, sati was declared a criminal act in 1829, a widow remarriage act was passed in 1856, and the age of consent for marriage was raised to ten in 1860 and subsequently to fifteen in 1929, where it stayed until independence in 1947. In 1874 widows were granted rights to their deceased husband's property.

The reformers also started schools for women to counter the efforts of the missionaries who they suspected were proselytizing and introducing unhealthy Western ideas. In 1854 grants were given by the government for opening women's schools. By 1882 there were 2,697 educational institutions for women, most at the primary level, one college, and several teacher training institutes with 127,066 female students (Mies 1980). The schools were strictly sex-segregated, and the goal of education was to produce better mothers and wives.

Although the reform movement was led by men who viewed women merely as objects of reform, it resulted in creating a small group of upper caste, educated women who, along with some English and Irish women, initiated the first wave of the women's movement in India. They did so by forming autonomous women's organizations. The first such organization, the Indian Women's Conference was formed in 1904. The most important one, the All India Women's Conference (AIWC), was formed in 1927.

The primary focus of these organizations was education and "upliftment of women." They accomplished their goals by reforming Hindu, and later Muslim, social practices, spreading literacy among the poor, starting income generation schemes, and promoting handicraft production. This phase of the movement has been called the "women's upliftment" phase (Everett 1979) or social feminism (Forbes 1982). It accepted traditional roles, the uniqueness of women, and the idea of "separate spheres" of life for men and women. This ideology stretched the boundaries of the women's sphere without challenging the notion itself.

### Nationalism and Women's Rights

The nationalist movement to free India from colonial rule began in 1887 with the setting up of the Indian National Congress. The Congress was initiated by a British civil servant to channel the discontent of the Indian elites. Its aim was to give some political representation to the Indian elite in the colonial government within British constraints. Over the later part of the nineteenth century the nationalist movement became increasingly radical and set its sights on full national liberation. The issue of women's suffrage was first launched in 1917. After initial reluctance, the nationalist movement supported the issue, as they saw women as important allies in their cause of national liberation. The nationalist movement was, however, divided over issues of property rights for women, purdah, and child marriage. Some factions of the nationalist movement were even opposed to women's suffrage.

It was with the leadership of Mahatma Gandhi (1869–1948) in the nationalist movement that both the nationalist and women's movements changed from a small elite base to a mass base. Gandhi focused on mobilizing women because he felt that his methods of struggle were more suited to the female temperament. He wrote, "Because the qualities which this new form of warfare is displaying are feminine rather than masculine, we may look on this life and death struggle of India to be free as women's war" (quoted in Everett 1979, 76). It was Gandhi who explicitly linked women's subordinate status in the family to India's subordinate status with Britain. He convinced women that they had a duty to transform themselves and their country, linking the political and personal. Unlike the early reformers, he also made women the subjects of their own destiny, capable of changing themselves.

To enhance women's participation, Gandhi chose issues that would be directly connected to women's daily lives and at the same time be an expression of foreign domination. Thus, in his *swadeshi* (support for home-made goods) movement he encouraged women to take up spinning *khadi* (homespun cloth) instead of buying foreign cloth. He portrayed a new image of women as morally superior individuals. Although he appealed to all women, his main support came from urban middle-class women. His legacy for women, however, was mixed. On one hand, he emphasized not only the right but the duty of women to fight for their own and their country's freedom. Yet, he believed that women should primarily be mothers and wives and be an educated influence on men in worldly affairs.

Despite Gandhi's mixed messages, women in the nationalist movement learned the language of political rights, which they applied to their own status in the family. Around this time, the Communist Party of India was formed, which explicitly supported equality for men and women not just politically, but also economically and socially. Both of these sources enabled women in the All India Women's Conference to articulate women's rights in the family as well as to revisit the issue of women's suffrage.

In 1934 AIWC introduced the Hindu code bill, which would bring equality in marriage and grant Hindu women divorce and inheritance rights. The nationalist movement refused to support this bill. Nationalist leaders argued that women's organizations were elitist, that they were influenced by Western ideas, and, therefore, that they did not represent the majority of Indian women (Jayawardena 1986). Thus, as long as the enemy was external, women received support, but as soon as male privilege in the home was threatened the women's movement was not supported.

Despite this rejection of the proposed Hindu code bill, at independence Article 15 of the Indian constitution guaranteed, under law, the full equality of women in economic and political realms (ICSSR 1975). Women were considered equal to men, but their rights to marry, divorce, and inherit were to be shaped by their religious communities. There was no uniform civil code established for all Indian women. This issue would come back to haunt the autonomous women's movement in the 1980s.

After independence, many women's organizations, like the All India Women's Conference (closely connected with the ruling Congress Party) and the National Federation of Indian Women (affiliated to the Communist Party of India), were in the forefront of passing legislation that would ensure some of the equality promised in the constitution. However, both the government and the movement organizations considered the women's question to be solved. Many of the women from the movement organizations were co-opted into government positions; the movement became institutional-ized, and the organizations lost their dynamism. From 1947 to the 1960s, only the communist and socialist parties made an effort to redefine the woman question. While they tried to mobilize masses of women in rural and urban India, they did so only around issues of equal wages, workplace safety, maternity and retirement benefits, and childcare.

Thus, the first wave of the women's movement in India led to constitu-tional equality, but it did not change the situation of most women within the family or society. Socioeconomic issues, primarily access to livelihood and equal pay for equal work, became the focus of the various grass-roots movements of the late 1960s, which led to the second wave.

## WOMEN'S RIGHTS TODAY

The woman question reemerged in the late 1960s and early 1970s in the context of economic and political crises in the country. State-sponsored eco-nomic development was geared toward economic growth instead of em-ployment for people. For example, the capital-intensive industries could absorb less than 10 percent of the millions of rural landless peasants who came to the urban areas for jobs. The rest had to eke out a living in the informal sector by street vending, providing domestic service, and producing food and clothes in their home to sell in the marketplace. The "green rev-olution" promoted capital-intensive agriculture, and the expansion of large mechanized farms led to increasing landlessness as small farms were bought out. These developments made subsistence extremely insecure for poor men and women. At the same time, Prime Minister Indira Gandhi was intent on consolidating her power in the Congress Party and did not respond im-mediately to the increasing misery of the poor.

Faced with the growing miseries of the poor and the inadequacy of bu-reaucratic party machinery in responding to them, young, college-educated men and women began organizing the poor in alternative ways. Unlike political parties, the new activists built nonhierarchical, participatory grass-roots organizations. They focused on caste, gender, and culture in addition to class as equally important forces of oppression. They also began with people's knowledge rather than with abstract theories or outside experts. Hundreds of men and women went into villages and urban slums to build grass-roots movements for economic and social justice. The second wave of the women's movement emerged as part of these grass-roots efforts (Desai 1989).

### Affiliated Women's Movements

In the early or what I term the "affiliated" phase of the second wave, primarily poor women organized around issues of economic and social justice within the labor, peasants', and tribal movements. Among the most militant and successful efforts were those of tribal women in Maharashtra, hill women in Uttar Pradesh, and poor, urban women in Gujarat. For example, tribal women in the *Shramik Sangathana* (Toilers' Union) in Maharashtra organized against alcohol-related violence. Along with urban middle-class activists, they participated in *shibirs* or camps to express their grievances around violence by drunken husbands and landlords, illegal alcohol production and consumption, and unequal pay. They came up with militant and innovative solutions such as public shaming of abusive men and destroying the illegal liquor stills in the villages to highlight women's right to freedom from violence.

Poor women in the Himalayan foothills organized against tree-felling by private contractors by hugging the trees in the now famous Chipko movement. They argued that the destruction of the forests impinged on their livelihoods, which depended on the forests for firewood, food, and herbal medicines. The Chipko women succeeded in highlighting women's unrecognized economic work and the right of poor women to common resources.

The Self Employed Women's Association (SEWA), a union of women working in the informal sector, emerged in 1972 from the Women's Wing of the Textile Labor Association in Ahmedabad when laid off women textile workers were faced with harassment. SEWA was the first union of informal sector workers that sought to extend the protection of labor laws to women working as street vendors, rag-pickers, and home-based manufacturers of various goods. SEWA established the first women's bank for poor, illiterate women. It also organized women into production, service, and distribution cooperatives to enable them to have greater control over their labor and products as well as freedom from harassment by middlemen and moneylenders.

In 1974 the Indian government released the report on the status of women in India prepared for the UN-sponsored International Women's Year. The report documented the deteriorating status of women in independent India, in particular their increasing unemployment and illiteracy rates and the declining sex ratio. The sex ratio refers to the number of men versus women in any country. India is one of the very few countries in the world where there are more men than women. This sex ratio began tilting in men's favor in the 1930s and has continued to do so in most decades. The imbalanced sex ratio reflects a preference for sons expressed through neglect, sex-selective abortions, as well as infanticide.

In response to this situation, the left parties and the activists of the workers', peasants', and tribal groups organized the first women's liberation conference in Pune. Over 700 agricultural laborers, porters, tribals, teachers, students, and bank employees participated. (Tribals are the indigenous groups of India who live in jungles and hills and were, until recently, geographically isolated from the mainstream.) Participants sang: "This is the call of women's liberation that reaches the skies! Reactionaries, exploiters take heed that times are changing." Issues such as childcare, violence against women, and unequal pay for agricultural and factory work were the focus of discussion and action. The year 1975 also saw the emergence of the first explicitly feminist groups, such as the Progressive Organization of Women in Hyderabad and the Stree Mukti Sangathana (Women's Liberation Organization in) Bombay. Most of the women who formed these groups were activists of the various grass-roots movements.

Much of this protest activity came to a halt with the declaration of national emergency in 1975, which lasted until 1977. Indira Gandhi declared a state of national emergency in June 1975 to control the various protest movements and the increasing discontent among the people and political parties. During the emergency, the national parliament was dissolved and all political and civil rights were suspended.

## The Autonomous Women's Movement

The "autonomous" phase of the second wave emerged after the emergency. This is the term used by urban women's groups formed after the emergency to define their political position vis-à-vis political parties and movements, particularly of the left. The autonomous movement formed when women activists from various protest movements of the 1960s and early 1970s created an informal network in which they discussed the subordination of gender issues to class/caste issues and the relevance of Western feminist discourses to the Indian situation. It was in these groups that activists arrived at the need for an autonomous women's movement, one led by women, in which women's issues and organizations are not subordinated to other issues and organizations (Patel 1985, 16). In 1978, forty movement women from New Delhi, Kanpur, Bangalore, Ahmedabad, Baroda, and Bombay came together and created an informal national women's network, or a women's movement community which continues today. This network forms the backbone of much discussion and organizing around women's issues.

What transformed networking into active mobilization were the political issues and opportunities provided by the termination of the emergency. As soon as the emergency was lifted in 1977, a new group of journalists, reasserting their democratic freedoms, began to report on cases of state-sponsored police atrocities against the poor and political activists. Police rapes of women were a common form of terror practiced during the emergency. Several civil liberties and democratic rights groups emerged throughout the country to redress the "excesses" of the emergency through legal channels.

In November 1979, in the course of their human rights activism, four law professors from the University of New Delhi came across the 1977 Supreme Court judgment in the Mathura case, which had first come to trial in 1972 (Kumar 1993). In 1972 Mathura, a fourteen-year-old tribal girl, had been raped by two policemen while in police custody. The policemen were acquitted by a local court, indicted by the Bombay High Court, and again acquitted by the Supreme Court in 1977 on the grounds that Mathura was not physically coerced—as evident from the lack of bruises on her body—and had a history of sexual activity. The law professors were so outraged by the blatant injustice of the case that they wrote an open letter to the Supreme Court in November 1979, condemning the judgment, pointing out the legal flaws and the sexist bias, and demanding an immediate reopening of the case. They circulated copies of this letter to groups and activists all over India, seeking to pressure the Supreme Court into reopening the case.

The circulation of this letter led to the formation of new groups and launched a new activist stage in 1980. Most of the autonomous groups arose at this time, for example, the Forum Against Rape in Bombay, Saheli in New Delhi, Vimochana in Bangalore, and Chingari in Ahmedabad. Many of these groups were composed of activists from the previous movement phase but also included middle-class professional women, academics, and women from the various left parties.

The autonomous groups organized protest marches throughout Indian cities and launched a public consciousness-raising campaign through slide shows, poster exhibitions, and street theater. They also sought changes in laws related to rape, dowry, and violence against women, and they started self-help groups for victims of violence. After the anti-rape campaign, the autonomous groups also launched campaigns against wife-battering, sex-selective abortions, the issue of sati (widow immolation), and dowry-deaths (Gandhi and Shah 1991; Kumar 1993). Dowry-deaths are murders, usually committed by the mother-in-law and sister-in-law, after the bride's family is unable or unwilling to give any more dowry. Dowry is a traditional, one-time exchange of money from the bride's family to the groom's family. Today dowries take the form of consumer goods like refrigerators, cars, and even flats. Thus, in today's consumerist society, a traditional practice is combined with modern desires leading to deathly consequences. After the death, the groom would marry again, and thus get another dowry from the new bride's family.

Such campaigns against rape, dowry-deaths, sex-selective abortions, and wife-battery have led to several legal and policy changes in addition to the major achievement of making such violence a public issue. Legal changes include revised rape, dowry, and anti-sati laws, a new national law that investigates as murder any death of a married woman within the first seven years of marriage, and a law in Maharashtra that bans the use of amniocentesis for sex-selective abortions. Policy changes to address the problems include new programs and resources at the national and state level. These programs address issues of violence and have created women's cells in the criminal justice system to support abused women.

The major gains and visibility of the autonomous movement in the early

1980s were challenged in the mid-1980s by Hindu and Muslim fundamentalists. The fundamentalists labeled feminists pro-Western imperialists who were threatening Indian culture. Among the major setbacks for the autonomous women's movement during this time was the Shah Bano case and the Protection of Muslim Women's Bill that followed in 1986. In 1985 the Supreme Court of India granted alimony to Shah Bano, a Muslim woman, under a penal law criticizing Muslim personal laws. Personal laws are laws relating to divorce, marriage, child custody, and inheritance. In India each religion has its own set of laws that apply to people who chose identity based on their religion. So Muslim personal laws apply to Muslims. Her husband protested this decision, saying that no such payment was required under Muslim personal laws. The case also angered Muslim fundamentalist groups who protested the Supreme Court judgment as interference in their religious matters. To appease the Muslims, Rajiv Gandhi, the then prime minister, introduced a bill in parliament that would exclude Muslim women from the civil laws of the land. Autonomous feminist groups organized against this bill but were not able to garner enough support to defeat it. The bill was signed into law in 1986.

Another major setback for the movement was the response to the sati of Roop Kanwar, an eighteen-year-old woman, in 1987. This murder, which made international news, revealed the modernity of tradition. Roop Kanwar's husband was a college-educated man, and her in-laws were urban educated folks who were also active in local politics. The husband died unexpectedly after a short illness, and his family decided that she should become a sati. Investigative reports indicated that when Roop Kanwar learned of their plans she tried to escape but was captured, drugged, and coerced to become a sati. Villagers from miles around came to observe the event, and the police, although alerted, claimed ignorance and stood by out of respect for tradition and Roop Kanwar's "decision" to become a sati. Overnight there were protests by anti-sati groups, mostly women's and other progressive movements, and pro-sati groups, primarily Rajasthani politicians and some Hindu fundamentalist groups who argued that sati was their cultural/religious heritage and "right."

Despite such setbacks the autonomous groups continue to grow and provide real services to women, as well as an alternative discourse on gender in India. Many of them meet every few years in the Indian Women's Movement Conference to discuss current issues and plan action across the country. Many of them also mobilized to go to the UN Fourth World Conference in Beijing to present the issues of women in India, especially the impact of globalization and structural adjustment on women under the new liberalizing economies. Today many autonomous groups along with other social movements are mobilizing women to take advantage of the new law that reserves 30 percent of seats in local government for women. Their main task, however, is to provide an alternative to the politics of Hindu fundamentalism, which has succeeded in mobilizing masses of women all around India.

### The Third Wave: From Autonomy to Sustainable Development

During the various setbacks of the autonomous movement in the mid-1980s, several grass-roots women's movements developed. They took the feminist insights of small, urban, autonomous groups to mass-based rural women and moved from issues of violence against women to issues of development (Omvedt 1993). Some of the major women's movements of this wave are the Stree Mukti Sangharsh (SMS [Women's Liberation Struggle]) and Shetkari Mahilla Aghadi (Farm Women's Front) in Maharashtra, the Coastal Women's Association in Kerela, and Jharkhand Nari Mukti Samiti (Jharkhand Women's Liberation Committee) in Bihar. All of these grass-roots women's movements are part of larger social movements in the area.

For example, the SMS is part of a larger movement, the Shoshit Shetkari Kashtakari Kamgar Mukti Sangharash (SSKKMS [Exploited Peasants', Toilers', Workers' Liberation Struggle]) of peasants and workers from several villages in the Sangli district. The movement initially organized protests around drought relief and then envisoned an alternative model of rural development, one based on people's knowledge and participation, equality between men and women, and people's cultural needs as opposed to the dictates of global capitalism (Mukti Sangharsh 1985, 1).

The issue that brought this movement to national attention was their success in building the Baliraja Memorial Dam. It is a small eco-friendly, people-friendly dam. Villagers conceived and built it with the help of the People's Science Movement, urban professionals and sympathizers who shared a commitment to "alternative development" based on environmentally sustainable, economically just and equitable, and culturally rooted practices. Small dams were seen as a means of raising the water table and preventing droughts in the future. Water from the dam is shared equally by men and women, small peasants, and the landless poor.

The activists overcame great resistance from state and local bureaucrats and politicians, and the dam was finally built. Not only was this a major breakthrough for alternative development, but it was also an example of gender justice and equity. Women were not only involved in all stages of the movement, but gender was an important aspect of all thinking and planning about the dam.

SMS has also organized women who have been deserted due to widowhood or abandonment by husbands. SMS activists mobilized these women through meetings and gatherings in villages. Articulating an identity of the *paritakta* (deserted woman) has enabled women to demand ration cards from the local government offices. In 1997 SMS and the women demanded housing plots for these women and access to fallow waste lands that could be cultivated and sustained ecologically. The state has agreed in principle to provide housing plots to the *paritakta*, and in several villages in the eastern part of the district has even given the land to the women. However, where the land is intensively cultivated there has been no concession, as there is no available land that can be used for the purpose.

In some villages where the state has granted permission to women to cultivate the fallow land, local villagers have encroached on the land and prevented the women from using it. In 1998 SMS filed a court case against the local encroachers. The integrated approach of SMS is evident in this issue as well. In addition to the demands made for housing, SMS has also proposed that the common land be used by women for sustainable development with the understanding that the women would share the output with either the private owners of the land or, in case of community or state land, with the village *panchayat* (local governments of five elected leaders based on a traditional council of village elders). Thus, the movement provided tangible as well as symbolic dignity to women who otherwise are invisible and stigmatized.

The Shetkari Mahilla Aghadi, affiliated with Shetkari Sangathana (Farmers' Union), is another rural women's movement which has a multifaceted program for women based on low-input sustainable agriculture, farming cooperatives, and granting land rights to women. Many of these programs are still run by men though they are targeted for women. Even so, with programs such as organizing women to run for local elections and Laxmi Mukti (Free Goddess Laxmi) the Aghadi is working on the issue of women's rights. The Laxmi Mukti program was launched to free the goddess of wealth from male control by granting men and women equal rights to wealth, primarily land. Villages in which 100 families had given equal land to men and women were declared Laxmi-mukti. Yet, it is the middle class and rich farmers' wives and daughters who are getting involved, and not the poor women.

The Coastal Fisher Women's Association along with the National Fishermen's Forum, has been in the forefront of protesting overfishing by the factory ships of multinational corporations. Not only has overfishing led to the depletion of the seas, but the export orientation of the factory ships has made fish unavailable to the local fisherfolks. Here again, women are making the links between the deterioration of the environment and the increasing nutritional poverty of the poor due to the liberalization and export orientation of the Indian economy. The protests by the movement led to banning of mechanized fishing for a year and also launched a world forum of fisherfolks organized against the exploitation of the seas for the benefit of Western consumers.

Many of these women's movements have also started mobilizing rural women to enter local politics. Several states have passed legislation reserving 30 percent of seats in local government for women. Since 1990 several local governments have had women members. In 1992 there were only twelve women panchayats in Maharashtra. Nine of the twelve were at the initiative of women, but all had support of men. Only four women had to contest elections; the others were unopposed (Datta 1996).

Water scarcity and the need for toilets and new schoolrooms were among the problems addressed by women's panchayats. Women in rural India typically spend many hours a day procuring good drinking water. In several villages, women leaders used the local resources to bring potable water to the community through a common tap. This had never been a priority for the male leaders. Thus, concrete changes are brought about in women's daily lives through their participation in electoral politics, which had been scorned by most radical movements in India. Now there is recognition that state power cannot simply be overthrown or taken over; one has to use it as well as challenge it.

The major contribution of the third wave had been providing what activists call concrete alternatives for poor rural women based on a critique of contemporary industrial, consumer-oriented development. These concrete alternatives are giving women control over resources, especially community resources such as land, water, and waste land. In addition, women have been provided with a knowledge and skill base to develop those resources for a sustainable livelihood.

## THE FUTURE OF WOMEN'S RIGHTS

The women's movements in India are dynamic, diverse, and multifaceted. While the first wave of the movement ended at independence, the second and third waves continue to grow and work with each other. The women's movements in India today are (1) providing insights into how gender is implicated in and integral to all contemporary issues such as globalization and sustainable development, and (2) demonstrating concrete ways of empowering women and other marginalized people. In doing so, the women's movements in India today are engaged in rearticulating the connection among economic, social, and political aspects of women's rights, and providing concrete alternatives to actualize those rights.

## BIBLIOGRAPHY

Bhai, Suresh, 1999. Rakshasutra Movement: A Women's Campaign to Save Uttarkhand Forest. *Manushi* 110: 25–28.

Datta, Bishakha. 1996. *And Who Will Make Chappatis?: A Study of All-Women Panchayats in Maharashtra, 1962–1995.* Pune, India: Alochana, Centre for Documentation and Research on Women.

Desai, Manisha. 1989. "From Affiliation to Autonomy: The Emergence of the

Women's Movement in Western India." Ph.D. dissertation, Washington University, St. Louis.

Everett, Jana. 1979. "Women and Social Change in India." New Delhi: Heritage.

Forbes, Geraldine. 1982. "Caged Tigers: First Wave Feminists in India." *Women Studies International Forum* 5, no. 6: 525–36.

Gandhi, Nandita, and Nandita Shah. 1991. *The Issues at Stake: The Theory and Practice in the Contemporary Women's Movement in India.* New Delhi: Kali for Women.

ICSSR. 1975. "Status of Women in India: Synopsis of the Report of the National Committee on the Status of Women." New Delhi: Allied Publishers.

Jayawardena, Kumari. 1986. *Third World Feminism and the Nationalist Struggles.* London: Zed Press.

Kumar, Radha. 1993. *The History of Doing: An Illustrated Account of Movements for Women's Rights and Feminism in India, 1800–1990.* New Delhi: Kali for Women.

Mies, Maria. 1980. *Indian Women and Patriarchy.* New Delhi: Concept.

Minault, Gail. 1981. *Extended Family and Political Participation in India and Pakistan.* Delhi: Chanakya.

Mukti Sangharsh. 1985. "Exploited Toilers' Peasants', Workers' Liberation Struggle: A Report and Appeal." Unpublished paper.

Omvedt, Gail. 1974. *Cultural Revolt in a Colonial Society.* Bombay: Scientific Socialist Education Trust.

———. 1993. *Reinventing Revolution: New Social Movements and the Socialist Tradition in India.* Armonk, NY: Sharpe.

Patel, Vibhuti. 1985. "Indian Women on Warpath." In *Reaching for Half the Sky: A Reader on the Women's Movement in India,* ed. Vibhuti Patel. Baroda: Antar Rashtriya Prakashan, 1–48.

Spender, Dale. 1982. *Women of Ideas and What Men Have Done to Them: From Aphra Behn to Adrienne Rich.* Boston: Routledge Kegan Paul.

# 9

# IRAN

## Emerging Feminist Voices

### Ziba Mir-Hosseini

## INTRODUCTION

### Profile of Iran

Iran is one of the largest countries of the Middle East (1,648,000 square kilometers) and has a population of over 60 million. It is the only country whose official religion is Shi'a Islam (to which 10 percent of all Muslims adhere). It was never colonized, but in 1907 Russia and Britain divided the country into two "zones of interest": the former controlled the north, and the latter the south. Iran experienced two revolutions in the twentieth century, in both of which independence, democracy, and the rule of law were the central demands. The Constitutional Revolution (1906–1911) put an end to absolute monarchy, and the revolution of 1978–1979 led to the establishment of an Islamic Republic and brought Shi'a clerics into power. Twenty years later, Iran is going through a crucial stage of transition from theocracy to democracy. The radical early discourse of the Islamic Revolution is gradually giving way to a more pluralistic one in which Islam is reconciled with democracy and human rights. The turning point in this transition was the 1997 presidential elections, won by the moderate government of Mohammad Khatami. In paradoxical ways, the creation of the theocratic state paved the way for the secularization of society. Challenged by an overwhelmingly young population (60 percent are under twenty-five), the theocratic nature of the state is now an issue that is widely debated in the press and within the ruling elite.

## A Case Study

Zahra is an eighteen-year old divorcée from Tehran. The daughter of a bus conductor, at age fifteen she entered an arranged marriage, which she welcomed as it seemed to offer some freedom and a better life with a husband with prospects. It was not long before she realized that this was not to be. Her husband stopped her from studying and meeting her friends and family. After a year, she left him and filed for divorce. After many court sessions, she got her divorce, but only after giving up her claim to what her marriage contract entitled her to: the *mahr* (dower, or marriage gift). She went back to school and now is studying hard to pass the university entrance exams. The competition is tough, and her chance of success is one in ten. Gender is no barrier. In 1998, 52 percent of those who entered university were female. Zahra wants to study law and to become a lawyer. She says that her divorce experience taught her that without knowing the law and how to use the legal system, women cannot attain their rights. She is from the new generation of women who have come of age during the Islamic Republic and who are learning to use the political vocabulary of the state to argue for their rights. Unlike women of previous generations, Zahra does not have to choose to be either Muslim or feminist: she can be both.

# HISTORY OF WOMEN'S RIGHTS

## The Beginnings

In Iran, as elsewhere in the Muslim world, women's demand for equal rights emerged in the context of anti-colonial and nationalist discourses. Cultural identity and loyalty were central: any dissent or criticism of patriarchal elements in Muslim society and culture could be construed as a kind of betrayal. Muslim women who acquired a feminist consciousness and advocated women's rights were under pressure to conform. They were faced with a painful choice between their Muslimness and their feminism. Leila Ahmed puts it eloquently:

It is only when one considers that one's sexual identity alone (and some would not accept this) is more inextricably oneself than one's cultural identity, that one can perhaps appreciate how excruciating is the plight of the Middle Eastern feminists caught between those two opposing loyalties, forced almost to choose between betrayal and betrayal. (1984, 122)

In this way, for many Muslim women acquiring a feminist consciousness and advocating women's rights became a curse rather than a cure. The curse, however, is losing its power. This chapter tells the story of this loss in Iran, where new discourses on women are emerging that are rooted in Islam and yet can be called feminist.

Let us take a minimalist definition of feminism: an awareness that women suffer discrimination because of their gender, as well as action aimed at changing the situation. In Iran, we can trace the roots of such feminism to the Babi movement in the mid-nineteenth century. The founder, Seyyed 'Ali Mohammad Shirazi, known as the Bab, called for radical reforms in religion and society, including equality and emancipation for women. Himself a cleric, the Bab had contained his call for reform within the bounds of Shi'i Islam, but the clerical establishment denounced it as heresy, and the movement turned into a revolutionary religion whose followers were brutally persecuted. One of the earliest and most influential followers was Tahereh, better known by her title Qorrat ol-'Ein (literally, Solace of the Eye). Born and married into clerical families, Tahereh was a renowned scholar and an eloquent speaker. She left her family to join the Babi struggle, and embraced the new faith with passion and boldness. When it was proclaimed, she uncovered her face to deliver her speech—an act of revealing to symbolize the coming of a new age. In 1852 an unsuccessful attempt by three Babis on the life of the newly crowned Naser ad-Din Shah led to a new wave of persecution, and Tahereh was among those executed.

Though Babism was defeated as a movement and ended up as a persecuted religion, calls for women's emancipation continued. Subsequent reformers no longer sought inspiration in religion. They now looked to the West, arguing that women's lack of education and absence from public life were what kept the nation in a state of backwardness. Women's emancipation became an integral part of the political discourse that led to the Constitutional Revolution of 1906–1911. Supported by a majority of clerics, the Revolution led to the creation of a parliament (Majles) and paved the way for women's presence in society and participation in politics.

The turbulent events of those years saw no woman leader as revolutionary and eloquent as Tahereh, but shortly after the granting of the Constitution in 1906, women from upper and middle classes began to form associations. These were extensions of male local societies, known as *anjoman*, which had become a conduit for grass-roots democracy during the Revolution. In Tehran alone, a dozen women's societies were formed. One of these was the Women's Freedom Society, whose meetings were attended by two daughters of Naser al-Din Shah, the monarch who had signed Tahereh's death warrant. One of them, Taj as-Saltaneh, left a memoir which is an eloquent critique of the patriarchal society in which she lived; it is one of many feminist writings of the period. Among the achievements of these women's societies were the establishment of girls' schools and the founding of women's journals. By 1910, when the first such journal, *Danesh* (Knowledge), appeared, over fifty girls' schools had already opened in Tehran. However, women failed to win suffrage: this was rejected by the Majles, whose conservative members questioned its Islamic legitimacy as well as that of the women's societies.

In the decade following the Constitutional Revolution, the growing gap between modernist and traditionalist forces rendered the Majles ineffective, and the government's inability to maintain order in the country caused widespread disillusionment. Most people yearned for a strong government able to put an end to foreign intervention, to carry out reforms, and to stand up to the conservatives who were invoking religion and tradition to impede progress. It was in such a climate that the army officer Reza Khan came to power in 1921; in 1925 the last Qajar monarch was deposed, and Reza Khan was declared Shah. He embarked on a project of nation-building and modernization, ruling with an iron hand until 1941, when he was forced by the Allied Powers to abdicate in favor of his son, Mohammad Reza.

Referred to as the founder of modern Iran, Reza Shah established a standing army, a secular educational system, and a modern judicial system, and initiated sociopolitical reforms. All these were done brutally: no political activities or groupings were tolerated, and all opposition and independent voices were silenced. The state took it upon itself to promote women's participation in society; their education was expanded and their employment in government organizations was encouraged. Yet, women's societies and journals were closed down, and neither the issue of female suffrage nor reform of the patriarchal rules of classical Islamic law was raised. Men's rights to unilateral divorce and polygamy were retained in the Family Law enacted between 1927 and 1935. This was now codified and grafted onto a modern legal system, in line with the state's modernization project.

The most drastic measure in the modernization of society was the ban on women's *hejab* (covering). (Today the minimally acceptable *hejab* is a headscarf and a long coat with long sleeves. For some clerics [but not in law], the only proper *hejab* is the *chador*. An acceptable compromise that has emerged since the Revolution, and is commonly worn by women officials, is the *maqna'eh* and rupush, a complete styled covering of the body, hair, and neck, leaving the face open and the hands free.) In 1936 a law required all women to appear in public without *hejab*; they could cover their hair by wearing European-style hats, but they could not wear *chadors*, or even scarves. Policemen had orders forcibly to remove women's *chadors* or scarves, and to arrest them if they resisted. While some women welcomed the unveiling law and saw it as a means to facilitate women's participation in society, many saw it as a direct invasion of their personal space. Many women stayed at home, either because they could not face coming out uncovered or because their families prohibited them from doing so. Gradually the measures taken to enforce the unveiling law were relaxed, and it was abandoned altogether in 1941. Its divisive impact continued to haunt society, however, and made the issue of *hejab* a sore point in Iranian politics, linking it firmly with state violence. It also cast a shadow over the other steps taken during Reza Shah's era to enhance women's access to education and participation in society.

Reza Shah's modernization project confronted reformists and modernists, both male and female, with a dilemma. They had to align themselves either with the modernizing state or with the opposition, which by now included a large section of the clerical establishment. While the first entailed accepting state repression, the second meant refusing the opportunity offered by the state for radical reform. Most people chose the former; the desire for change and reform overcame doubts about the means for achieving them. Nevertheless, the dilemma was not resolved, and positions were no longer as clear-cut as they had seemed at the turn of the century. Political discourses began to change, and with them the terms of the "woman question."

After Reza Shah's abdication in 1941, there followed a period of relative political freedom, during which the Majles became active again. In 1951 the popular nationalist government of Mohammad Mosaddeq nationalized the oil industry, which brought a confrontation with the British, who had acquired the oil concession under the Qajars. The young Shah sided with the British and was forced to go into exile. In 1953 Mosaddeq was toppled by a military coup staged and financed with British and American help. The Shah returned and resumed his father's modernization program, though less brutally. The growing oil revenues allowed the state to become progressively less dependent on political participation and to keep ahead of popular demands for reform.

The state began a process of co-opting and controlling women activists and their organizations. In order to continue their activities, they had to come under umbrella of the High Council of Iranian Women's Organizations, presided over by the Shah's twin sister, Ashraf Pahlavi. In 1963 the Shah introduced a radical program known as the White Revolution. This program included female suffrage and the creation of a female literacy corps for rural areas. Soon afterwards, the High Council was allocated a special budget and was renamed the Women's Organization of Iran. By the early 1970s, it had offices all over the country, providing health and educational services for women. It was involved in a campaign to change the divorce laws, initiated by a group of women lawyers and aired in a women's magazine, *Zan-e Ruz* (Woman of Today). In 1967 the Family Protection Act was passed, abolishing men's unilateral right to divorce, restricting polygamy, and giving women equal access to child custody. No divorce could be registered without a certificate from the new civil courts; every divorcing couple was required to come before a judge, who was sometimes a woman (Afkhami 1984; Sanasarian 1982).

The main beneficiaries of these legal reforms were educated urban women, rather than the large majority of women who were uneducated and lived in rural areas. Their significance was certainly lessened by their identification with the Shah, who was becoming dictatorial and unpopular. The opposition, both secular and Islamic, distanced themselves from the Shah's policies, seeing his modernization project as a denial of the religious and cultural identity of the nation. Because of its Western baggage, feminism too became a synonym of decadence, and any demand or tendency that could be labeled feminist was seen as a betrayal of Islamic ideals and an adoption of foreign ones (Hoodfar 1999; Paidar 1995).

## Feminism Rejected

After the establishment of the Islamic Republic in 1979, the development of the woman question went through several phases. The first was marked by women's mass participation in demonstrations during the Islamic Revolution. Hundreds of women's groups mushroomed all over the country, in mosques, government offices, factories, schools, and so on.

Ranging from small and spontaneous to large and organized, these groups represented the three main ideological tendencies, Islamic, nationalist, and Marxist, which together brought about the fall of the Pahlavi dynasty. Some of them were affiliated with underground political organizations during the old monarchy; others were formed during the Revolution.

These women's groups did not have mass support, nor did they voice any new feminist demands. Women active in them were aware of, and opposed to, the gender bias in orthodox interpretations of Islamic law, which were becoming evident in the Revolutionary Council's decisions and the religious leaders' announcements, but in general they subordinated their feminist aspirations to the wider goals of the parent organization. Political groups, whether Islamist, leftist, or nationalist, saw the issue of women's rights as secondary to wider anti-imperialist goals and interests.

Partial and important exceptions in this early phase were two women's groups, the Women's Society of the Islamic Revolution and the National Union of Women. The former, adhering to an Islamic ideology, began as a loose coalition of individual women activists with varying Islamic tendencies who came together during the 1978 upheavals. They took over the pre-revolutionary, state-sponsored Women's Organization of Iran, whose offices and communication facilities were appropriated during the Revolution. After the revolutionary government axed the organization's budget, a rift opened between women activists and the government; the organization broke up and its members dispersed and continued their activities elsewhere. One of them, Azam Taleqani, daughter of Ayatollah Taleqani, was elected to the first Majles, established the Islamic Institute of Women of Iran, and published the journal *Payam-e Hajar* (Message of Hagar). Another, Monir Gorji, an activist and preacher, was promoted by the Islamic Republican Party and became the only woman representative in the Assembly of Experts, which ratified the Constitution. A third, Zahra Rahnavard, wife of Mir Hossein Musavi (who later became prime minister), took part in the Islamization of the press in the Ettela'at Publishing Institute, transforming its weekly women's magazine *Ettela'at-e Banuan* into the Islamic *Rah-e Zeinab*.

The National Union of Women emerged in the aftermath of International Women's Day on March 8, 1979, when thousands of women demonstrated in Tehran and Shiraz. Many women were disturbed by the dismantling of the pre-revolutionary legal reforms, in particular the declaration on February 26 that the 1967 Family Protection Law (which had curtailed men's access to divorce and polygamy) was non-Islamic. Ayatollah Ruhollah Khomeini's statement on the eve of the demonstrations, requiring women working in government offices to observe the "Islamic code" of dress, also made *hejab* an issue. The authorities ignored these demonstrations, and radio and television (by now under the control of the Islamic forces) denounced them as agitation by promiscuous women and agents of the previous regime. Women continued demonstrating in protest, but they were attacked and harassed by groups of men drawn from the urban poor and religious zealots. Yet the scale of the women's protest was such that the Provisional Government had to modify Khomeini's statement on *hejab* and to promise to set up new family courts to protect women's rights. Adhering to a Marxist-feminist ideology, the Union grew into a national organization with centers in most provinces, and became the largest semi-autonomous organization. However, its activities were curtailed and then halted in 1981 with the ascendancy of the clerical forces. Many members of secular women's organizations were imprisoned or departed to the West (Tabari and Yeganeh 1982).

With the onset of war with Iraq in 1980, the radicals gradually gained the upper hand, the left and national forces were repressed, and a process of Islamization began. While women kept their suffrage rights, many pre-revolutionary legal reforms were suspended. Men's rights to unilateral divorce and polygamy were reinstituted. Women's rights to divorce and child custody were limited, and women were forbidden to study mining and agriculture, to serve as judges, and to appear in public without *hejab*. Many women who at the beginning genuinely, although naively, believed that under an Islamic state women's position would automatically improve became disillusioned. These included those women who had played instrumental roles in discrediting secular feminists and in Islamizing the existing women's press and organizations, such as Zahra Rahnavard, Azam Taleqani, and Monir Gorji.

After this phase, the contradictions in the early revolutionary discourse on women gradually emerged. This discourse made gender a central issue of an Islamic polity; it made the private public, and the personal political, and in this way politicized every aspect of women's lives. Yet, it remained adamant in adhering to the Shari'a and in treating women differently. These contradictions were enshrined in the Constitution of the Islamic Republic. For instance, on the one hand, the Constitution puts men and women on the same footing in matters such as protection in law, rights to vote and to be elected, access to education, and employment (Articles 3, 20). On the other, it subordinates these rights to the supreme rule of the Shari'a, which restricts women and treats them as second-class citizens (Articles 4, 91, 93).

Meanwhile, as the coalition of forces that had brought about the Revolution collapsed, the religious authorities came to rely on popular support, including large numbers of women. This gave an opportunity for political activity to so-called traditional women, who until then had seen politics as beyond their realm. The long drawn-out war with Iraq and the accompanying rapid price inflation forced women into the labor market, and the state's moralistic rhetoric and compulsory veiling made women's activity outside the home respectable in the eyes of religious and traditional families. As public space became more Islamic, thus morally correct and safe, these families could no longer thwart their women's wishes to go out to study and work. Likewise, the unwritten gender codes governing Majles proceedings, which assumed that female members' constituencies consisted solely of women, also became a strong lobbying force in defense of women's rights. Women parliamentarians devoted all their energies to women's issues; despite their small number (four in the first three Majles, nine in the fourth, and thirteen in the fifth, convened respectively in 1979, 1983, 1987, 1992, and 1996), they were able to ensure the airing of women's grievances.

The Islamic Republic was now caught by its own rhetoric: its official discourse advocated domesticity and motherhood as ideal roles for women; the Constitution promised to guard the sanctity of the family; yet the return to Shari'a provisions which gave men a free hand in divorce and polygamy in effect subverted the very sanctity of the family as understood by women, thus negating the Constitution's promise. Where the gender policies of the Pahlavi regime had faced a Shari'a-based opposition, those of the Islamic Republic now had to deal with a secular and liberal opposition, both inside and outside Iran. In this way the government and those women active in its sponsored organizations had to engage with feminist discourses—and in denouncing them came to adopt some of their elements (Afshar 1998; Hoodfar 1999; Kian 1997; Mir-Hosseini 1999).

The end of war with Iraq in 1988 heralded a new era of "Reconstruction" and the emergence of an independent press that carried a critique of official discourses and policies. A new phase in the woman question began with the resumption of debates that had earlier been harshly suppressed, but this time in an Islamic format and framework. Conducted publicly in the women's press, these debates paved the way for a shift in official gender discourses and the enactment of legislation to confront the inequity of men's Shari'a rights.

The shift was most evident in a number of new laws and policies: many of the earlier restrictions on subjects women could study were removed (1986); family planning and contraception became freely available (1988);

divorce laws were amended so as to curtail men's right to divorce and to compensate women in the face of it (1992); and women were appointed as advisory judges (1992). In short, by the early 1990s many of the early decisions of the revolutionary regime with regard to women had been modified or were at least being debated—a notable exception being the *hejab* regulations (Ramazani 1993).

## WOMEN'S RIGHTS TODAY

### A New Feminist Voice

In some ways these modifications represented the official, establishment side of the debates. There was another side, however, aligned with a new trend of thought in postwar and post-Khomeini Iran intent on creating a worldview to reconcile Islam with democracy and modernity. This trend sought a dialogue with secular thinkers and offered a different interpretation of Islam that had the potential to change the terms of the Islamic Republic's discourses on women. This is so because it not only challenged orthodox notions of gender in Islam but also questioned the very Shari'a legitimacy of the laws enforced by the Islamic Republic.

These views were first aired in *Zanan* (Women), a women's magazine whose appearance marked the onset of another phase, in which one could talk of the emergence of a new and distinctive "feminist" voice. Shahla Sherkat, founder and editor of *Zanan*, had played an important role in the Islamization of the women's press in the early years of the Republic. In 1982 she was invited to join the Kayhan Publishing Institute as editor of *Zan-e Ruz*, the most popular and outspoken women's magazine in the pre-revolutionary era. She remained editor until 1991, when she left because of unresolved disagreements over the ways in which gender issues were being addressed. The first issue of *Zanan* appeared seven months later, in February 1992.

Two features of *Zanan*'s feminism and line of argument were novel. First, unlike previous discourses (both Islamic and secular) on women in Iran, *Zanan*'s did not subordinate women's issues to a wider political project, but advocated them in their own right. Sherkat, having subscribed to the new regime's early position on women, had been involved in its translation from rhetoric into policy. During this process she came to confront its inherent contradictions, and became aware that she could find support in feminism, regardless of its Western baggage, while in patriarchy, regardless of its Islamic credentials, she could only meet resistance.

Second, *Zanan* advocated a brand of feminism that took its legitimacy from Islam, yet made no apologies for drawing on Western feminist sources and collaborating with Iranian secular feminists to argue for women's rights. It argued that there is no logical link between patriarchy and Islamic idealism, and no contradiction between fighting for women's rights and remaining a good Muslim. Unlike the mass of post-revolutionary apologetic literature, *Zanan* did not attempt to conceal or rationalize the gender inequalities of Islamic law, but sought to address them within the context of Islam itself (Mir-Hosseini 1999; Najmabadi 1998).

Among the early contributors to *Zanan* were a female lawyer, Mehrangiz Kar, and a male cleric, Seyyed Mohsen Sa'idzadeh, whose articles on women's Islamic, legal, and political rights featured regularly in the journal. These articles took issue with the very premises of the official Islamic discourse on women, laying bare their inherent gender biases. Sa'idzadeh's articles, written in the language and mode of argumentation of Islamic jurisprudence, transported *Zanan*'s message into the heart of the clerical seminaries but also forced the authorities there to respond. *Zanan*, in effect, Islamized notions such as the legitimacy of women's choices and their demands for equal treatment, and became a forum to which both Islamic and secular feminists contributed. *Zanan* had an influence well beyond its small political base, and even induced its own counter-discourse, articulated by both clerics in Qom and women with close links to the political elite and the government. In 1992 the Propagation Office of the Qom Seminaries launched *Payam-e Zan* (Women's Message), a monthly journal that aimed to provide an answer to the woman question within the Islamic framework. In 1993 appeared the first issue of *Farzaneh* (Wise), a quarterly edited by Massoumeh Ebtekar and Mahboobeh Ommi and published by Monir Gorji's Centre for Women's Studies and Research. With articles in English and Persian, *Farzaneh* was the first women's studies journal in Iran; aiming to bring the woman question into the academic domain, it advocated a top-down approach, feminism from above. Gorji's outspoken articles, engaging in Koranic exegesis to show that the Koran does not sanction gender discrimination, were a far cry from her earlier timid objections, as the only woman deputy in the 1979 Assembly of Experts, to impositions on women in the name of Islam.

Ebtekar and Ommi played active parts in Iran's official preparations for the 1995 Women's Conference in Beijing, orchestrated by Shahla Habibi, the president's adviser on women's affairs and head of the Women's Bureau. While women in *Zanan* declined to participate because of the hands-on approach of the government, those in *Farzaneh* organized workshops in Iran to familiarize women's nongovernmental organizations (NGOs) with the working of United Nations conferences and took part in the international meetings at which the Conference Document was shaped. Ebtekar became a member of the Iranian delegation in Beijing.

In this new phase—marked by factional politics and the intensification of struggles between traditionalist and modernist interpretations of Islam—women's issues acquired an unprecedented urgency. This time, however, there were signs that women were gaining ground in political terms, and that the media, in particular the women's press, had become a forum for protest and for solidarity between secular and religious women. More women joined the modernist forces; some who until then had previously considered women's issues unimportant joined the debate by the mid-1990s. More women than before stood in the Majles elections of 1996, and some of them defeated candidates backed by conservatives, not only in Tehran and other large cities but also in smaller ones. Among them Fa'ezeh Rafsanjani, younger daughter of the then president, polled the second highest vote in Tehran; even higher, it was rumored, than Ahmad Nateq-Nuri, conservative choice for the forthcoming presidential elections. She ran on a platform of promoting women's participation in politics, society, and sport. Although the thirteen women deputies were no great increase from the nine in the previous Majles, they became more vocal on women's issues and set up a Women's Commission. Likewise, women's votes were among the decisive factors in the 1997 presidential elections, when Mohammad Khatami, the candidate of the moderates, gained an overwhelming victory over the conservative candidate, Nateq-Nuri. The women's press, in particular *Zanan*, played a role in informing women of the gender views and policies of the two main candidates (*Zanan* 34, May 1997).

The 1997 presidential elections, in particular, showed the importance of gender issues in the politics of the Islamic Republic. Among the messages from that election that the authorities cannot afford to ignore were women's demands for social justice and equal opportunities. No political figure can afford to alienate the new generation of women, who have come of age in the Islamic Republic and are demanding equal opportunities under the Shari'a on all fronts.

## THE FUTURE OF WOMEN'S RIGHTS

It is too early to predict the future of the women's movement in Iran. Evidently, as before, its fate is entangled with wider socioeconomic and political developments. What is certain is that the 1979 Revolution brought home to women from all walks of life the harsh reality of subjection to the Shari'a when applied by the machinery of a modern state. Paradoxically, Islamization and segregation policies designed to keep women at home became a catalyst for their increased participation in society and brought about a critique of the fundamental gender assumptions of Islamic law. For the first time, it has become possible to question its patriarchal elements without being accused of heresy.

Although Iranian women, like other Muslim women, have always been aware of gender inequality, feminism—as consciousness if not as a movement—was conceived at the beginning of the twentieth century during the Constitutional Revolution. Its gestation took place during the rule of two Pahlavi shahs, when a modern nation-state came into being, but a natural birth was delayed by its appropriation by the Pahlavi state, whose undemocratic nature and identification with the West sullied the positive legal measures it took to improve women's position in society. This made it difficult for women to use existing political structures and vocabulary to express feminist demands. Besides, the very fact that such demands were articulated by women from the middle and upper classes limited the movement's grassroots expansion. The Islamic Revolution of 1979 deepened the perceived chasm between Islam and feminism, and the early rhetoric and policies of the Islamic Republic made it impossible to be both Muslim and feminist. The state now relied on women from religious and lower middle classes in spreading and enforcing its gender ideology and policies.

In time, many Iranian women—both religious and secular—were forced to reexamine and redefine the relation between their faith and their feminism. A new phase of the politics of gender in Iran began and a new gender awareness was fostered. A crucial element of this type of politics was that it created a space where a critique of gender biases in Muslim societies could be sustained in ways that were previously impossible. Women started to use the Islamic Republic's own political vocabulary and discourse to demand equal rights. An indigenous—locally produced—feminism was born. It was a difficult and painful birth. It takes time for the wounds to heal. Iranian women have yet to come to terms with their multiple identities, in particular with their sexuality, and to challenge their patriarchal culture in a coherent way. While women's sexuality is dealt with extensively in classical Islamic texts, it is largely bypassed in modern texts and is very much veiled in women's writings. The notable exception remains Forugh Farrokhzad (1935–1967), whose poetry is an explicit acknowledgment of her own sexuality (Milani 1992). This silence, as I have argued elsewhere, is significant and can be seen as a reaction to Islamic discourses and an attempt to carve a space within them where women can be perceived as social beings (Mir-Hosseini 1999).

At the close of the twentieth century, the context and dynamics of the woman question in Iran are different from what they were a century earlier, when the issue entered the political discourse of the emerging nation-state. But one basic fact has not changed. The issue continues to be defined by the state, and it is still a site where the forces of traditionalism and modernity fight their gendered battles.

## BIBLIOGRAPHY

Afkhami, Mahnaz. 1984. "Iran: A Future in the Past. The 'Prerevolutionary' Women's Movement." In *Sisterhood Is Global*, ed. Robin Morgan. Garden City, NY: Anchor Books.

Afshar, Haleh. 1998. *Islam and Feminisms: An Iranian Case Study*. London: Macmillan.

Ahmed, Leila. 1984. "Early Feminist Movements in the Middle East: Turkey and Egypt." In *Muslim Women*, ed. Freda Hussain. London: Croom Helm.

Hoodfar, Homa. 1999. "The Women's Movement in Iran: Women at the Crossroads of Secularization and Islamization." *Women Living Under Islamic Laws—The Women's Movement*, Series No. 1.

Kian, Azadeh. 1997. "Women and Politics in Post-Islamist Iran: The Gender Conscious Drive to Change." *British Journal of Middle Eastern Studies* 24, no. 1: 75–96.

Milani, Farzaneh. 1992. *Veils and Words: The Emerging Voices of Iranian Women Writers.* Syracuse: Syracuse University Press.

Mir-Hosseini, Ziba. 1999. *Islam and Gender: The Religious Debate in Contemporary Iran.* Princeton: Princeton University Press.

Najmabadi, Afsaneh. 1998. "Feminism in an Islamic Republic: Years of Hardship, Years of Growth." In *Islam, Gender, and Political Change*, ed. Yvonne Yazbeck Haddad and John Esposito. Oxford: Oxford University Press.

Paidar, Parvin. 1995. *Women and the Political Process in Twentieth-Century Iran.* Cambridge: Cambridge University Press.

Ramazani, Nesta. 1993. "Women in Iran: The Revolutionary Ebb and Flow." *Middle East Journal* 47: 409–28.

Sanasarian, Elizabeth. 1982. *The Women's Rights Movement in Iran.* New York: Praeger.

Tabari, Azar, and Nahid Yeganeh, eds. 1982. *In the Shadow of Islam.* London: Zed Press.

# 10

# ISRAEL

## The Myth of Gender Equality

### Chava Frankfort-Nachmias

## INTRODUCTION

### Profile of Israel

The state of Israel has its roots in Zionism—the nationalist movement founded in 1896 to reclaim Palestine as a homeland for the Jewish people. Established by Eastern European Zionists who immigrated to Palestine early in the twentieth century, Israel emerged as a state in 1948 after it had won a war against its Palestinian Arab neighbors. Subsequently, Israeli society has become a homeland to millions of Jewish immigrants from different countries and diverse backgrounds. During the three years following the establishment of the state, mass immigration doubled the size of the Jewish population, which was approximately 600,000 in 1947. Today there are over 5.5 million people in Israel, with a Jewish majority comprising about 82 percent of the nation's population. The remaining 18 percent are non-Jews, mostly Arabs. Israeli Jews are evenly divided between those of European (Western) origin and those originating from Middle Eastern countries. Israel is an industrialized urban society with about 90 percent of its population living in urban areas. It has a Western-style democracy with a multiparty parliamentary system. The parliament (Knesset) of 120 members is elected by proportional representation from party lists. Israel has a technologically advanced market economy with considerable government participation.

## A Case Study

Gila Shoham is forty-two, married with three children, ages nineteen, fourteen, and seven. She has worked part-time since her children were born and is now working as a legal secretary, a job she has held for a decade. Despite her part-time position, Gila has received the same workers' benefits and social security, as well as the benefits of tenure, as full-time workers in her office. However, Gila's salary is lower than the salary of men in similar positions, and her opportunities for promotion and higher pay are rather limited. Yet, Gila sees herself as a wife and a mother first, with her obligation to her family taking precedence over her commitment to and expectations of her job. She spends a great deal of her time tending to family affairs and has primary responsibility for housekeeping and childcare. Her parenting role became even more demanding since her oldest son began compulsory military service. During his weekends and furloughs at home, Gila is busy pampering her soldier son. She is accustomed to this role from years of catering to her husband who combines a demanding career with an obligation—shared by most Israeli men under fifty—to serve in the military reserve at least thirty days each year. Gila's family obligations are not unusual in a country where the family is perceived as a safe haven for its soldiers. In a society where family comes first and where being a wife and a mother is sometimes seen as a national obligation, women like Gila Shoham have limited choices despite a history of progressive women's rights legislation.

## Overview of Women's Rights Issues

The first scholarly book on contemporary Israeli feminism is *Calling the Equality Bluff: Women in Israel* (Safir and Swirski 1991). The title is symbolic of the most significant characteristic of feminism in Israel: the sharp contrast between legislation on women's equality and reality (Yishai 1997, 18). While the status of women has received attention since the establishment of the state, with some impressive landmarks, most efforts have been confined to the institutional level rather than converted into action (Yishai 1997; Swirski and Hasan 1998).

Despite progressive legislation gender inequality is evident at all levels of society in Israel: in the family, the labor force, politics, and the military. Israeli women are excluded from the center of political power. They work in a highly segregated labor force and occupy a highly traditional role in the family. How do we account for this paradox? Answering this question requires taking a critical look at the most central institutions of Israeli society: family, work, politics, and the military. The framework used in this chapter to analyze gender equality in Israel applies only to Jewish women. While Israeli Palestinian women are Israeli citizens, their gender status is not affected by the same forces that shape the status of Jewish women.

## HISTORY OF WOMEN'S RIGHTS

Israel is considered among the "first wave countries" where women gained political rights, including the right to vote, early in in the twentieth century (Yishai 1997; Swirski and Hasan 1998). Suffrage was granted by the British government in the late 1920s, about twenty years before the establishment of the state. The struggle for gender equality was led by a minority of revolutionary Jewish women who emigrated from Russia to form a new egalitarian society in Palestine. These women fought for the right to work and established the Women's Workers Movement, an important feminist force in the Jewish community. After independence in 1948, gender equality was inscribed in the Declaration of Independence, and in the 1950s the Israeli Knesset passed the Women's Equal Rights Law, which entitled women to legal equality (Raday et al. 1995; Berkovitch 1997). In the 1970s a new women's movement developed, inspired by immigrants from the United States and other English-speaking countries. The movement led to the establishment of shelters for battered women, rape crisis centers, and other feminist organizations (Swirski and Hasan 1998). During the 1970s, various steps were taken by the government to address women's issues. In 1975 Prime Minister Yitzhak Rabin appointed a commission on the status of women, which presented its findings and recommendations in 1978. Following the recommendations of the commission, various government agencies were established to promote women's equality (Yishai 1997). The 1980s were marked by the development of liberal feminism in Israel, with feminist organizations as well as more traditional women's organization focusing on legislation and political participation. During this period, the Israel Women's Network, a nationwide organization for women, was established.

## WOMEN'S RIGHTS TODAY

### The Family

Although Israel has been characterized as a developed, urban-industrial democracy, it is a family-oriented society with strong traditional-patriarchal elements more typical of agrarian societies. The divorce rate in Israel in 1994 was 4 per 1,000, while only 6 percent of households were headed by a single parent (CBS 1994). The fertility rate, which was 2.62 for Jewish women in the years 1990–1994, is higher than in most urban industrialized countries (Swirski and Hasan 1998). Marriage and children are the norms for women in Israel and are not seen as a choice. The pressure for women to find their identity and security in marriage produces a society where approximately 98 percent of the women are or have been married.

There are several explanations for the centrality of the traditional family in Israeli society. The first explanation is the Jewish religious tradition, which historically has emphasized the family as a means of ensuring individual and communal survival (Yishai 1997; Golan 1997). The majority of Israelis, orthodox, conservative, or secular Jews, adhere to the basic tenets of the Jewish tradition. These values have been sustained by contemporary historical events. In the aftermath of the Holocaust, the majority of Israeli Jews found themselves with truncated families, with many first generation Israelis never knowing their grandparents. The family became a means to establish permanence and stability and to create a new family history.

### The Religious Influence

The strong religious influences on the Israeli family can be observed not only in the private sphere but in the public arena as well. In 1953 the state gave the orthodox rabbinical courts complete jurisdiction over matters of personal status, such as marriage and divorce. Religious law takes priority over matters of personal status and at present there is no mechanism under the jurisdiction of civil law that allows individuals to marry or divorce. This legislation has had adverse effects on the status of women in the family and in the larger society. The Jewish religion, with its patriarchal attitudes toward gender roles, does not consider men and women equal before the law. According to Jewish religious law (Halakha), the marriage ceremony is a unilateral ceremony where the woman is "purchased" by the husband. Moreover, Jewish women cannot get a divorce without the consent of their husband even when they are abused or abandoned by the husband (Yishai 1997; Swirski and Hasan 1998). It is estimated that there are approximately 10,000 women in Israel whose husbands will not grant them a divorce. The status of women in religious courts is no better than the status of the mentally deficient, the insane, or the convicted criminal. Women cannot sign documents, be witnesses, or testify (Swirski and Hasan 1998). Considering women's inferior status, it is not surprising that in a prayer recited by the orthodox Jewish male every morning, thanks is given to God for not creating him a woman.

### Security Issues and Militarization

The second reason for the importance of the family is the centrality of the army and security issues in Israeli society. Since the establishment of the state in 1948, Israel has fought five wars and has been engaged in an ongoing conflict with its Arab neighbors. Consequently, soldiering, the army, and national security have dominated the public discourse (Herzog 1998). The unspoken consensus that Israel faces a constant security threat continues to prevail despite Israel's military and economic resilience (Herzog 1998). This siege mentality has reinforced the already strong family tradition in Israeli society. The family is seen as a safe haven for husbands, sons, and brothers who face a demanding and long military duty (usually three to five years plus one month a year until they turn fifty).

The militarization of Israeli society has created a male-oriented culture in which women are expected to nurture their men who are called up to serve their country and who give up their lives if necessary. The metaphor of the "crowded nest" has been used to describe the typical Israeli family, where "the female hovers over the males, preoccupied with combating real and imaginary enemies and attending to their needs" (Yishai 1997, 242; Safir and Swirski 1991; Herzog 1998). These "duties" have been internalized by women, who are seen as the front-line "soldiers," serving their country by catering to the needs of men.

The family remains at the center of the Israeli woman's life even when her children leave home to serve in the army. During this period, the family is seen as an important source of support for its soldier. The woman is expected to nurture her soldier son or soldier daughter by laundering and ironing uniforms, preparing meals during family visits, and baking cakes for the children to take back to the army. This period only serves to reinforce the Israeli woman's traditional role in the family (Azmon 1993, 1–13; Herzog 1998).

The task of being a wife and a mother is thus seen as falling in the public rather than the private sphere. Having a family, preferably with many children, became a national priority encouraged and rewarded by state authorities. In the 1950s, David Ben-Gurion, the first prime minister of Israel and a leading proponent of a high birthrate, announced a prize for families with ten children or more (Safir and Swirski 1991). State subsidies are granted for large families (those with four or more children) to cover the cost of daycare and summer camps, and there is a political lobby that represents the rights and interests of large families (Safir and Swirski 1991).

The combined influence of the Jewish religion and the institutionalization of security issues has served as a significant mechanism sustaining the traditional family, the gendered division of labor within the family, and, consequently, gender inequality (Herzog 1998; Azmon 1993, 1–13). Numerous studies have confirmed the unequal division of labor between men and women in the Israeli family (Yishai 1997; Safir and Swirski 1991). Childcare is considered the mother's responsibility; and although the founders of the state, influenced by socialist ideals, expected women to work, the assumption was that they would work part-time so that they could fulfill their duties as wives and mothers. Married women are expected to be home when their spouse and children come home between one and four in the afternoon. Husbands are rarely equal partners in managing the house and at best are expected lend a hand (Safir and Swirski 1991).

Ironically, the centrality of the family in Israeli society, coupled with early socialist ideology, has resulted in progressive legislation designed to protect women in their multiple roles as workers, wives, and mothers (Safir and Swirski 1991). However, despite these gains, the gendered division of labor and the perception that women's role is secondary to men's have made

Israeli women dependent on men and severely limit the choices open to them.

### Women and Work

The "myth of equality" in Israel and the sharp contrast between formal legislation and its implementation is best illustrated in the area of women and work. Israel is noted as one of the most progressive nations in its labor legislation as it relates to women (Yishai 1997). However, while they enjoy economic equality before the law, Israeli women are employed in a highly segregated labor market where pay and other benefits are unequally distributed.

Labor legislation relating to women dates back to the 1950s. Labor law provisions reflected Israeli culture's dual commitment to a socialist philosophy in which everyone is engaged in productive labor on one hand, and a strong family orientation in which women are perceived as homemakers and mothers on the other (Raday 1991; Berkovitch 1997). This duality is manifested in legislation and institutional arrangements that support the working mother model as long as the family is given priority (Azmon 1993, 1–13). Consequently, a strong legal foundation was created to ease the integration of family and work. The main thrust of this legislative effort was the provision of protection to working mothers. For example, women are given a three-month maternity leave and the right to take up to one year of leave without pay (Raday 1991). In addition, measures were also taken to provide working mothers with publicly subsidized daycare and preschool services.

Progressive legislation and general public support for women's employment outside the home contribute to a relatively high labor participation rate among Israeli women. Between 1976 and 1996 the proportion of women in the labor force rose from 32 percent to 46 percent. Among women ages thirty-five to forty-four the rate in 1996 was 68 percent. Education is highly correlated with women's labor participation rate. Whereas 68 percent of women with sixteen years of education or more were in the labor force in 1996, the rate was only 28 percent for women with less than a high school education (CBS 1996, Table 12.5).

The upward trend in women's employment can be also attributed to restructuring of the Israeli economy and demographic trends in Israeli society. First, the expansion of the economy in the 1980s resulted in a demand for qualified workers in education and in financial and business services. At the same time, growing defense needs absorbed men from the civilian sector, thus opening new employment opportunities for women (Azmon 1993). Furthermore, the availability of childcare facilities has made it possible for women with young children to be in the labor force (Yishai 1997). In 1996, 59 percent of women whose youngest child was under one year of age and

79 percent of women whose youngest child was between ten and fourteen were in the labor force.

The strong family orientation in Israel and the pressure exerted on women to put family obligations first have motivated many women to work part-time. The proportion of women working part-time in 1996 was 36 percent. Moreover, women constitute close to 70 percent of all part-time workers in the labor force. However, it should be noted that, in contrast to other countries, part-time workers receive the same workers' benefits and social security as well as the benefits of tenure as full-time workers (Azmon 1993, 11–13; Yishai 1997).

While the legal infrastructure facilitates the integration of work and family for women, it also perpetuates the stereotype of women as the primary homemakers and secondary employees and ignores the need to guarantee equal opportunity for women in the labor market (Raday 1991). The current policies support a highly segregated system in which the majority of women are on career tracks where the opportunities for promotion and higher pay are limited (Israeli 1991).

As in most industrialized countries, Israeli women and men are concentrated in different jobs and occupations, a fact that accounts for women's poor position in the labor market. Women tend to concentrate in a small number of traditionally "feminine" occupations. In 1996 Israeli women were heavily concentrated in education (75 percent) and social work and nursing (75 percent). In contrast, they constituted less than 30 percent of the work force in agriculture, industry, and construction.

What are the consequences of gender segregation in the workplace? In societies where people's jobs and occupations determine their location in the status system in terms of income and prestige, gender segregation in the workplace contributes to women's lower pay and lesser social power (Reskin and Padavic 1994, 46). Israeli women have "more limited career choices, fewer promotional opportunities, and inferior wages and fringe benefits" than Israeli men (Yishai 1997, 154). Despite the fact that the proportion of women in management positions has almost doubled in the last twenty years, women occupied only 20 percent of management positions in 1996 (CBS 1996). Moreover, women in all positions earn considerably less than men. In 1996 the average hourly wage for women employed full time was 80 percent that of men. The gender gap in earnings increases with level of education. The hourly wage of women with only four years of education or less was almost equivalent (95 percent) to that of men with the same level of education. In contrast, educated women (sixteen years of education or more) earn 27 percent less than men with the same level of education (CBS 1996).

The income differentials in Israel are attributed not only to a segregated labor market but also to direct discriminatory practices of employers. In Israel, fringe benefits such as overtime pay, cars, and travel allowances account for about 40 percent of take-home pay. Employers tend to differentially allocate such benefits to men and women in essentially similar jobs. Because of the weight of fringe benefits in the overall pay package, such practices tend to widen the pay gap between men and women.

### The Employment Opportunity Law

From the mid-1970s through the early 1980s a series of lawsuits contested discrimination against women in the labor market. These efforts culminated in the Equal Employment Opportunity Law, passed by the Knesset in 1988. The law made discrimination on the basis of sex in the workplace illegal. Specifically, the law prohibits discrimination in job advertising, conditions of employment, job training, and promotion as well as dismissal and severance pay (Yishai 1997). A prohibition against sexual harassment was also included. In 1996 the law was further expanded to define fringe benefits as income and to prohibit unequal allocation of these benefits for similar jobs.

Clearly, the unequal status of women in the labor market has been an important part of the legislative agenda in Israel. Beginning in the 1950s and culminating in the 1980s and 1990s, serious efforts have been made to fight gender discrimination in the workplace. Yet, despite these legislative attempts to reduce inequality, Israeli women continue to be employed in a segregated labor market. Furthermore, women continue to have limited access to training and promotion opportunities and earn considerably less than men do. Feminist scholars have argued that recent legislation introduced to fight discrimination in the workplace has not been effective because it does not include affirmative action in its definition of equality, nor does it have provisions for enforcement (Yishai 1997; Raday 1991). Another factor accounting for the ineffectiveness of the new legislation is the reluctance of women to sue employers. While a few landmark cases have been fought in the labor courts, the majority of women are unwilling to pay the economic and psychological price involved in suing their employers.

Finally, the perception of women as wives and mothers, and thus as secondary breadwinners, continues to reinforce the traditional stereotype of females as needing protection in the workplace even when this limits their ability to compete equally (Raday 1991). Without a fundamental change in social norms regarding women's equal status in the labor force, employment legislation will be limited to providing legal rights rather than promoting gender equality in the workplace.

### The Military

The problem of national security has dominated the public discourse in Israel in the pre-state era and since the establishment of the state in 1948. The unspoken consensus that Israel faces a constant external threat has made security the highest priority issue on the national agenda for more than fifty years.

In a nation preoccupied with security, the military has become a major institution. Israel was the first and still remains the only country with compulsory conscription of Jewish citizens of both sexes. Military service is perceived as both an obligation and a right and as a defining Israeli experience and a key to Israeli identity (Herzog 1998; Golan 1997). The central role of the army in Israeli life has created a macho culture, which fosters the myth of male superiority and female dependence and contributes to the perpetuation of gender inequality (Azmon 1993, 11–13). Although the image of women clad in uniform and carrying rifles on their shoulders has been touted by Israeli public opinion campaigns as proof of an egalitarian approach, this egalitarian image is a myth (Yishai 1997).

Despite compulsory conscription of both men and women, the Israeli Defense Force (IDF) is probably the most gendered institution in Israeli society. Women serve in the military for a shorter period than men and are automatically exempted from service if they marry or become pregnant or if they are religiously observant. All women who serve in the Israeli military belong to the Women's Corps, which is entirely separate from other units in the IDF. The acronym for the Women's Corps, Chen, means charm, suggesting the traditionally feminine characteristic emphasized in the Corps. Women are expected to "raise the morale" of the male fighter and create for him "a home away from home" (Sharoni 1992). Furthermore, during basic training women receive cosmetic guidance to help them emphasize their feminine characteristics and neat appearance (Yuval-Davis 1982; Sharoni 1992).

The prime illustration of women's unequal status in the IDF is their exclusion from all jobs involving combat. While women are sometimes on the front lines in various support positions, they are sent to the rear at the first sign of hostilities. The unequal status of women with their male counterparts begins with basic training, with men shooting hundreds of bullets during three weeks of basic training compared with only one clip of thirty-two bullets shot by women (Beth-Halachmy 1996). A Jerusalem councilwoman put it this way: "[A] woman has a better chance of hitting a terrorist with her handbag than with a bullet" (quoted in Beth-Halachmy 1996). Women's exclusion from combat duty severely limits their job opportunities in the military. Occupations in the IDF are severely segregated along gender lines, with most female soldiers assigned to clerical or similar positions, mostly providing support to male commanders (Sharoni 1992). In 1976 only about 30 percent of all jobs in the IDF (out of a total of about 700) were filled by women, and approximately 65 percent of women soldiers held secretarial, administrative, and clerical jobs.

When the IDF was first established, the state recognized the right of women to serve in all jobs on a voluntary basis. As time passed, equality disappeared. The only considerations are army efficiency and economic ones. Jobs are opened and closed to women on this basis. As a result the IDF lags behind other armies, which are more resourceful in absorbing women (Bloom 1991, 135). Following the recommendation of the Commission on the Status of Women, the range of jobs open to women expanded considerably, from 30 percent to about 70 percent by the end of 1994. While nearly 90 percent of all combat jobs are still closed to women, the IDF has successfully experimented with assigning women as instructors in artillery and tank corps. However, these jobs account for less than 4 percent of women conscripts.

Despite the progress that has been made regarding women's status, the IDF remains a deeply gendered institution. Women soldiers are still the secretaries, the clerks, the telephonists, the nurses, the teachers, and the social workers of the IDF (Yishai 1997). As recently as 1981, the Israeli military attorney general ruled that coffee making and floor washing are considered legitimate duties of military secretaries, the majority of whom happen to be women (Sharoni 1992; Yuval-Davis 1982).

Gender inequality in the IDF has far-reaching implications in Israeli society. Due to the dominance of national security in the public discourse, the military plays a central role in the formation and recruitment of political and economic elites. High-ranking officers, upon retirement at the age of forty-five, are routinely recruited for political posts and management positions in business and industry. In 1995 women constituted only 12.4 percent of the officers in the professional services (IWN 1997). Their small numbers and exclusion from combat duty severely limit women's opportunities for promotion on the military ladder and their ability to link into the "old boy network" so crucial to recruitment and advancement of post-military careers (Azmon 1993, 11–13; Golan 1997). Thus, while men are able to translate their military service into better positions in the labor market, women are rarely in a position to do so (Herzog 1998).

The IDF, with the preferential treatment it accords to men and its highly segregated and gendered nature, reproduces and reinforces the gendered division of labor and the masculine-macho culture of Israeli civil society. Its centrality and dominance and the important role it plays in creating an Israeli identity render legitimacy to gender inequality and limit women's access to power.

## Women and Politics

The myth of gender equality in Israel has been reinforced by the image of Golda Meir, the late prime minister, who was cited as proof positive that Israel had no need for feminism. However, Golda Meir, who rose through the party ranks after years of hard work, was a glaring exception. As with other institutions, women's political representation is shaped by social and cultural forces and by the relative predominance of patriarchy. A major impediment to women's political representation in Israel is the preoccupation with national security and the influence of religion on public affairs (Yishai 1997, 54; Herzog 1998).

In Israel, as in most other countries, women are underrepresented in elected bodies at all levels and branches of government, including the Knesset, the government on the local level, and in the bureaucracy. Since 1948, when elections of the first 120-member Knesset took place, the number of women members has fluctuated between a low of eight and a high of twelve. The 1999 elections brought a distinct improvement in the representation of women, whose numbers rose from nine in the Fourteenth Knesset to fourteen in the Fifteenth Knesset. Despite this improvement, the proportion of women legislators has consistently remained below 12 percent. In this respect, however, Israel does not differ much from most nations in the West, with the exception of the Scandinavian countries (Azmon 1993).

Even when elected, Israeli women have very little power relative to men. A woman has hardly ever belonged to either the Foreign and Security Affairs Committee or the Finance Committee, the two most powerful committees in the Knesset (Yishai 1997, 30). Similarly, women are underrepresented in the cabinet. For example, not a single woman was included in the late 1980s cabinet, which had twenty-six ministers (Yishai 1997, 32). While the situation changed somewhat in the 1990s, the 1996 Netanyahu cabinet included only one woman. Even the 1999 elections, which brought a distinct improvement in the representation of women in the Knesset, did not result in a much better representation in the newly formed cabinet. Only two women were included in the newly formed cabinet led by Ehud Barak.

In many countries, while women are excluded from the centers of power in national legislative institutions, their representation at the local level is considerably higher. The focus of local governments on matters of traditional concern to women as well as family constraints has attracted women to the local political arena. In Israel, the proportion of women elected to local political bodies has gradually risen, from 4.2 percent in 1950 to 10.9 percent in 1993 (IWN 1997). However, despite this increase in their relative representation on the local level, women's representation is still very small, with only three women heading local councils out of a total of sixty-three and not a single female mayor prior to the 1998 elections. The public sector is another arena in which Israeli women are underrepresented. In 1995 women constituted 60 percent of those employed in the public sector, yet 80 percent of all those employed at the lower ranks were women, while they constituted barely 10 percent of the four highest ranks in the government bureaucracy (Yishai 1997).

Finally, as in other countries, women's limited political power is correlated with their unequal gender status in other social and economic institutions. Israeli feminists agree that an increase in political representation at all levels of government is essential for the removal of some of the major impediments to gender equality in Israel. However, despite the organization of a women's network which has been relatively successful in mobilizing broad coalitions of women, the predominant patriarchal culture and the increased influence of the orthodox religious parties remain serious obstacles to the political representation of women in Israeli society.

## THE FUTURE OF WOMEN'S RIGHTS

Israel combines two worlds: on the one hand, it is a liberal society characterized by democratic institutions, principles of equality, justice, and freedom, and a relatively free flow of communication; on the other hand, it is characterized by a high level of familialism, the strong influence of religion and tradition, and military involvement in government and civil society.

This duality has resulted in relatively progressive legislation in women's issues coupled with gender inequality, which is evident in all major institutions of society. Israeli women are discriminated against in the workplace and the military and are excluded from the center of political power. In the family, the role of Israeli women is similar to the role occupied by women in traditional and agrarian societies. With security at the top of the national agenda, gender equality has not been high on the list of priorities for most Israelis, who consider equality for women of secondary importance at best.

The election of a more progressive government in 1999 and its commitment to jumpstarting the peace process have given many social observers and feminists cause for optimism. Certainly peace may result in the diminished importance of the military, a decline in the centrality of the family, and the depoliticization of motherhood and mothering. However, as long as the ongoing conflict continues to dominate the national discourse, the combined influence of religion and the institutionalization of security issues will persist as powerful barriers to gender equality in Israel.

## BIBLIOGRAPHY

Azmon, Yael. 1993. "Women and Politics: The Case of Israel." In *Women in Israel*, ed. Yael Azmon and Dafna N. Izraeli. New Brunswick, NJ: Transaction Publishers.

Azmon, Yael, and Dafna N. Izraeli, eds. 1993. *Women in Israel*. New Brunswick, NJ: Transaction Publishers.

Berkovitch, Nitza. 1997. "Motherhood as a National Mission: The Construction of Womanhood in the Legal Discourse in Israel." *Women's Studies International Forum* 20: 605–19.

Beth-Halachmy, Sharon. 1996. "Principles of Gender Equality in Israeli Law: The Military Example." Unpublished paper.

Bloom, Anne R. 1991. "Women in the Defense Forces." In *Calling the Equality*

*Bluff: Women in Israel*, ed. Marilyn P. Safir and Barbara Swirski. New York: Pergamon Press.

Central Bureau of Statistics (CBS). 1994. *Statistical Abstract of Israel*. Jerusalem: Office of the Prime Minister.

———. 1995. *Statistical Abstract of Israel*. Jerusalem: Office of the Prime Minister.

———. 1996. *Statistical Abstract of Israel*. Jerusalem: Office of the Prime Minister.

Golan, Galia. 1997. "Militarization and Gender: The Israeli Experience." *Women's Studies International Forum* 20: 581–86.

Hazelton, Leslie. 1977. *Israeli Women: The Reality Behind the Myth*. New York: Simon and Schuster.

Herzog, Hanna. 1998. "Homefront and Battlefront: The Status of Jewish and Palestinian Women in Israel." *Israel Studies* 3: 61–84.

Israeli, Dafna N. 1991. "Women and Work: From Collective to Career." In *Calling the Equality Bluff: Women in Israel*, ed. Marilyn P. Safir and Barbara Swirski. New York: Pergamon Press.

The Israel Women's Network (IWN). 1997. *Women in Israel: Information and Data*. Jerusalem: The Israel Women's Network (in Hebrew).

Raday, Frances. 1991. "Women, Work and the Law." In *Calling the Equality Bluff: Women in Israel*, ed. Marilyn P. Safir and Barbara Swirski. New York: Pergamon Press.

Raday, Frances, C. Shalev, and M. Liban-Kooby, eds. 1995. *Women's Status in Israeli Law and Society*. Tel-Aviv: Schocken (in Hebrew).

Reskin, Barbara, and Irene Padavic. 1994. *Women and Men at Work*. Thousand Oaks, CA: Pine Forge Press.

Safir, Marilyn P. 1991. "Religion, Tradition and Public Policy Give Family First Priority." In *Calling the Equality Bluff: Women in Israel*, ed. Marilyn P. Safir and Barbara Swirski. New York: Pergamon Press.

Safir, Marilyn P., and Barbara Swirski, eds. 1991. *Calling the Equality Bluff: Women in Israel*. New York: Pergamon Press.

Sharoni, Simona. 1992. "Every Woman Is an Occupied Territory: The Politics of Militarism and Sexism and the Israeli-Palestinian Conflict." *Journal of Gender Studies* 1: 447–62.

Swirski, Barbara, and M. Hasan. 1998. "Jewish and Palestinian Women in Israeli Society." In *Women in the Third World: An Encyclopedia of Contemporary Issues*, ed. Nelly P. Stromquist. New York: Garland.

Yishai, Yael. 1997. *Between the Flag and the Banner*. New York: SUNY Press.

Yuval-Davis, Nira. 1982. *Israeli Women and Men: Divisions Behind the Unity*. London: Change Publications.

# 11

# JAPAN

## Democracy in a
## Confucian-Based Society

### Linda White

## INTRODUCTION

### Profile of Japan

Japan is a highly efficient modern society and one of the safest in the world. The population of its 4 major and nearly 3,900 smaller islands is 125,931,533 (*World Almanac* 1999). Rapid industrialization began in Japan in the mid-nineteenth century when its 250-year isolation was broken by international trade and Westernization. The largest city and the capital of Japan is metropolitan Tokyo, which has a population of over 25 million people. The symbolic head of state is Emperor Akihito. The prime minister of the parliamentary democracy is Yoshiro Mori, a member of the Liberal Democratic Party, the dominant party in Japan, which has held a majority of seats in the National Diet (parliament) almost continuously since the party was formed in 1955.

### A Case Study: Akiko, a Single Mother

Family is the key battleground of women's rights issues in Japan. Although the 1947 revised Civil Code and Constitution virtually abolished the patriarchal family system that denied most rights to women in the family, remnants of the system still haunt many Japanese women. Akiko Kubota was born in 1955, ten years after the end of World War II, and raised in a seven-person household that included mother, father, paternal grandparents, an aunt, and one brother. Her parents were skilled laborers who did not push her academically. She attended a junior college in Tokyo (as did more than half of all women high school graduates who entered schools of higher education in the 1970s—19.9 percent attended junior college, and 12.5 percent attended four year universities) and upon graduation began working as a bank clerk.

Akiko met her future husband at the bank. When they married, she quit her job, in keeping with the policy at her bank. At the time she was twenty-five years old. According to Akiko, that is just the way things were done then. We did not ask why, she said, we just agreed. She was given a very small separation payment and became a housewife. During the next several years she gave birth to two children but found that she was unsatisfied with her husband and had little in common with him. Akiko divorced her husband when her children were three and five years old. She began working part-time and applied for government assistance as a single mother. Although she thinks that her husband would have made regular alimony payments if she had insisted, she did not ask him to do so. She did not want her new lifestyle and childrearing methods to be limited by the expectations that she feared would be attached to his alimony payments. While her children were still quite young Akiko moved to Canada for a year at the invitation of a Canadian friend who thought she might enjoy a view of politics from a new perspective. The trip turned out to be a turning point in her life; when she returned to Japan she had the skills and confidence to open an English language school, not the typical variety, but one dedicated to feminism and environmentalism.

Single-mother households like Akiko's make up only 1 percent of all households in Japan, where the divorce rate is still relatively low. However, two ever more common household types are on the increase in Japan: the "pseudo-single-mother family" where a father is legally present but so busy he is rarely involved with family life; and the "domestic divorce," which means that a husband and wife continue to live together for the sake of convenience despite having ended their conjugal relationship (Fujimura-Fanselow and Kameda 1995). These trends suggest that some major fault lines exist beneath the calm surfaces of Japanese domestic life.

### Overview of Women's Rights Issues

A series of laws have been written in the postwar period that give Japanese women increased rights. The 1947 Constitution granted women equal rights under the law and made major revisions to the definition of family in the Civil Code. In 1983 the government revised the Nationality Law to allow women for the first time to pass their nationality on to their children when not married to a Japanese man. In 1985 the Equal Employment Opportunity Law was passed, increasing job opportunities for women. In 1991 the Child Care Leave Act was passed, granting up to one year of unpaid leave to mothers or fathers after the birth of a child. But despite these important legal gains and improvements in opportunities for women, many unresolved legal and attitudinal problems remain regarding women's rights in the family, women's employment opportunities, the care of the elderly, which falls almost exclusively on the shoulders of women, and issues related to health and sexuality.

## HISTORY OF WOMEN'S RIGHTS

During the feudal Tokugawa period (1603–1868) it is widely agreed that the position of women in the family and in society at large was dependent upon their location in the highly stratified five-tier class system (Ueno 1987). Women in peasant households and small merchant households tended to hold significant power over other females in the household, and when married to the head of household shared responsibility for many economic and political decisions of the family. In samurai households (the elite class of society), on the other hand, power was more exclusively held by the male head of household, who in most cases had numerous wives, none of whom had significant power or control over her own children or household.

Modern Japan begins with the transformation that occurred around the middle of the nineteenth century. When Commodore Matthew Perry arrived in Yokohama in 1853 and demanded that Japan open its ports to trade with the United States, many in the country knew that change was inevitable. In the first several decades of the Meiji period (1868–1912) the new government, made up of former samurai who had been at odds with the Tokugawa forces, worked to modernize Japan by developing a modern military, an industrial infrastructure, and an educational system and rhetoric that would turn uneducated peasants into national subjects (Gluck 1985). In 1871 Japan created the Ministry of Education, and the following year made four years of education compulsory for males and females of all classes and backgrounds.

The position of women in society became an important topic for Meiji period intellectuals writing in the early 1870s, some of whom believed that women's roles reflected a society's overall level of civilization. Thus, among some of the key male Meiji thinkers, including Yukichi Fukuzawa, Arinori Mori, and Masanao Nakamura, in order for Japan to become a civilized and modern nation, the position of women needed to be improved (Sievers 1983). These thinkers attacked the traditional family system and argued for equality between husbands and wives in marriage and divorce. They were adamant opponents of concubinage (a system which allowed men to have legal wives and mistresses under one roof), the common practice among the upper levels of society. However, they did not advocate equality of the sexes outside of the home.

It was the same Nakamura who coined the expression "Good Wives, Wise

Mothers," the intractable model for Japanese womanhood that, according to Dorinne Kondo (1990), still motivates Japanese women's life choices, such as choosing to work in low-paying part-time jobs rather than full-time jobs that would take them away from their perceived duties in the home. Nakamura, greatly influenced by his experience living in Europe, proposed that Japanese women, rather than being considered intellectual inferiors to men who were unfit to educate their own children, as they had been during the feudal period, should take it upon themselves to "provide religious and moral foundations of the home, educating their children, and acting as the 'better half' to their husbands" (Sievers 1983, 22). The new claim for women's intellectual equality and moral superiority was placed squarely and completely in the service of their husbands and children as educators and moral role models in the home. In addition, the samurai household system was applied to the entire country in the Meiji Constitution, which emphasized the Confucian-based hierarchy within the family and the importance of filial piety and patrilineal descent. The hierarchy is epitomized in the old saying, "When she is young, she obeys her father; when she is married, she obeys her husband; when she is widowed, she obeys her son," from the Doctrine of the Three Obediences, written by the Chinese philosopher Lieh Tzu and cited in Japan as early as the twelfth century (Robins-Mowry 1983).

## Women in the Movement for Freedom and Popular Rights

Beginning in the 1870s a democratic movement known as the Movement for Freedom and Popular Rights took shape and began to question the absence of individual rights in rapidly modernizing Japan. The movement rallied for political reform that would increase authority to local governments and establish a constitution that would guarantee basic civil rights and grant suffrage to all landowners (Bowen 1980). While the movement was made up primarily of men, in 1882 an extremely articulate young woman named Toshiko Kishida (1863–1901) joined and gave a speech entitled "The Way for Women," outlining an agenda for Japanese women (Sievers 1983). Kishida believed in rationality and felt that "the exclusion of women from the task of nation building was irrational" (Sievers 1983, 35). According to Kazuko Tanaka (1977), Kishida was the first woman to insist on equal rights for both the sexes in Japan. Kishida's intelligence, beauty, and passion are said to have inspired other women to begin discussing the question of women's rights and the question of women's roles in the newly developing nation. One such recruit, Hideko Fukuda (1865–1927), became a very important advocate for women's rights.

After she heard Kishida speak, she wrote, "[L]istening to her speech, delivered in that marvelous oratorical style, I was unable to suppress my resentment and indignation . . . and began immediately to organize women and their daughters" (Sievers 1983, 36). Fukuda, like Kishida, spoke publicly and worked for the equal rights of women. In addition to arguing for women's equal rights in the family, Fukuda argued that women must achieve economic independence (Tanaka 1977). Kishida and Fukuda were members of the liberal movement that rooted much of its philosophy in works by European thinkers such as Herbert Spencer and John Stuart Mill. They longed for democracy and a notion of rights which was not part of the Meiji government's agenda for its people. These notable women are remembered for articulating a critique of Japanese patriarchy and for advocating a society where women could move beyond the Confucian edicts to remain obedient, subservient, and harmonious within a rigid power hierarchy.

However, the movement was squashed by the authoritarian government. Many of the leaders of the popular rights movement were arrested in the early 1880s and treated as revolutionaries who threatened state control (Sievers 1983). By 1884 the movement had been virtually silenced. Kishida went on to become a journalist, but the intensity and passion of her public speeches were not matched in her articles for a more conservative readership (Sievers 1983). Fukuda continued to play an important role in Japanese leftist politics until her death in 1927. The feminist enthusiasm aroused during this period was frustrated first by the demolition of the popular rights movement, then by the virtual exclusion of women from politics when in 1890 the government enacted a law prohibiting women from organizing politically or attending political meetings (Sievers 1983).

## The Influence of Christianity

An expansion in the roles of women was promoted by Christian missionaries who came to Japan in the 1860s and 1870s. Their primary concerns included the abolition of prostitution, the replacement of polygamy with monogamy, and the education of women to be independent thinkers who could help forge Japan's modernization (Tanaka 1995). Missionaries opened schools for girls, increasing the availability of education to a wider sector of society. However, up until and well into the Meiji period the idea that women were better off unlettered was widely held (Hara 1995). The Tokyo Women's Christian Temperance Society, founded in 1886, demanded the abolition of polygamy and licensed prostitution. Chapters of the organization were set up throughout the country, providing one arena in which women could develop ideas and strategies for social and legal change for the position of women in society. In the 1920s the association, renamed the Japan Women's Christian Temperance Society, supported the suffrage movement. While only a very small percentage of Japanese people have ever professed Christianity (at present about 1 percent), its standards for women were as progressive as any in the country in the late nineteenth and early twentieth centuries.

### Women and Labor

One of Japan's first and most successful export industries in the modern period was textiles. Both silk and cotton were produced in Japan beginning in 1872, when the first silk mill was constructed by the government. Women and, in many cases, girls as young as twelve years old made up more than half of all workers. At first daughters of samurai were trained in silk and cotton textile production, and then, as the demand for workers grew, girls from the poorest families were sent to the mills (Tsurumi 1990). By 1911 the number of women in the textile industry reached 476,000, around 60 percent of textile workers (Sievers 1983).

Conditions for women workers were notoriously rough. Accounts of malnutrition, a high rate of tuberculosis among workers, isolation from family support, and sexual harassment were widely reported. But many poor families suffering from Meiji period tax reforms could not afford to feed their children, and the opportunity to get cash for the service of their daughters was very tempting. In many cases a financial transaction between employer and father occurred before a girl was sent to work off her family debt for two or three years (Tsurumi 1990). Female workers in many different textile mills went on strike during the late nineteenth and early twentieth century, beginning with a strike of 100 women at a silk factory in 1886 in response to the owner's plan to increase already long working hours and reduce already low wages. The Factory Law of 1911, written to control overly harsh working conditions, limited hours of work to twelve per day with two days off per month. Working women of this period were never able to organize strong unions or national organizations that might have helped them improve their working conditions.

### Bluestockings

In 1911 a group of women led by Raichoo Hiratsuka who called themselves the "new women" started a society called Seitoo sha (Bluestockings), named after the Bluestockings of England (a label applied to an eighteenth century women's literary group and then to those who patterned themselves after the original group). These women started what was to be a remarkable journal questioning the role of women in Japanese society. Raichoo was a well-educated young woman from an upper-middle-class family, and her organization attracted other bright, privileged young female writers. While the original intention of *Seitoo* was to showcase women writers who were often excluded from other journals and to encourage women's creative expression generally, it quickly became a voice for feminist views. In the issues of *Seitoo*, the group's publication, writers used poetry, fiction, and prose to present and discuss themes including motherhood, women's education, marriage, women's sexuality, prostitution, abortion, and socialism. One of their contributors, Akiko Yosano (1878–1942), wrote a poem for the journal that has become a standard-bearer of women's power in Japan, "The Day the Mountains Move."

> The day the mountains move has come,
> I said, though no one would believe.
> They have merely dozed a while,
> But long ago, they burned with fire and roamed.
> It hardly matters if you don't believe.
> But this alone you must trust:
> All those sleeping women
> Are now awake and moving.

The Bluestockings raised new and important issues about the individual, women's sexuality, and the tension between marriage and identity for women (Sievers 1983).

Japan's years of colonial expansion throughout Asia, which began with the Manchurian incident in 1931, depended on the cooperation of women. Recent feminist scholarship in Japan has focused on the ways in which women's political agendas were co-opted by the nationalist government, which was willing to give women some access to the public sphere if they cooperated with the war effort (Ueno 1996). This stifled feminist activity for almost twenty years.

## The New Women's Association

In the early twentieth century Japanese women were excluded from political participation, lacked the right to vote, and in many cases were employed under horrendous working conditions in factories or as prostitutes in and outside of Japan. Throughout the years that the Bluestocking journal had flourished, women continued to be excluded from political meetings. Gaining access to political meetings was high on the agenda of the New Women's Association, formed in 1920 by Hiratsuka Raichoo, Fusae Ichikawa, and Mumeo Oku (Robins-Mowry 1983). The association held meetings around the country, working on issues of equality, protection of motherhood, education, and women's suffrage (Robins-Mowry 1983). In 1922 the group was successful in amending Article Five of the Meiji Constitution, which had prohibited women's participation in political organizations, thereby opening the doors for women's expanded political action. Several of the key women in this organization retreated from feminism soon after this victory. Oku, for example, became involved in charities and the consumer movement and left feminist politics for good. However, Ichikawa went to the United States in 1921 to study labor organization, and when she returned to Japan continued to be a very important force for suffrage and women's issues generally. The New Women's Movement dissolved in 1922, but within its short history it made important gains for Japanese women by bringing together Bluestocking literary types, socialists, and housewives, and helping them set an agenda for Japanese women, which started with gaining the right to political organization (Sievers 1983).

### Postwar Changes

The end of the war in August 1945 ushered in a period of rapid change for Japanese women and society in general. While Japan experienced its first and only foreign occupation, the American-led Allied forces attempted to bring about profound social and political change in Japan. In the move to democratize Japan, the Allied forces considered improvement in the status of women a key objective. Fusae Ichikawa, the prewar suffragist, renewed her campaign for women's suffrage after the war and found a more receptive audience in the government. In 1946, even before the new Japanese Constitution was promulgated, the election laws were changed to include women. Given many women's complete lack of understanding of the voting process only the year before, 67 percent was considered a great turnout (Robins-Mowry 1983). Of the seventy-nine female candidates who ran for the House of Representatives, thirty-nine were elected.

Equal rights for women were established in Article Fourteen of the Japanese Constitution, proclaimed in 1946. The article guarantees equal rights to citizens regardless of race, creed, sex, social status, or family origin. In a further effort to reorder social relations and eliminate inequalities in Japanese society, the Constitution states that marriage is to be based on equality and the consent of both individuals, a move away from the Japanese family system, which emphasized continuity and mutual obligation over individual choice in matters of marriage. The changes implied in the new Constitution were far-reaching, and many in Japan were not ready for them. While Japanese women had been granted equal rights, they had not been socialized to expect them. Fully realizing the implications of the Constitution continues to be a project for women in Japan more than fifty years after it was promulgated.

### WOMEN'S RIGHTS TODAY

The 1960s student movement in Japan gave birth to a movement known as *uman ribu*, or "women's lib." Women who had protested the war in Vietnam and the status quo in Japan began questioning inequality between the sexes at home, in schools and the workplace, and in the student movement. Led by Mitsu Tanaka, women held public protests, started newsletters, and attracted the mass media to their cause. Tanaka drew attention to the way men in the student movement had treated women in her manifesto "Benjo kara no kaiho" (Liberation from Toilets), suggesting that men had treated women in the movement as little more than toilets, a place to release bodily fluids. Between 1970 and 1975 many grass-roots organizations were started to focus on specific issues such as the birth control pill, changes in the abortion law, the institution of marriage, and lesbianism.

In the mid-1970s the first women's studies courses were taught in Japan, and some of the women who had been involved in early 1970s activism began to enter the academic world. At the same time the 1975 United Nations women's conference in Mexico City led many women to organize anew and to make new demands of the Japanese government. Although Japanese women were now guaranteed equal rights in the Constitution (unlike women in most other societies), more and more Japanese women were beginning to feel the contradictions between their high level of education and their limited opportunities in the workplace (Mackie 1988). The four United Nations women's conferences have played a major role in women's activism and governmental initiatives regarding women since 1975. The UN documents, such as the World Plan of Action developed in Mexico City in 1975 and Forward-looking Strategies for the Advancement of Women developed in Nairobi, have served as a model to stimulate resistant governmental agencies, and Japanese activists have taken the texts of these documents, to legislators and others in the government to encourage alignment with the UN goals.

Although the women's movement in Japan is not vast, and in many ways is far from highly visible, scores of women's voices respond daily in the media to the slightest issue that concerns women. When something profound occurs, such as the engagement and subsequent marriage of the Crown Prince to the highly educated and highly ranked diplomat Masako Owada in 1994, or an imminent change in employment laws, an all-out feminist debate transpires in the mainstream as well as alternative media. Japanese feminists are far from quiet, and they are increasingly entering more and more professions.

### Family Issues

Multiple lawsuits have arisen to address discrimination against women and children in aspects of current family law. For example, all married couples must register their new households/relationships at government offices and choose one common surname. This is a problem for young Japanese women who would like to keep their maiden names but find the norm of taking their husbands' names and the pressure of the law more than they can combat. As of 1990, 98 percent of new marriages were registered under the husband's surname (Kinjo 1995). The Family Registration Law also requires parents to register family births and deaths and grants different legal rights for legitimate and illegitimate children. Lawsuits argue that this practice is unconstitutional because it discriminates against some children. While some small victories have been made, the judicial process is notoriously slow. These details of the family system support the underlying ideology that holds that families are understood as ongoing patrilineal lines, that women marry into male households, and that women are worthy of no rights in the family.

## Employment Issues

Employment has been a very important issue for Japanese women. The great majority of Japanese women have always worked in their family's business, which until the twentieth century was overwhelmingly agriculture. As late as 1930, 50.3 percent of all households in Japan were agricultural (Smith 1959). Between 1960 and 1975 the percentage of agricultural workers dropped from 32.6 to 13.9 percent (Tanaka 1995). Today Japan's agricultural roots can be found throughout the nation, but there is a continuing trend toward urbanization, and it is difficult to find young people (male, and especially female) willing to carry on family farms. Women now make up 40 percent of the labor market, though many are part-time or temporary employees. Since 1983 over 50 percent of married women have worked outside of the home (Ueno 1987). However, a majority of women leave work to have children and later reenter the work force, in most cases in different jobs with less security and fewer long-term prospects. Many of these reentrants take part-time jobs, which are defined by the Labor Ministry as those requiring less than thirty-five hours a week. But as Dorinne Kondo (1990) has shown, part-time work is defined more by expectations about commitment to job and company than by the actual number of hours worked. Thirty-one percent of all female workers in Japan work part-time (Fujimura-Fanselow and Kameda 1995). While many women find that part-time work fits their understandings of their primary obligations to their families and children, other women find it hard to find good full-time jobs with job security and benefits when they return to the labor force after having children.

The Equal Employment Opportunity Law (EEOL) of 1985 has eradicated some of the blatant discrimination encountered by women in hiring and forced retirement. Akiko's forced retirement at the bank, for example, is no longer the norm. However, women still lack access to the resources available to male employees. Looking at lawsuits filed in 1995 for wage discrimination, Mori (1999) found that the underlying wage and salary system in many Japanese companies, one based on the idea of paying a living wage, pays differently for a father of three than for a single woman. Thus, potentially, two people doing the exact same job can be paid quite differently because of gender and number of dependents (Mori 1999). For Japanese companies this deeply rooted ideology can rationalize a great deal of discrimination. The EEOL is understood by many feminists as a law passed in haste in order to comply with the UN-sponsored Convention on the Elimination of All Forms of Discrimination Against Women (CEDAW) and to assuage international disapproval of sexism in Japan. Furthermore, in their haste, legislators were able to pass a law on equal rights that includes no penalty for violation. Given the widespread discrimination in many Japanese corporations and the lack of sanctions for violation, the new law has been met with criticism and has been marred by controversy from the day it went into effect in 1986.

In 1991 the Child Care Leave Act was enacted in response to the very low birthrate in Japan, which dipped to 1.53 in 1990 (Kinjo 1995). This act allows a father or mother to take one year of unpaid leave upon the birth of a child. Much attention has been given to the problem of sexual harassment, which has been so much a part of the fabric of Japanese company life that it is very hard for many men to understand. There are still no laws regarding harassment on the books, though many lawsuits have been filed.

## Reproductive Issues

During the past twenty years Japanese women have struggled to gain reproductive rights. While abortion has been widely available since the immediate postwar period, it is granted through a clause in the problematic Eugenics Protection Law, drafted in 1947 to allow abortion of "undesirable" fetuses. There are clauses allowing abortion for other reasons, and most Japanese women today use the clause on economic constraints to qualify for abortion. However, during the past twenty years activists have disagreed about the law. Some want it abolished because it grants abortions for many reasons, but not based on a woman's right to self-determination; others fear that abolishing the law could bring about new constraints on the easy availability of abortion. A further concern for women's health in Japan has been lack of access to the birth control pill, which was not legalized there until 1999.

## Regional and Global Issues

During World War II the Japanese government authorized its military to open camps of forced prostitution for its armies in China, Korea, and Southeast Asia. These camps were filled with women who were kidnapped or bought from their families. At the end of the war, this system was abolished, and the many women who had suffered in the camps were sent home. Back in Tokyo rumors of the camps were vociferously denied. Only in the late 1980s and 1990s did the story of the former "comfort women," as they were called in Japanese, become a political issue. With cooperation among women throughout Asia, Japanese activists played an important role in putting pressure on their government to acknowledge the system and make reparations. In 1995 the government officially apologized and helped set up a nongovernmental fund to make reparations. This was only a half-way measure, but nonetheless a sign of progress from the resistant Japanese government. In addition to continuing to support former "comfort women," groups like the Asian Women's Association work on the effects of Japanese investment in Asia that negatively impact women and the environment. Japanese women have been educating themselves about the effects of the "Japanese economic miracle" on neighbors throughout Asia.

Japanese women face other kinds of serious problems, including overwork as employees who as wives and daughters are also called upon to take care of their elderly in-laws and parents in a rapidly graying society that expects filial piety in the form of nursing and custodial care for the elderly. Domestic violence and rape continue to be serious and underreported problems in Japan. Inequality in education is a serious problem being studied by scholars concerned about women's low career ambitions related to the guidance of their teachers and social pressures to become marriageable young women. Japanese women have been well organized since the early part of the century regarding consumer issues related to pricing, health, and taxes. In addition women have played a major role in the environmental and peace movements in Japan.

## THE FUTURE OF WOMEN'S RIGHTS

In the 1990s Japanese women were blessed with many opportunities. They are citizens of a wealthy nation with a highly efficient educational system and a social welfare system that provides not only universal health care but extensive social benefits for all. They have equal rights by law, and they have gained many legal advantages in the past twenty years. However, discrimination is rampant, and attitudes prevalent about ambitious, rebellious women are extremely negative given the strong Confucian value of accepting one's position in society and conforming to societal norms. Japanese women have responded in many ways to the rapid changes in their society since the end of World War II. In recent years the pressure to marry and have children has lessened to some extent, and many young women are delaying the age of marriage, marrying and choosing not to have children, or never marrying at all. Others insist on new expectations within marriage and spend a good deal of time finding or influencing the attitudes of men who can live with women who plan to be equals within marriage.

In recent community meetings around the country, the problem of male responsibility in the home has been a popular topic. It seems that in the past Japanese men had been given permission, even instructions, to bring home the paycheck and keep out of the way of their wives. Now that women are increasingly interested in working outside of the home or developing interests outside of their roles as wives and mothers, they are looking to their husbands to become more involved in housework and childcare. Helping younger Japanese men adjust to the new expectations of Japanese women seems to be a central goal among female activists. While legal changes have abolished the Confucian underpinnings of Japanese society, the cornerstones of Japan's Confucian legacy—filial piety, hierarchy, gender inequality, and male-centered households—will not just slip away.

## BIBLIOGRAPHY

Bowen, Roger. 1980. *Rebellion and Democracy in Meiji Japan: A Study of Commoners in Popular Rights Movement*. Berkeley: University of California Press.

Buckley, Sandra. 1994. "A Short History of the Feminist Movement in Japan." In *Women of Japan and Korea*, ed. Joyce Gelb and Marian Lief Palley. Philadelphia: Temple University Press, 150–86.

———. 1997. *Broken Silence: Voices of Japanese Feminism*. Berkeley: University of California Press.

Fujieda, Mioko. 1995. "Japan's First Phase of Feminism." In *Japanese Women: New Feminist Perspectives on the Past, Present, and Future*, ed. Kumiko Fujimura-Fanselow and Atsuko Kameda. New York: Feminist Press, 323–42.

Fujimura-Fanselow, Kumiko, and Atsuko Kameda. 1995. *Japanese Women: New Feminist Perspectives on the Past, Present, and Future*. New York: Feminist Press.

Gluck, Carol. 1985. *Japan's Modern Myths: Ideology in the Late Meiji Period*. Princeton: Princeton University Press.

Gordon, Beate Sirota. 1998. "Celebrating Women's Rights in the Japanese Constitution." *U.S.-Japan Women's Journal*, English Supplement, 14: 64–83.

Hara, Kimi. 1995. "Challenges to Education for Girls and Women in Modern Japan: Past and Present." In *Japanese Women: New Feminist Perspectives on the Past, Present, and Future*, ed. Kumiko Fujimura-Fanselow and Atsuko Kameda. New York: Feminist Press.

Kaneko, Sachiko. 1995. "The Struggle for Equal Rights and Reforms: A Historical View." In *Japanese Women: New Feminist Perspectives on the Past, Present, and Future*, ed. Kumiko Fujimura-Fanselow and Atsuko Kameda. New York: Feminist Press, 3–14.

Kawashima, Yoko. 1995. "Female Workers: An Overview of Past and Current Trends." In *Japanese Women: New Feminist Perspectives on the Past, Present, and Future*, ed. Kumiko Fujimura-Fanselow and Atsuko Kameda. New York: Feminist Press, 271–94.

Kinjo, Kiyoko. 1995. "Legal Challenges to the Status Quo." In *Japanese Women: New Feminist Perspectives on the Past, Present, and Future*, ed. Kumiko Fujimura-Fanselow and Atsuko Kameda. New York: Feminist Press, 353–64.

Kondo, Dorinne. 1990. *Crafting Selves: Power, Gender and Discourses of Identity in a Japanese Workplace*. Chicago: University of Chicago Press.

Mackie, Vera. 1988. "Feminist Politics in Japan." *New Left Review* 167: 53–76.

Mori, Masumi. 1999. "Gender Discrimination in Wages and Employment Practices in Japan." *U.S.-Japan Women's Journal*, English Supplement, 16: 103–37.

Robins-Mowry, Dorothy. 1983. *The Hidden Sun: Women of Modern Japan*. Boulder, CO: Westview Press.

Rodd, Laurel Rasplica. 1991. "Yosano Akiko and the Taisho Debate over the 'New Woman.' " In *Recreating Japanese Women, 1600–1945*, ed. Gail Bernstein. Berkeley: University of California Press, 175–98.

Sievers, Sharon. 1983. *Flowers in Salt: The Beginnings of Feminist Consciousness in Modern Japan*. Stanford, CA: Stanford University Press.

Smith, Thomas C. 1959. *The Agrarian Origins of Modern Japan*. Stanford: Stanford University Press.

Tanaka, Kazuko. 1977. *A Short History of the Women's Movement in Modern Japan*. Tokyo: Femintern Press.

———. 1995. "The New Feminist Movement in Japan, 1970–1990." In *Japanese Women: New Feminist Perspectives on the Past, Present, and Future*, ed. Kumiko Fujimura-Fanselow and Atsuko Kameda. New York: Feminist Press, 343–52.

Tsurumi, Patricia. 1990. *Factory Girls: Women in the Thread Mills of Meiji Japan*. Princeton: Princeton University Press.

Ueno, Chizuko. 1987. "The Position of Japanese Women Reconsidered." *Current Anthropology* 28, no. 4: 75–84 (supplement).

———. 1996. "The Making of a History of Feminism in Japan." *Asian Journal of Women's Studies* 2: 170–91.

# 12

# NIGERIA

## Women Building on the Past

### Victoria B. Tashjian

### INTRODUCTION

#### Profile of Nigeria

With nearly 111 million inhabitants in 1998, Nigeria is the most populous nation in Africa. More than 250 ethnic groups are found within its 356,000 square miles, though three alone account for a majority of the population: the Hausa in the north, the Yoruba in the southwest, and the Igbo in the southeast. Islam is the primary religion in Nigeria's north, while Christianity predominates in the south. Many Nigerians also practice African traditional religions, either solely or in conjunction with Christianity or Islam. Since gaining independence from Britain in 1960, Nigeria has switched repeatedly between military and civilian rule. With the election of the former general Olusegun Obasanjo as president in 1999, Nigeria has returned to democratic governance once again after fifteen years of military rule. Nigeria's gross domestic product is the second largest in Africa, in part because of its extensive oil production. Its per capita income of $1,300 annually, however, is approximately Africa's average. In keeping with the experience of many people across the African continent, the standard of living for Nigeria's citizens has declined markedly since the 1980s, when the government implemented austerity programs designed to jump-start the Nigerian economy. Also in keeping with many other African countries is Nigeria's crippling burden of international debt, which hampers economic development (Ramsay 1999, 52–55).

### Overview of Women's Rights Issues

The ethnic and religious heterogeneity of Nigeria's population makes it very difficult to generalize about the status of women, particularly since so many of the social and economic issues commonly understood to determine women's rights are deeply affected by cultural norms, which vary across Nigeria's many ethnicities. The fact of British colonization in the fairly recent past further muddies the waters: for example, Nigerian law draws heavily upon English common law as well as upon Islamic and customary law. Furthermore, as in all countries, women do not constitute a monolithic category in Nigeria. They are sometimes divided not only by ethnicity or religion, but also by class, occupation, and rural versus urban residence, among other factors.

## WOMEN AND POLITICAL AUTHORITY

### Women and Political Authority in Nigeria Historically: A Brief Overview

Historically, many women in what is now southern Nigeria exercised significant political authority. Precolonially, the western Igbo had parallel political institutions consisting of separate male and female strands of political authority. In these dual systems, women typically wielded authority over those aspects of life deemed of great concern to women, such as markets, women's crops, and marital disputes. Men held authority not only over those spheres considered of greatest concern to men, but also over areas that affected the entire community, such as military decisions (Okonjo 1976, 48–54). Yoruba women also held political offices precolonially, likewise with a focus upon issues particularly significant for women, and were consulted by male office holders on important decisions affecting the community as a whole, though their counsel could be ignored (Denzer 1994, 10–12).

In the precolonial period many women also wielded power through collective bodies. Igbo women, who formed associations based on age grades or membership in a particular family by virtue of birth or marriage, utilized a number of tactics to exert their will and safeguard both their individual and collective interests (Van Allen 1972, 169–171; Okonjo, 1976, 51–55). If women disliked a decision or action taken by men in the community, they might strike or boycott. For example, if Igbo men did not clear the paths that women took to market, women of that community might refuse to cook or have sexual relations with their husbands until the men had fulfilled their customary responsibility (Van Allen 1972, 170). Through their collectives Igbo women also had at their disposal an institution called "sitting on" or "making war on" a man or woman, which allowed them to sanction individuals as well as groups. If a man severely mistreated his wife, for example, the women of the community would go to his house,

dancing, singing scurrilous songs which detailed the women's grievances against him and often called his manhood into question, banging on his hut with the pestles women used for pounding yams, and perhaps demolishing his hut or plastering it with mud and roughing him up a bit . . . The women would stay at his hut throughout the day, and late into the night, if necessary, until he repented and promised to mend his ways. Although this could hardly have been a pleasant experience for the offending man, it was considered legitimate and no man would consider intervening. (Van Allen 1972, 170)

Thus did southern women collectively exert far more authority than they could individually. In the north, many Muslim women did not exercise extensive political authority at the onset of colonialism since Islamization at an earlier date had already stripped them of most public roles.

Unfortunately, the political empowerment of Igbo and Yoruba women declined rapidly under colonialism, and southern Nigerian women have not yet regained the level of political authority they possessed precolonially. The British, who began colonizing Nigeria in the mid-nineteenth century, believed that women's place was firmly in the home. They sometimes literally did not see or, when they saw, chose not to recognize, southern Nigerian women's substantial political authority. Colonial authorities simply refused to acknowledge and interact with either individual female office holders or women's collectives, with the result that women's political authority faded into the background and withered.

### Women and Political Authority in Nigeria from Independence to the Present

Nigerian independence from colonial rule, which came in 1960, has not yet led to women's political reempowerment. Women have been completely underrepresented in all of the governments, civilian and military, since independence. In fact, though all southern women did gain the right to vote in 1957, as independence neared, women in northern Nigeria had to wait until 1976, when a military government instituted a universal enfranchisement of women that civilian governments, fearing the opposition of northern men, had lacked the political will to effect (Mba 1989, 76).

Nigerian women's lack of political access is most commonly attributed to party politics that marginalize women. Funmilayo Ransome-Kuti, an internationally known Nigerian nationalist and women's rights activist, faced this discrimination. In the 1950s, she was deeply involved in the party politics that developed as Nigerian independence neared. An active member of the National Council of Nigeria and the Cameroons (NCNC), a prominent political party, she held important party offices that could be expected to lead to party nomination for a federal seat. Challenging the absence of female candidates for federal elective offices, Ransome-Kuti repeatedly sought such nomination from the NCNC. After being passed over in the 1954 and 1956 federal elections, she finally succeeded in receiving NCNC nomination for a seat in 1959. However, male party members who opposed her candidacy—they wanted to give the reward of nomination to an individual who was their close friend and relative—replaced her with a male nominee. To her deep anger, the party refused to seriously investigate her sidelining (Johnson-Odim and Mba 1997, 111–115). Sadly, her experience has proved to be anything but unusual. Women have not only had very limited success in electoral politics since independence. For most of the years since 1960 military rather than civilian governments have ruled Nigeria, and women in military regimes, like women in the military, are rarities.

Because of the many impediments to their office holding, women's most prominent formal political activity from the nationalist period of the 1950s to the present has actually come in what are referred to as the "women's wings" of Nigerian political or ruling parties, entities whose very existence makes clear the second-class status of women in Nigerian politics. These wings typically serve the party's interests rather than their own, focusing on the mundane tasks of registering women and then getting out their vote for what are overwhelmingly male party candidates, while remaining marginalized from positions of authority or policy-making in the party (Mba 1989, 81).

Given the very limited political voice women have been able to gain through party politics, it is not surprising that the idea of reserving seats for female office holders has been raised repeatedly, but unsuccessfully, by Nigerian women's groups. The Nigerian Women's Union, founded in 1949 and headed by Ransome-Kuti, immediately called for reserved seats, while in recent years organizations such as the Women Empowerment Movement, Gender and Development Action, and National Council for Women's Societies have sought women's proportionate representation in elective and appointive offices (Johnson-Odim and Mba 1997, 101; Denzer 1999, 3).

It is also not surprising that women's grass-roots organizations, drawing on traditions of collective action like the Igbos' "sitting on" a man, have continued to be an important locus for women's political activism as women have been marginalized in mainstream Nigerian politics. This was the case in colonial Nigeria, as it has been since independence. For example, in the Women's War of 1929 Igbo women protested colonial taxation by "sitting on" colonial officials. More recently, in 1984–1985 market women in the southwestern city of Abeokuta, working together in recognition of their common occupational interest, challenged government taxes levied on the self-employed; "for hours they rained abuses and poured scorn on the state's administration" (Mba 1989, 86). Following the Third World Conference on Women, held in Nairobi in 1985, Nigerian women have also turned in greater numbers to a newer kind of collectivity, forming nongovernmental organizations (NGOs) to press for various improvements in women's lives (Assié-Lumumba 1998, 540).

What is sadly notable in most of these organizations, however, is their very limited ability to effect meaningful change in Nigerian politics or in Nigerian women's lives. The 1984–1985 protests, for example, did not cause the government to rescind the objectionable tax on market traders (Mba 1989, 86). Moreover, NGOs have received sustained criticism for their limited agendas and results. The reasons for NGO shortcomings are numerous. Some, particularly those formed or headed by first ladies, do not challenge problematic state policies because of their very close ties to ruling parties. For example, although the Better Life for Rural Women Program, formed in 1987 by Mrs. Maryam Babangida, then the first lady, did focus substantial attention and resources on the plight of rural women, it could not be openly critical of governmental policies detrimental to the status of women (Assié-Lumumba 1998, 540). Another drawback lies in the fact that professional women from the upper and upper middle classes, a distinct minority among Nigerian women, head most NGOs, and too frequently their agendas have focused on goals peripheral to the needs of the majority of women. It is thus not surprising that their organizations have not engendered the mass support necessary to their success (Mba 1989, 86; Denzer 1999, 3). Finally, women's thorough political marginalization has alienated a majority of women from political involvement or interest, allowing mainstream political parties to conclude that it is unnecessary to respond to the agendas of politically active women.

## WOMEN AND WORK

### Women's Work

Today, as in the past, Nigerian women expect to work, and work hard. In common with women across sub-Saharan Africa, most grow up assuming that they will be primarily responsible for their own financial well-being rather than dependent solely upon a husband for economic support. Sub-Saharan African women dominate the labor force in the fields of agriculture, market trading, and the small-scale production for sale of items such as foodstuffs, prepared food, beer, and many handicrafts. This gendered division of labor, found broadly across sub-Saharan Africa today, holds true for Nigerian women with the important partial exception of agriculture. In much of sub-Saharan Africa, in striking contrast to the rest of the world, women do the bulk of agricultural labor and are the primary producers of food, cultivating approximately 70 percent of all food crops. In Nigeria, however, a relatively scant one-third of working women labor in agriculture

(Stichter 1995, 263) because two of the country's largest ethnic groups, the Yoruba and the Hausa, concentrate farming in male hands: the Yoruba have long considered farming a male activity, while the Muslim Hausa practice purdah, the seclusion of women in the home, which effectively precludes all but the poorest Hausa women's participation in agriculture.

Like women across Africa, Nigerian women also bear responsibility for the domestic work of food preparation, childcare, laundry, and, in the rural areas where almost two-thirds of Nigeria's population resides, the gathering of firewood and water. This domestic labor, though highly time-consuming, physically demanding, and critical to social reproduction, is unremunerated and generally unrecognized in formal labor statistics. Because of their double burden of work both inside and outside the home, on average Nigerian women labor many more hours daily than do Nigerian men.

### Women and Work in Nigeria Historically: A Brief Overview

Nigerian women's participation in the work force is not of recent standing. For example, in the nineteenth century Yoruba women were widely noted for their extensive involvement in commerce. In addition to dominating market trading, they played key roles in long-distance trade, where successful women traders had the income to employ workers, and the authority to set prices and head up large caravans which controlled the movement of trade goods. They also dyed cloth, brewed beer, made a variety of products including soap, beads, pottery, and mats, and processed palm and other nut and vegetable oils. Although they did not cultivate agricultural products, they did assist with harvesting and processing crops (Denzer 1994, 3–7). Despite purdah Hausa women traded from their homes, circumventing the restrictions of seclusion by using children, who are free to travel outside the home, as their intermediaries in business.

The colonial period proved to be a mixed bag for women in terms of work. New opportunities certainly opened up: the growth of cities led to larger markets for prepared foodstuffs, beer brewing, and market trading. On the other hand, the colonial period caused women who farmed, like the Igbo, to bear far heavier workloads since they now had to grow cash crops in addition to food crops. Most women did not profit from this increased agricultural labor, since men dominated the ownership of cash crops and could insist that their wives and daughters work for them without pay. Furthermore, men now gave women far less assistance in cultivating foodstuffs as they turned their energy and the land they controlled to the more lucrative export crops. Outside of agriculture, women were excluded from many of the new occupations. They were barred not only from jobs like truck driver or road worker, but also from most of the new clerical positions requiring literacy. Women thus had very limited opportunities to benefit from the increasingly important cash incomes provided by these wage jobs.

### Women and Work in Nigeria from Independence to the Present

Women have continued to face a very heavy workload and substantial economic marginalization in the years since Nigeria gained its independence. Nigerian women are underrepresented in the better-paying professional sector, which has opened up to Nigerians since 1960. As of 1992, 7.3 percent of Nigerian women worked in professional, technical, administrative, or clerical occupations, compared to 12.2 percent of Nigerian men (Stichter 1995, 263). Women's underrepresentation in these jobs is linked to their limited access to higher education: though close to 50 percent of the students enrolled in Nigerian primary and secondary schools in the 1980s and 1990s have been girls, they account for only 25 percent of the students enrolled beyond the secondary level (Assié-Lumumba 1998, 536; Neft and Levine 1997, 365). Women who do attain high levels of education and professional jobs tend to be clustered in health care, education, and the law (Neft and Levine 1997, 366). In the fields of production, mining, and transportation, because of attitudes which discriminate against them, women make up an even smaller percentage of workers than they do in the professions: 5.8 percent of working women are found in these fields, compared to 16.4 percent of working men (Stichter 1995, 263).

As a result of these limitations, the vast majority of Nigerian women continue to work in agriculture or the informal sector of the economy, and market trading continues to be their primary source of employment. Close to one-half of Nigerian women who work are still found in this single occupation (Stichter 1995, 263). Though for most women market trading is not a highly lucrative field, it is critically important as their primary source of income. Drawing on the history of women's collectives, women who work in market trading have formed occupation-based voluntary associations that have demonstrated a striking ability to protect their economic niche against periodic governmental efforts to break their domination of the sale of foodstuffs and many other domestic goods. Through their occupation-based associations market women also provide credit and training to new market traders and enforce order in the market by setting prices for commodities and regulating competition between traders.

## MARRIAGE, KINSHIP, AND DOMESTIC LIFE

### Key Factors Affecting Domestic Life in Nigeria

It is very difficult to generalize meaningfully about Nigerian women and family life since ethnicity and religion affect domestic relations profoundly. This truth is reflected in the fact that Nigerian law today recognizes three distinct types of marriage: those solemnified according to customary, Islamic, and civil law (Center for Reproductive Law and Policy [hereafter

CRLP] 1997, 82). Women's rights in marriage differ according to the form of marriage they have entered into. For example, laws pertaining to divorce, child custody, and a widow's or child's right to inherit property from a husband or father vary depending on the kind of marriage. Therefore, it must be stressed that those of the following statistics from the 1990s which apply to the country as a whole, rather than to particular subgroups within Nigeria, will not describe the life circumstances of all Nigerian women. Half of Nigerian women first marry by age sixteen, though this statistic is skewed by the north, where more than 50 percent of girls marry between twelve and fifteen years of age. Half of Nigerian women also bear children by age twenty. Just over 40 percent are in polygynous marriages, that is, unions in which their husbands are married simultaneously to one or more other wives. This figure too is affected by the greater prominence of polygyny in the Muslim north at 50 percent of marriages, although polygyny is still common among all religions and ethnicities in Nigeria (CRLP 1997, 75, 85; Neft and Levine 1997, 365).

It is also important to point out that in Nigeria, as in much of Africa, ties of kinship—ties between people related by patrilineal, matrilineal, or bilateral descent—rather than ties of marriage are of paramount social and economic importance. It is through kinship that individuals most frequently gain access to the important economic resources of land and housing, and the important social resources of familial support and ritual and political influence (Denzer 1994, 5). Furthermore, kinship ties will last a lifetime, while marriages come and go. Consequently, a woman's relationships to her kin are typically more enduring and significant than relationships of marriage.

Whether defined by kinship or marriage, Nigerian families are characterized by the expectation that women will play a subordinate role in domestic life. The exact forms of this patriarchy vary considerably across ethnic, religious, and regional lines. In daily life it is most commonly manifested in women's obligations to cook and clean, serve husbands and fathers first and reserve the best food for them, and defer to men in most household decision-making. Many women are also obligated to provide unremunerated labor on farms owned by their husbands or male kin. Additionally, family resources are more likely to be directed to males than to females; for example, the births of sons are often celebrated far more lavishly than the births of daughters, and the higher education of sons is a far greater priority than the higher education of daughters. Furthermore, in some of Nigeria's states husbands have authority over whether a wife works, and in what occupation, or whether she holds a passport. Some states also restrict women's ability to own property (Women's International Network 1992, 11).

## Women and Domestic Life in Nigeria Historically:
## A Brief Overview

While recognizing that before British rule women in many parts of what is now Nigeria held significant political and economic authority, most argue that patriarchy characterized domestic life in the precolonial period and continues up to the present (Denzer 1994, 20, 36; Wariboko 1995, 370). However, in her pathbreaking and provocative work on the Igbo, Ifi Amadiume (1997) argues for recognition of the prominent domestic authority vested in Igbo women precolonially. Alongside a patriarchy located in the ancestral family house which was controlled by men, she asserts a parallel matriarchal basis to precolonial Igbo society rooted in what she terms the "matricentric" female-headed domestic unit of mother and children that formed a productive and economic as well as residential entity. Such households arose because in Igbo marriages, each woman and her children shared a single house within a larger compound which also contained the houses of any co-wives, as well as the husband's own dwelling (Amadiume 1997, 18–19, 109–143).

Though the precise level of domestic authority held by women precolonially remains uncertain, there is no doubt that in the colonial years women experienced both gains and setbacks in domestic life. On the positive side, it became far easier for women to divorce husbands, and women promptly chose divorce in rapidly increasing numbers. Divorce became easier at this time because women who wished to terminate marriages gained the option of having their cases heard in British forums, which often granted women a far more sympathetic hearing of marital disputes than the customary venues did. British officials backed divorces sought by women for a variety of reasons, especially their antipathy toward polygyny and types of marriage that they saw as tantamount to slavery (Byfield 1996, 46). Colonial and Christian mission courts also tended to favor women over husbands in cases involving child custody and inheritance by widows. They worked to end childhood betrothals of girls and forced marriages of women, thereby limiting the authority not only of husbands but also of male and senior female kin (Denzer 1994, 8; Byfield 1996, 45–46).

On the other hand, where Christian missionaries established a firm foothold, notably in southern Nigeria from the mid-nineteenth century, the colonial encounter had negative as well as positive effects on women's domestic lives. Missionaries strongly encouraged converts to form marriages that mirrored the norms of Victorian Britain, and such marriages disempowered women in highly significant ways. For example, women who had expected to work—and consequently enjoy substantial economic independence and autonomy—faced strong mission pressures to limit their lives to the private sphere of the nuclear family home. While most converts could not afford to do so, well-to-do couples often followed these mission dictates, and as a result elite women were left far more financially and socially dependent upon husbands than they had previously been (Mann 1985, 77–91; Denzer 1994, 17).

## MATERNAL CARE AND REPRODUCTIVE RIGHTS

Attitudes widely held across Nigeria promote high rates of childbearing, and a 1990 survey indicated that more than half of Nigerian women want to have more than four children (Pearce 1995, 251). Some of these women, though, would like more control over the spacing of their children or over the total number of their children, and, of course, women who wish to bear fewer than four children also want these controls. Yet, these women face significant obstacles to reproductive choice. First and foremost, women's subordinate status in marriage makes control of fertility very difficult to achieve if their husbands do not support this goal. Very limited access to health care facilities that provide not merely contraceptives, but a broad range of effective reproductive services, is a second significant barrier.

The result of these realities is a high rate of population growth, currently just under 3 percent a year. In 1988 the government formulated the National Policy on Population for Development, Unity, Progress and Self-Reliance to slow Nigeria's population growth by providing accessible and affordable family planning services, including contraception. However, in the 1990s only 6–7 percent of the population routinely practiced contraception, one of the lowest rates in the world (CRLP 1997, 78–79; Neft and Levine 1997, 369). Further, abortion is illegal in Nigeria except when pregnancy endangers a woman's life. In all other circumstances, women who have abortions face jail terms of seven years, while abortion providers face imprisonment for fourteen years (CRLP 1997, 81–82).

The criminalization of abortion, the reality that many women's economic security still lies in having many children, and the social pressures that encourage women to bear many children lie behind the fact that as of the early 1990s, Nigerian women gave birth to an average of six children over the course of their lives. Deaths resulting either directly or indirectly from pregnancy and childbirth are a key health issue for Nigerian women. Approximately 1 percent of pregnant Nigerian women die as a result of any given pregnancy—a rate that is among the highest in the world and leads to the stark reality that a Nigerian woman has a one in sixteen chance of dying during pregnancy or childbirth. The illegal abortions which women, particularly young women with unwanted pregnancies, resort to are estimated to account for close to 50 percent of these maternal deaths (CRLP 1997, 75–76; Neft and Levine 1997, 370). Beyond maternal mortality directly related to pregnancy, unsafe abortions, and childbirth, Nigerian women face serious health problems that stem from the significant nutritional toll that can result from having numerous pregnancies in rapid succession. Given these circumstances, it is notable that most governmental attention to reproductive health in Nigeria has focused on efforts to control fertility rather than attempts to decrease the very real risks Nigerian women face during pregnancy and childbearing.

## VIOLENCE AGAINST WOMEN

It is difficult to gauge the precise extent of domestic violence in Nigeria. Legal sanctions against domestic violence exist in the form of criminal laws against assault, under which charges can be brought against husbands, and in the form of divorce laws, which allow a woman to divorce a husband who has been found guilty of "grievously injuring her or attempting to seriously injure or kill her" (CRLP 1997, 84). However, domestic violence is rarely reported to the police, who generally see it as a private matter in which the state should not intervene, and it is even more rarely prosecuted. Indeed, the legal code in the north, which is separate from the legal code in southern Nigeria, expressly permits husbands to "correct" wives physically so long as that "correction" is not "unreasonable" and does not result in "the infliction of grievous hurt" (CRLP 1997, 85). Though the extent of domestic violence in Nigeria, as elsewhere, is impossible to quantify precisely, it is reputed to be common, particularly in rural areas and among individuals of low socioeconomic status (Odujinrin 1993, 161).

Likewise, statistics on the incidence of rape in Nigeria are not readily available. As with domestic violence, rape is rarely reported to the police, though, according to Nigerian law in both the north and the south, a rape conviction carries a sentence of life imprisonment. Nigerian law does not provide any direct remedy against marital rape except in the case of an estranged spouse, although it is theoretically possible for women to press charges on the basis of assault laws (Neft and Levine 1997, 372; CRLP 1997, 84–85).

Female genital mutilation (FGM), also referred to as female circumcision, has received significant attention both inside and outside of Africa over the last two decades. FGM involves the surgical removal of portions or all of the clitoris, labia minora, and labia majora, and can be carried out at any point from a few days after an infant's birth to the time of a woman's first pregnancy. The many serious physical and psychological problems that can result from FGM include life-threatening infections and loss of blood stemming from the operation itself, chronic urinary and reproductive tract infections, severe pain with menstruation and intercourse, obstructed childbirth, a diminished or destroyed capacity for sexual pleasure, and more. It is estimated that almost one-half of Nigerian women have undergone FGM.

Efforts to eradicate FGM have been undertaken with increasing frequency in recent years, both in Nigeria and in other countries around the world where it is practiced. During this time the practice of FGM in Africa has received considerable—many would argue undue—attention in the United

States, Canada, and western Europe, with a prejudicial tendency in these parts of the world to interpret it as an indication of an innate backwardness and misogyny on the part of African peoples. In the United States, this curiosity culminated in the early 1990s in suggestions by some members of Congress that U.S. foreign aid should be tied to a country's willingness to pass anti-FGM laws. It is the belief of many African women working to eradicate FGM that at best these external efforts are ineffectual, while at worst they smack of an intrinsic belief in Western superiority and a heavy-handed interference by ill-informed outsiders. Instead, they would argue that FGM eradication efforts must be rooted in a deep understanding of the many local factors that help to perpetuate its practice in various parts of the world, most of which are grounded in a broad-based gender oppression of women. Thus, for example, in Nigeria as in many societies where FGM is conducted, mothers face great pressure to see to the circumcision of their daughters since an uncircumcised woman is unmarriageable, and generally nonmarriage is not a viable life path. Consequently, Nigerian groups pushing for an end to FGM, such as the Inter-African Committee of Nigeria on Harmful Traditional Practices Affecting the Lives of Women and Children, and the National Association of Nigerian Nurses and Midwives, typically stress the procedure's serious health risks while also pushing for far broader measures aimed at raising the educational levels and social and economic status of women, since these efforts will have the long-term effect of empowering women so that they may choose an alternate course (Thomas 1998; CRLP 1997, 82).

## THE FUTURE OF WOMEN'S RIGHTS

Precolonially, many women in what is now Nigeria enjoyed relatively high political and economic status. They have experienced a serious erosion of their standing over the past 100 and more years, first under colonial rule and subsequently under the governments of independent Nigeria. Women's loss of political authority is particularly problematic since it removes from them one of the major mechanisms for effecting change available in the modern state: political standing. This reality allows for the diminishing of women's status in all spheres, which is reflected in the concentration of women in low-paying jobs, the erosion of women's domestic authority, and women's relative lack of access to higher education. Nigerian women have continued their history of collective action in attempts to safeguard and improve their positions. A greater ability to routinely appeal to and articulate the needs of all women, not just elite women, would heighten the effectiveness of these organizations. It remains very difficult for them to succeed, however, in the face of women's substantial political marginalization; though they have made gains for women, Nigerian women's organizations operate in a notably hostile political environment.

## BIBLIOGRAPHY

Amadiume, Ifi. 1997. *Reinventing Africa: Matriarchy, Religion and Culture*. London: Zed Books.

Assié-Lumumba, N'Dri. 1998. "Women in West Africa." In *Women in the Third World: An Encyclopedia of Contemporary Issues*, ed. Nelly P. Stromquist. New York: Garland.

Awe, Bolanle. 1992. *Nigerian Women in Historical Perspective*. Lagos: Sankore Publishers.

Byfield, Judith. 1996. "Women, Marriage, Divorce and the Emerging Colonial State in Abeokuta (Nigeria), 1892–1904." *Canadian Journal of African Studies* 30, no. 1: 32–51.

Callaway, Barbara J. 1987. *Muslim Hausa Women in Nigeria: Tradition and Change*. Syracuse: Syracuse University Press.

Center for Reproductive Law and Policy, Inc. (CRLP) and International Federation of Women Lawyers (Kenya Chapter). 1997. "Nigeria." In *Women of the World: Laws and Policies Affecting Their Reproductive Lives. Anglophone Africa*. New York: Center for Reproductive Law and Policy.

Dawit, Seble, and Salem Mekuria. 1993. "The West Just Doesn't Get It: Let Africans Fight Genital Mutilation." *New York Times*, December 7.

Denzer, LaRay. 1994. "Yoruba Women: A Historiographical Study." *International Journal of African Historical Studies* 27, no. 1: 1–39.

———. 1999. "The Persistence of Nigerian Women's Political Inequality." *Northwestern University Program of African Studies News and Events* 9, no. 3 (Spring): 2–3.

Johnson-Odim, Cheryl, and Nina Emma Mba. 1997. *For Women and the Nation: Funmilayo Ransome-Kuti of Nigeria*. Urbana: University of Illinois Press.

Mann, Kristin. 1985. *Marrying Well: Marriage, Status and Social Change Among the Educated Elite in Colonial Lagos*. Cambridge: Cambridge University Press.

Mba, Nina Emma. 1982. *Nigerian Women Mobilized: Women's Political Activity in Southern Nigeria, 1900–1965*. Berkeley: Institute of International Studies, University of California–Berkeley.

———. 1989. "Kaba and Khaki: Women and the Militarized State in Nigeria." In *Women and the State in Africa*, ed. Jane L. Parpart and Kathleen A. Staudt. Boulder: Lynne Rienner.

Neft, Naomi, and Ann D. Levine. 1997. "Nigeria." In *Where Women Stand: An International Report on the Status of Women in 140 Countries, 1997–1998*. New York: Random House.

Odujinrin, O. 1993. "Wife Battering in Nigeria." *International Journal of Gynaecology and Obstetrics* 41, no. 2: 159–64.

Okonjo, Kamene. 1976. "The Dual-Sex Political System in Operation: Igbo Women and Community Politics in Midwestern Nigeria." In *Women in Africa: Studies in Social and Economic Change*, ed. Nancy J. Hafkin and Edna G. Bay. Stanford: Stanford University Press.

Pearce, Tola Olu. 1995. "Case Study: Monitoring the Impact of Contraceptive Technology in Nigeria." In *African Women South of the Sahara*, ed. Margaret Jean Hay and Sharon Stichter. 2nd ed. Harlow, England: Longman Group UK.

Ramsay, F. Jeffress. 1999. *Global Studies: Africa*. 8th ed. Guilford, CT: Dushkin/ McGraw-Hill.

Smith, Mary. 1955. *Baba of Karo: A Woman of the Moslem Hausa*. New York: Philosophical Library.

Stichter, Sharon. 1995. "Some Selected Statistics on African Women." In *African Women South of the Sahara*, ed. Margaret Jean Hay and Sharon Stichter. 2nd ed. Harlow, England: Longman Group UK.

Thomas, Irene M. 1998. "Nigeria: Strategies and Tactics for Prevention and Eradication of Female Genital Mutilation." *Women's International Network News* 24, no. 4 (Autumn): 30–31.

Van Allen, Judith. 1972. " 'Sitting on a Man': Colonialism and the Lost Political Institutions of Igbo Women." *Canadian Journal of African Studies* 6, no. 2: 165–81.

Wariboko, Waibinte E. 1995. "The Status, Role and Influence of Women in the Eastern Delta States of Nigeria, 1850–1900: Examples from New Calabar." In *Engendering History: Caribbean Women in Historical Perspective*, ed. Verene Shepherd, Bridget Brereton, and Barbara Bailey. New York: St. Martin's Press.

Women's International Network. 1992. "Country Reports on Human Rights Practices: Nigeria." *Women's International Network News* 18, no. 2 (Spring): 11.

# 13

# OJIBWE

## Women of the Western Great Lakes

*Lisa M. Poupart*

## INTRODUCTION

### Profile of the Ojibwe Nation Reservations in the United States

In their traditional language, the Ojibwe people refer to themselves as the "Anishinabe." They are most often referred to as the Ojibwe or Chippewa. While the Ojibwe people share a common history, culture, and language, the members of the Nation were separated and placed on reservations throughout the western Great Lakes in the late 1800s and early 1900s. In the United States, the Ojibwe have reservations in the states of Michigan, Minnesota, and Wisconsin. There are also Ojibwe reserves in Canada. Approximately half of the U.S. American Indian population lives on reservations, while others live in urban areas throughout the country.

The Ojibwe Nation has the third highest population of all U.S. federally recognized American Indian nations, with 103,826 enrolled members. Like other American Indian nations, the Ojibwe experience high rates of poverty and unemployment. In 1990, 30.9 percent of American Indian adults and 37.6 percent of American Indian children lived below the poverty level (Reddy 1993). Unemployment rates on Ojibwe reservations are staggering. On the Bad River Ojibwe reservation in northern Wisconsin, the unemployment rate is 81 percent (Tiller 1996). On the White Earth Ojibwe reservation in Minnesota, the unemployment rate is significantly lower at 24.8 percent; however, the per capita income is only $4,917 (Tiller 1996). The impact of poverty and unemployment experienced by American Indians is further reflected in their high suicide rate. For American Indian males ages fifteen to twenty-four, the suicide rate is 40.7 per 100,000, and for those ages twenty-five to thirty-four the rate is 49.6 per 100,000 (Reddy 1993).

Each of the Ojibwe reservations in the United States has its own tribal government that was formed under the federal Indian Reorganization Act (I.R.A.) of 1934. Each Ojibwe tribal government has an elected council composed of a chairperson, vice-chair, and other officers. The traditional governing structures of American Indian nations, like the governing clan system of the Ojibwe, were outlawed in the 1800s and are not recognized by the federal government. Today the sovereign authorities of the modern tribal governments are severely restricted, as American Indian nations fall under federal and sometimes state jurisdiction.

### A Case Study

Author and activist Ishkwegaabawiikwe (Winona LaDuke) has guided the way in resisting the Western domination of Ojibwe people and other indigenous nations throughout the world. A member of the White Earth Ojibwe Nation, LaDuke has led the indigenous struggle for environmental justice on American Indian lands and has written about the deadly corporate exploitation of energy resources on reservations. She formed the White Earth Land Recovery Project, an organization committed to reclaiming lands reserved for the White Earth Nation in an 1867 treaty, but from which they were dispossessed. The White Earth Recovery Project has struggled to regain 1,000 of the original 837,000 acres lost (Walljasper 1998).

Demonstrating the continued political leadership roles of Ojibwe women, in 1996 and 2000 LaDuke was Ralph Nader's vice-presidential candidate on the Green Party ticket in the national presidential elections. In 1989 she co-founded the Indigenous Women's Network, an organization whose mission is to increase the visibility of Native women and empower them to participate in political, social, and cultural processes while working toward improving the conditions of Native communities (Indigenous Women's Network 1994, ii). LaDuke lives on the White Earth Reservation in Minnesota with her two children. She is the author of *Last Standing Woman*, a novel that explores the history of the White Earth Ojibwe through three generations of women who struggle for cultural survival (University of Minnesota 1999).

### HISTORY OF OJIBWE WOMEN'S RIGHTS

#### Precontact History

Prior to European and American colonization, American Indian women were honored within their traditional societies and occupied balanced and valued social, economic, political, and spiritual roles. In their traditional tribal communities, women occupied autonomous positions as leaders, healers, teachers, decision-makers, and warriors. Within many traditional American Indian communities, family lineage was traced through the women, who also owned the crops and homes. However, the traditional roles and status of American Indian women changed dramatically upon European invasion. As tribal people were introduced to and, in many cases, forced to accept Western culture, the subordinate, disempowered social, economic, and political position of Western women became a reality for many Indian women. This chapter explores the impact of colonization on the rights of Ojibwe women in the western Great Lakes region of the United States.

Like other American Indian nations, traditionally the Ojibwe placed primary emphasis on the community over that of individuals and subgroups within the Nation. The primacy of community remains an important cultural value today for Ojibwe people. Thus, an examination of Ojibwe women's rights can only be explored within the larger framework of understanding the historical and contemporary experiences of the Ojibwe Nation as a whole. One cannot isolate the experiences of Ojibwe women from the experiences of the Nation as a collective. Thus, throughout this chapter, Ojibwe women's rights will be explored as the combined experiences of the Nation.

In precontact Ojibwe society, women were central figures in the cosmology of the Nation. The significance of Ojibwe women within traditional tribal spiritual beliefs was further reflected within the daily life of the Nation. While Ojibwe women and men often performed separate and distinct gender roles and duties within their communities, those of the women were held in high regard and were not viewed as inferior to those of the men.

Balanced roles and relationships between Ojibwe women and men were a reality because human beings were viewed in terms of their shared differences from and similarities with each other, as well as with other living beings. Perceived differences between humans, including differences in biological sex, were viewed in terms of how those variations reflected each other. Such differences were viewed as symmetrical, or as mirroring each other in metaphysical balance.

The complementary view of the differences between women and men is exemplified in the traditions of the Ojibwe, where variations in the economic, political, and social roles of women and men were not prioritized or privileged. Among the Ojibwe, balanced social, political, and economic relationships existing between women and men in traditional communities were interwoven in intricate spiritual beliefs that permeated nearly every aspect of life. Spiritual beliefs structured government and family units, and guided and informed the daily practices of childrearing, healing, teaching, basket making, and the gathering and consumption of plants, animals, and water. The significance of female entities in traditional spiritual beliefs provides insight into the role of women in daily life.

The Ojibwe supreme deity, Gitchi Manitou, was neither female nor male but, rather, female *and* male—a balance of all that existed in the universe. In addition, traditional cultures like that of the Ojibwe recognized individual spiritual deities and entities embodied as either female or male, equal to each other and each playing an integral role in the spiritual beliefs and practices of the tribe. Female spirit beings have significant roles in the traditional spiritual beliefs of nations like the Ojibwe. For example, Geezhigoquae (Sky Woman) is viewed as the procreator of the Nation. Among the Ojibwe it is believed that after Gitchi Manitou created the universe, great floods covered the Earth, killing all land and animals, including humans (Johnson 1990b, 1995). During these floods, the water animals invited Geezhigoquae from the heavens to visit upon the back of Turtle. With the help of Muskrat, a handful of Earth was collected from below the waters, and Turtle transformed into an island, upon which Geezhigoquae gave birth to the Ojibwe people (Johnson 1990b, 1995).

The valued role of women as procreators in some traditional tribal societies was premised upon women's cycles of creation. Throughout many traditional communities, women were highly regarded for their roles as perpetuators of the tribe. In his book *My Elders Taught Me*, John Boatman describes the primacy of female beings in the nations of the western Great Lakes region, including the Ojibway.

My Elders taught that, by design of the Great Spirit, female beings have primacy over males. Their preeminence is due to the female's integral and intimate participation in the continually manifesting sacred cycle of creation, destruction, and re-creation. As a result, all female beings symbolize and embody a portion of Great Spirit's life-giving force. (1992, 61)

This belief is echoed in the written account of an oral history Educator and leader Edward Benton-Benai (Lac Court Oreilles Ojibwe) retells the story of Gitchi Manitou's emissary Waynaboozhoo. Benton-Benai (1988) tells us that upon Waynaboozhoo's journey on Earth, Nokomis (Grandmother Moon) spoke to him of her role and the role of women. Nokomis told Waynaboozhoo that

it was her purpose to watch over i-kway'-wug (women) of the Earth and guide their lives. She told him of the powers of the Moon and how the Moon was symbolic of womanhood and the cycle of oon-da-di'zoo-win' (birth). She explained that woman was used by the creator to cast the light of knowledge on man just as the Moon casts its light on the Earth. Alone, man is backwards and undeveloped. He need[s] the light that woman give[s] to make him whole. (37)

Women within traditional Ojibwe communities were distinguished as the providers and keepers of subsequent generations; in essence, they were viewed as the guardians of the future.

The lives of all living beings were recognized and respected by tribal members, and the importance of living in balance with all beings was emphasized. Humans did not dominate other humans, nor did they dominate nature. Nations like the Ojibwe believed that to respect living beings meant to live in balance with the universe and that disrespect of living beings could invoke the spirit world (Boatman 1992; Johnson 1990a, 1990b).

The complementary and honored roles of Ojibwe women within traditional society were also mirrored in the daily practices of social life. Ojibwe women of the western Great Lakes were respected for their role as mother and for providing primary care for children. As mothers, women were viewed as providing the most significant function in daily life, as they were the sole providers of initial sustenance for each member of the Nation (Boatman 1992).

Within traditional life, the day-to-day tasks of men and women were often strictly divided by sex. Priscilla Buffalohead (1983) explains that although Ojibwe women had duties that were different than those of the men, women's roles were not denigrated but were viewed respectfully, as they balanced the roles of men. She states that the daily duties of men and women sometimes overlapped, with men and women working together "having separate duties in the same general activity" (238). For example, Buffalohead explains that in canoe building, men and women worked together at separate tasks, whereby "men fashioned the frame of the birch-bark canoe and made the paddles while the women sewed the back to the frame with spruce roots and applied the pitch or gum to the sewn areas to create watertight vessel" (238). This demonstrates the gender balance inherent in all aspects of Ojibwe life, for the work performed by women and men was viewed as equally important and was, in many cases, dependent upon the other.

## Changes Due to Contact

The traditional roles and status of American Indian women changed dramatically after the European invasion. As tribal people were introduced and, in many cases, forced to accept Western culture, the subordinate, disempowered social, economic, and political position of Western women became a reality for many American Indian women, including many Ojibwe women. In her book *Chain Her by One Foot*, Karen Anderson (1991) provides a comprehensive discussion of the status of Huron and Montagnais women of the Northeast due to colonization. Like the Huron and Montagnais, the Ojibwe came into contact early with Europeans. The impact of Christian missionaries and involvement with the fur trade devastated traditional lifeways and altered the status of women within those nations.

The disempowerment of American Indian women upon French contact was largely due to the economic exploitation by the French, whereby French men were ordered by the monarchy not to bring women to the "New World," but to intermix with Indian women to produce a new race of subjects for the crown (Anderson 1991). Anderson further contends that the biracial offspring of French and Indian unions were viewed as a "natural resource, like any other resource that might provide masters with riches . . . and would defend the country against all other monarchs' claims" (1991, 35–36). Thus, the French largely believed that the "native population had to be tamed, civilized and intermarried with French peasant stock" (Anderson 1991, 35).

Like the French, in order to control and exploit the indigenous people, Spanish and English colonizers sought to alter the status of women in traditional Indian cultures, as well as the relationships that existed between women, men, and children. Conversion to Christianity and formal European schooling imposed these formations upon Indian people. Christian missionaries broke apart tribal spiritual beliefs that honored women. Missionaries eroded traditional values and roles with exposure to patriarchy through Christian beliefs that revered male dominance and deemed women and children as mere property. Reflecting their own perceptions of Western women, Christian missionaries constructed Indian women as evil, morally corrupt, and consorts of the devil (Anderson 1991).

Through indoctrination into Christianity and Euro-American culture, many American Indian people learned and internalized the devalued Western view of women. As Anderson states:

With christianization a great deal of anger was directed towards women. Women were identified as responsible for any unpleasantness, insecurity or danger that members of society, especially men, found themselves in. A great deal of energy was then directed toward controlling women, and they became the legitimate brunt of hostility—both of their own self-loathing and of men's loathing and mistrust. (1991, 163)

In addition to the changing status of American Indian women prompted by missionaries, changing Indian economies and colonial and U.S. assimilation efforts further eroded the traditional status of women across nations. As the complementary economic roles of women and men in traditional economies were devastated by the fur trade, reduction of plains buffalo herds, loss of land, famine, and Western assimilative efforts, the social and political relationships between women and men altered dramatically.

As many tribal economies were devastated women lost their traditional roles in the production of the means of existence. Among the Ojibwe, the valued and balanced traditional roles of women and men were dramatically altered by the fur trade, as French traders often coveted the pelts obtained by the men in their hunts over the goods and services provided by women

(Devens 1992). The European market demand for furs and Christian conversion efforts operated simultaneously to create economic and social hierarchies that valued men's roles over women's within nations involved in the fur trade. Additionally, the balanced social roles of Ojibwe women were further eroded as indigenous lands were stolen and individual bands were removed to reservations (Shkilnyk 1985). As Anastasia Shkilnyk (1985) observes of the Grassy Narrows in Ontario, Ojibwe women no longer performed their traditional gardening and harvesting duties because of depleted or changed soil conditions and limited space on the reservation.

As all nations became assimilated into a capitalist economy, they were introduced to a wage economy and the split between public and private domains. American Indian men gained wage-labor jobs, while Indian women were removed from roles benefiting the entire community and placed into private household service (Leacock 1979). Moreover, many American Indian women were deprived of the traditional highly valued role of childrearing, as Indian children were systematically removed and placed in off-reservation boarding schools. Thus, Ojibwe women were also deprived of the mothering role that was once so valued within their traditional communities. Shkilnyk (1985, 158) contends that Ojibwe women at Grassy Narrows have been "the silent victims of modernization" as they have "borne the brunt of the shock of being ripped out of a meaningful cultural setting" and placed in one that has offered valued opportunities only to males.

The Western market economy prioritized and valued the work of American Indian men over the domestic work of Indian women. This was reinforced in the boarding schools, where American Indian girls were restricted to training in domestic duties and devalued within those roles, while Indian boys learned a trade. Not only did the educational and economic systems provide valued work for American Indian men, but the wage-labor system privileged Indian males because it "enabled them to control" the traditional domestic roles of women as unpaid labor (Jamieson 1981, 138). In this subordinate position many Ojibwe women, like American Indian women from other nations, became largely dependent upon Indian men for economic support within the home.

Like other American Indian women, the marginalization of many Ojibwe women resulting from economic exclusion is further escalated by the dependent relationship between nations and the federal government. American Indian women are dependents within the home and outside of the home as well. This internal and external dependency places Indian women among the economically "poorest of the poor" in Western society (Jamieson 1981, 138). Hence, the devastation of traditional Indian economies and assimilation into the U.S. capitalist system facilitate and advance the disempowered status of American Indian women.

## WOMEN'S RIGHTS TODAY

### Economic Deprivation and Dependency as Continued Genocide

Since contact, traditional tribal cultures and lifeways have been devastated by Western imperialism. Nations were stripped of authority to govern as they had for thousands of years. Instead, Euro-American government imposed Western systems upon American Indian people and continues to administer nations paternalistically. Additionally, the theft of indigenous land, whether through forced military removal or governmental assimilationist efforts, has devastated tribal cultures. Traditionally all nations were socially, spiritually, and economically connected to their physical environments. For many nations, loss of land meant the end not only of traditional economies, but also of those spiritual beliefs and practices firmly connected to the Earth. Loss of spirituality, given the theft of tribal lands and Western conversion attempts, has in many cases meant the loss of the very foundation of traditional Indian cultures.

Today, the Ojibwe, like other American Indian nations, continue in depressed economic, political, and social situations. The disempowerment of nations and the establishment of the U.S. federal trust relationship, whereby the federal government has deemed nations its wards, have placed American Indian nations in a complicated position of dependency upon their oppressors. This relationship aids in the continued genocide of nations.

As the Western colonial empire expanded throughout the "New World," American Indian nations like the Ojibwe were decimated, while survivors moved into remote, undesirable locations where they remain excluded from the profits reaped from traditional land bases. Iris Young suggests that economic marginalization resulting from such systematic racism is perhaps the most dangerous form of oppression, for through it a "whole category of people is expelled from useful participation in social life and thus potentially subjected to severe material deprivation and even extermination" (1990, 53). Recognizing the inhumanity of this deprivation, imperialist governments like the United States often offer services or welfare payments to groups they deprive. Young further adds that such provisions "produce new injustice by depriving those dependent on [them] of rights and freedoms that others have" (1990, 54).

The increased economic dependency of American Indian nations enabled U.S. authorities to disempower Indian nations by executing laws and policies designating Indians wards of the state and by giving the federal Bureau of Indian Affairs patriarchal control over Indian lands, resources, and matters including education and health care (Snipp 1986a, 1986b). As American Indian nations became increasingly marginalized and reliant on governmental aid, tribal resources including timber, water, oil, and minerals were appropriated for the sole benefit of the non-Indian economy. Such exclusion serves to further deprive nations and ensure their dependency.

Today, American Indian women largely occupy a disempowered role within society and are among the most marginalized within both Indian and white communities. American Indian women living on and off reservations are more impoverished and less educated and have a shorter life expectancy than the general U.S. population (Lujan 1995). American Indian women living on reservations are particularly susceptible to "victimiz[ation] by federal, state, and religious institutions such as the Bureau of Indian Affairs, the Indian Health Service, universities, the legal system and specific laws" (Lujan 1995, 13), given their disempowered social, political, and economic status.

The dependent status of American Indian women has led to systematic abuse by the Indian Health Service (IHS). Several authors document this abuse. Dine (Navajo) author Carol Lujan contends that American Indian women and children "residing on reservations who are dependent upon the Indian Health Service for health care are in a vulnerable situation and considered fair game for medical research programs" (1995, 17). Similarly, Jicarilla Apache/Isleta/Laguna author Myla Vicenti Carpio (1995) documents the involuntary sterilization of American Indian women by the IHS and IHS contract health care providers, which occurred throughout the 1970s. Both Carpio (1995) and Lujan (1995) discuss the violation and exploitation of American Indian women by medical science, underscoring that such practices are not uncommon today as Indian women continue to be subject to contemporary forms of genocide at the hands of the federal government.

In addition to the oppression experienced by American Indian women within the dominant culture, today they may also be exposed to other forms of violence in their own homes and communities. Although violence was virtually nonexistent in traditional Indian families and communities, today American Indian women and children continue to experience violence within the dominant culture and its institutions, and also within their own families and tribal communities.

Through the processes of colonization, American Indian people have internalized white patriarchy. As traditional cultures were devastated Western power structures privileging men and objectifying women and children were internalized. Constructions of women and children as powerless commodities were also internalized. Within tribal communities today, many American Indian women and children are subordinated and oppressed by their own people.

Today, American Indian women are sometimes subject to overt sexism even in the practice of more traditional beliefs and religious ceremonies. Traditionally, many women did not attend ceremonies during particular times and did not partake in specific religious practices because they were perceived as closely connected to the spirit world, and thus too spiritually powerful. Today the traditional absence of American Indian women from certain rituals, including drumming circles and sweat lodge ceremonies, is sometimes perpetuated by the sexist and discriminatory practices of Indian men—those who no longer view women's nonparticipation as a recognition and reverence of women's close connection to the spirit world, but instead exclude women on the basis of subordination.

As American Indian people internalized Western patriarchal power hierarchies, violence, as an exercise of power over those more marginalized, has become familiar within Indian homes and communities. Largely eroded within many nations, traditional American Indian economies, spiritual practices, and family/community structures no longer guard individuals from marginalization and violent exercises of authority. As Western culture, language, religion, and economic structures were imposed upon tribal people, many traditional, extended, and matriarchal families eroded and were replaced by male-dominated familial structures.

Within these Western patriarchal family structures, American Indians recreate the power structures of the dominant culture. That is, Indian men have privilege and authority over Indian women, and Indian fathers and mothers have privilege and authority over children, whereby each may exert violence as a socially acceptable operation of Western patriarchal power. Like other disempowered individuals in the dominant culture, then, American Indian men may assert male authority violently in their homes and communities against women and children, and Indian women may assert parental authority violently against children.

Today, American Indian women persist in the world of the white man. Despite continued marginalization and mass attempts to destroy traditional cultures and identities, Indian women have taken primary roles in resisting genocide and preserving indigenous cultures for future generations.

### The Persistence of Ojibwe Women Today

In spite of a 500-year campaign by Western imperialists to colonize the lands and minds of Indian people, many nations resisted total assimilation and maintained portions of their traditional cultures. American Indian women continue on today in their roles as tribal leaders, teachers, healers, and activists. Women from numerous nations assume an active role in recording and preserving the history and traditions of their people for future generations (Forbes 1996). Like American Indian women from all nations, Ojibwe women continue to preserve their cultures by leading struggles to assert land claims and treaty rights, reaffirm tribal sovereignty, and stop the toxic contamination of reservation lands by government and corporations.

Today throughout the western Great Lakes Ojibwe women continue to assert tribal treaty rights to hunt, fish, and gather on public lands in territories that were ceded to the government throughout the 1800s. In the 1980s and 1990s, after these rights were affirmed by the federal courts, Ojibwe men exercised their off-reservation spear fishing rights, while Ojibwe women maintained a strong presence at the boat landings despite the presence of hundreds of non-Indian protestors who attempted to halt the exercise of these rights with acts of violence and racial aggression.

## THE FUTURE OF WOMEN'S RIGHTS

In the new millennium, Ojibwe women from Wisconsin, particularly members of the Sokaogon (Mole Lake) Band, continue to lead opposition to Anaconda Minerals/Exxon's proposed sulfide mine that would potentially lethally harm the wild rice beds, lake waters, fish populations, and ground water supply that are central to the continued cultural survival of the Sokaogon Ojibwe people.

Further, individual Ojibwe women continue to play critical roles in the assertion of Native rights and persist today in their work as writers and poets. The writings of Kimberly Blaeser (White Earth), Louise Erdrich (Turtle Mountain), Winona LaDuke, and Denise Sweet (White Earth) serve as testimonies to the contemporary struggles and persistence of Ojibwe women and culture. The writings of each of these authors offer a convergence for the telling of the authors' life experiences as Ojibwe women and as an emergence of their voices as acts of resistance.

Despite a 500-year Euro-American campaign to colonize the lands and minds of Indian people, American Indian nations in the United States today have resisted and continue to struggle for cultural survival. Perhaps native authors M. Annette Jaimes and Theresa Halsey (1992, 311) have best captured this truth in their presentation of a traditional Cheyenne saying: "A people is not defeated until the hearts of its women are on the ground."

## BIBLIOGRAPHY

Anderson, Karen. 1991. *Chain Her by One Foot: The Subjugation of Women in Seventeenth-Century New France.* New York: Routledge.
Benton-Banai, Edward. 1988. *The Mishomis Book: The Voice of the Ojibwe.* St. Paul: Little Red School House.
Boatman, John. 1992. *My Elders Taught Me: Aspects of Western Great Lakes American Indian. Philosophy.* Lanham, MD: University Press of America.
———. 1993. *Wisconsin American Indian History and Culture: A Survey of Selected Aspects.* Madison: University of Wisconsin Press.
Buffalohead, Priscilla K. 1983. "Farmers, Warriors, Traders: A Fresh Look at Ojibwe Women." *Minnesota History* 48, no. 6: 236–44.
Carpio, Myla T. Vicenti. 1995. "Lost Generation: The Involuntary Sterilization of Indian Women." M.A. thesis, Arizona State University.
Champagne, Duane. 1989. *American Indian Societies: Strategies and Conditions of*

*Political and Cultural Survival.* Cultural Survival Report 32. Cambridge, MA: Cultural Survival.

Devens, Carol. 1992. *Countering Colonization: Native American Women and the Great Lakes Missions, 1630–1900.* Berkeley: University of California Press.

Forbes, Jack D. 1996. "The Native Intellectual Tradition in Relation to Race, Gender and Class." *Race, Gender and Class* 3, no. 2 (Winter): 12–34.

Indigenous Women's Network. 1994. *Indigenous Woman* 2, no. 2.

Jaimes, M. Annette, and Theresa Halsey. 1992. "American Indian Women at the Center of Indigenous Resistance in Contemporary North America." In *The State of Native America: Genocide, Colonization and Resistance,* ed. M. Annette Jaimes. Boston: South End Press, 311–44.

Jamieson, Kathleen. 1981. "Sisters under the Skin: An Exploration of the Implications of Feminist-Materialist Perspective Research." *Canadian Ethnic Studies* 13, no. 1: 130–43.

Johnson, Basil. 1990a. *Ojibway Ceremonies.* Toronto: McClelland and Stewart, 1982; reprint, Lincoln: University of Nebraska Press, Bison Books.

———. 1990b. *Ojibwe Heritage.* Toronto: McClelland and Stewart, 1976; reprint, Lincoln: University of Nebraska Press, Bison Books (page references are to reprint edition).

———. 1995. *The Manitous: The Spiritual World of the Ojibwe.* New York: HarperCollins.

Leacock, Eleanor. 1979. "Women's Status in Egalitarian Society: Implications for Social Evolution." *Current Anthropology* 19, no. 2: 247–55.

Lujan, Carol Chiago. 1995. "Women Warriors: American Indian Women, Crime and Alcohol." *Journal of Women and Criminal Justice* 7, no. 1: 9–33.

Reddy, Marlita, ed. 1993. *Statistical Record of Native North America.* Detroit: Gale Research.

Shkilnyk, Anastasia. 1985. *A Poison Stronger than Love: The Destruction of an Ojibwa Community.* New Haven: Yale University Press.

Snipp, C. Matthew. 1986a. "American Indians and Natural Resource Development: Indigenous Peoples' Land, Now Sought After Has Produced New Indian-White Problems." *American Journal of Economics and Sociology* 45, no. 4: 457–74.

———. 1986b. "The Changing Political Status of American Indians: From Captive Nations to Internal Colonies." *American Journal of Economics and Sociology* 45, no. 2: 145–57.

Tiller, Veronica Velarde, ed. 1996. *Tiller's Guide to Indian Country.* Albuquerque: Economic Department of Administration, U.S. Department of Commerce.

University of Minnesota. 1999. *Voices from the Gaps: Winona LaDuke.* Web site: http://voices.cia.umn/authors/winonaladuke.

Walljasper, Jay. 1998. "Celebrating Hellraisers: Winona LaDuke." *Mother Jones Magazine/MoJo Wire.* Foundation for National Progress. http://bsd.mojones.com.

Young, Iris Marion. 1990. *Justice and the Politics of Difference.* Princeton: Princeton University Press.

## ADDITIONAL RECOMMENDED READINGS

Allen, Paula Gunn. 1986. *The Sacred Hoop: Recovering the Feminine in American Indian Traditions.* Boston: Beacon Press.

Blaeser, Kimberly. 1993. *Trailing You*. Greenfield, NY: Greenfield Review Press.

Broker, Ignatia. 1983. *Night Flying Woman: An Ojibwe Narrative*. St. Paul: Minnesota Historical Society Press.

Erdrich, Louise. 1984. *Love Medicine*. New York: HarperCollins.

———. 1986. *The Beet Queen*. New York: Holt.

Jones, Gina, Maryellen Baker, and Mildred "Tinker" Schuman. 1988. *The Healing Blanket: Stories, Values and Poetry from Ojibwe Elders and Teachers*. Salt Lake City: Commune-A-Key Publishing.

LaDuke, Winona. 1997. *Last Standing Woman*. Stillwater, MN: Voyageur Press.

Sweet, Denise. 1997. *Songs for Discharming*. Greenfield, NY: Greenfield Review Press.

Also recommended are volumes of *Indigenous Woman*, a publication of the Indigenous Women's Network, P.O. Box 174, Lake Elmo, MN 55042.

# 14

# UNITED STATES
## "The Great Work Before Us"
### Cheryl Toronto Kalny

## INTRODUCTION

### Profile of the United States

The United States has a representative form of government with a bicameral legislature. The population is 272,639,608 (as of July 1999) (United States Government 1999), three-quarters of which lives in urban areas. It is an ethnically diverse nation composed of white (83.5 percent), black (12.5 percent), Asian (3.3 percent), and Amerindian (1 percent) citizens. The high life expectancy (averaging seventy-six years), the 97 percent literacy rate, and an unemployment rate of 4 percent are indications of a high quality of life enjoyed by many Americans.

The United States has a diverse and technologically advanced economy which, since World War II, has contributed to the creation of a two-tier labor market. Workers on the bottom tier, many of whom are women and minorities, often fail to receive pay increases, health insurance, and other benefits (Brinton 1996). While per capita income in the United States is among the highest in the world, averaging $31,500, approximately 13 percent of Americans live below the poverty line today.

### A Case Study

Amelia Chamberlain was an eleventh-grade high school student, living in Queens with her mother and sisters in a small apartment, when she won a contest. Each year, Barnard College sponsors an essay competition for girls in the New York public schools, the theme of which is "A Woman I Admire." In 1995 Amelia's essay, entitled "Mama's Dark World," won first prize. Her essay described the life of not only her own working mother, but also of millions of other single mothers struggling to raise their families today with fewer and fewer social supports. Every night at 10:00 P.M., Amelia awakens her mother for work. Her mother rises from her bed on the living room couch, after as little as four or five hours of sleep, to go to her night job. Amelia writes that she and her sisters worry that their mother pushes herself too hard, but her mother always says, "We need the money." Watching her go to work each night, Amelia wonders how her mother will be able to keep doing it all (Sidel 1996).

## THE EARLY HISTORY OF WOMEN'S RIGHTS

The fight for women's rights in the United States began early in the nineteenth century and was rooted in the evangelical groups and volunteer associations of middle- and upper-class women. Bound by the social strictures of the "domestic code" or "separate spheres" ideology, which barred women from wage labor and restricted them to home and hearth, women of means formed benevolent societies to combat a host of social and moral ills confronting an increasingly urban, industrial America. Forming female associations, fund-raising, petitioning governmental bodies, and other forms of activism were considered acceptable, indeed Christian, acts when done on behalf of unfortunate others such as prostitutes, orphans, and the poor.

Indeed, in the eighteenth and nineteenth centuries, the voices of upper- and middle-class women were often the only ones raised in defense of poor immigrant women. One such powerless female, whose name surfaced in connection with a prostitute being prosecuted in St. Paul, Minnesota, in 1910, was seventeen-year-old Annie Blase. Annie, the eldest daughter in an abusive alcoholic household, was recruited by a male procurer to work in a house of prostitution. When police raided the brothel, Annie was arrested. Instead of finding justice as an abused minor in the courts, however, Annie's "character" was used to mitigate the sentence of her male recruiter, who received a reduced sentence. A court-appointed doctor testified that she was "a moral degenerate who would lead a life of shame no matter what" (Kalny 1989, 134–35). Annie's case is representative of the plight of powerless women everywhere and at every period of time, including the late twentieth century United States, where poor and voiceless women continue to be held more accountable than male defendants, even for the actions of men perpetrated against them.

Several decades of moral and public crusades waged by organizations such as the Magdalen Society and the Society for the Relief of Poor Widows with Small Children culminated in women's active participation in the abolition movement that took shape in the 1830s. Abolitionist women honed their public speaking skills and their courage stumping the country for more than twenty years, addressing often hostile crowds. They forged under fire an absolute dedication to a cause, and equally as important, they also learned the political necessity of bridge building. All of these lessons would prove invaluable when women in the United States began to organize for their own rights in the middle of the nineteenth century. Embarking, in the words of the first women's rights declaration, upon "the great work before us," they launched what would become a 150-year struggle for women's rights in the United States. That struggle continues into the twenty-first century.

## THE HISTORY OF POLITICAL RIGHTS

The first woman's rights convention was called in 1848 at Seneca Falls, New York. It was organized by a coalition of women, Elizabeth Cady Stanton, Lucy Stone, Lucretia Mott, and Susan B. Anthony, already experienced in the abolition, temperance, and property law reform movements. Their initial meeting produced a Declaration of Sentiments which, as noted by Eleanor Flexner (1975), outlined the major issues and initiatives that would occupy activist women into the next century: higher education for women, entrance into the professions and trades, custody and property rights, and suffrage—the goal which would dominate the women's rights movement for the next seventy years. Many came to believe, in the years after Seneca Falls, that winning the vote was the key to rectifying the whole complex of social and institutional oppressions that limited women's lives. Despite sharing this common ideology, however, the participants at the Seneca Falls Convention parted ways after the Civil War on questions of methods, means, and membership. Differing philosophies would eventually and unfortunately lead to the formation of two separate woman's rights organizations, often working at odds with one another.

The battle over the passage of the Fifteenth Amendment, granting the voting privilege to freed black males, split abolitionist women into opposing camps. The American Woman Suffrage Association, founded in 1869 by Lucy Stone, supported the Fifteenth Amendment. It retained ties with and support from old allies in the Republican Party, and favored a state-by-state referendum on the voting question. Stanton and Anthony established the National Woman Suffrage Association and used their newspaper, the *Revolution*, to urge female suffrage as a way to elevate the status of wealthy, educated women over that of freed slaves and immigrant men. Their organization endorsed the broad spectrum of issues introduced at Seneca Falls, insisted on an all-female leadership base, and worked for a federal suffrage amendment.

After several decades of divided and unsuccessful efforts, the two organizations merged in 1890. The new National American Woman Suffrage Association (NAWSA) intensified state campaigns, elected new national leaders Carrie Chapman Catt and Anna Howard Shaw, and forged critical connections with the growing women's club movement sweeping the country at the turn of the twentieth century, and with the even larger Woman's Christian Temperance Union. The rise of the Progressive Movement in these same years also strengthened and supported women's demand to participate in the electoral process in order to support social reform (O'Neill 1989).

It was the intervention of World War I, however, and women's overwhelming participation in volunteer work and service to the nation, which finally swung not only the Wilson administration, but also public opinion in favor of female suffrage. The House of Representatives passed a woman suffrage amendment in January 1918, which was approved by the Senate in June 1919. The thirty-sixth state needed for ratification of the amendment voted in favor of female suffrage in August 1920, and the woman's vote became legal after more than seventy years of hard work.

Following the passage of the Nineteenth Amendment, named in honor of Susan B. Anthony, the woman's rights movement, which had never enjoyed extended solidarity, split once more into opposing factions. The NAWSA, largely depleted of members after the vote was won, was reborn in the League of Women Voters. The League's goals remained the same throughout the twentieth century: to educate voters on issues and candidates, and to support legislation friendly to women and children. An even smaller group, under the leadership of Alice Paul, transformed the 1916 Women's Peace Party into the National Woman's Party (Lunardini 1986).

Paul and her followers proposed an Equal Rights Amendment (ERA) to the Constitution in 1923, designed to combat discriminatory state laws and to erase sex as a legal classification. Their brief document asserting that "[m]en and women shall have equal rights throughout the United States" provoked a storm of controversy even amid women's groups, some of whom feared the repeal of protective legislation reformers had worked long and hard to enact. Others opposed protective legislation as discriminatory and exclusionary to women in the workplace. The largest woman's organization of the time, the General Federation of Women's Clubs, endorsed the ERA, while the League of Women Voters, the American Association of University Women, the Young Women's Christian Association, and dozens of trade union groups opposed its passage throughout the 1920s and 1930s. The ERA failed in 1953 to win the needed two-thirds majority vote.

## POLITICAL RIGHTS TODAY

With the reemergence of a feminist movement in the late 1960s, the ERA was revived and pushed forward during the 1970s. In 1972, both the House and Senate passed the ERA, but opposition was mounting in the form of right to life and "pro-family" movements coalescing with right-wing Phyllis Schlafly's Stop ERA campaign (Schlafly 1978). The ERA was once more portrayed as a threat not only to American society, but to women's rights as well. In 1982 it was again defeated, this time having failed ratification by only three states.

Traditional interpretations have held that the only link between the suffrage movement at the beginning of the century and the emergence of a new women's liberation movement in the late 1960s was the ERA. During the intervening decades, according to this interpretation, the woman's rights movement was largely dead. More recent historical analysis, however, has argued that winning the vote was not the end of women's activism, but the beginning of modern feminism (Cott 1987). The lessons learned by women during the long suffrage campaign proved, in the long run, to be as valuable as achieving the vote.

Since the vote was won, women's voting patterns have continued to fluctuate. Disappointingly few women voted in the elections of the 1920s, particularly women of color in the South and immigrant women in the northern industrial centers. The Great Depression of the 1930s, however, mobilized large numbers of women to go to the polls, and to vote overwhelmingly for Democratic candidates. Nevertheless, not until the 1980s did women start outnumbering men at the polls.

Gender differences also exist in attitudes about such issues as war, the environment, gun control, national health care, affirmative action, and racial discrimination, with women consistently supporting more liberal positions (McGlen and O'Connor 1998, 69–71). Moreover, in the last decades of the twentieth century, women voters in the United States were twice as likely as men to vote for Democratic candidates, except in cases where female Republican candidates were supportive of social programs or women's issues.

Throughout most of this century, women represented less than 5 percent of the members of Congress or of state legislatures. Publicized as the Year of the Woman, 1992 galvanized female candidates, who won an unprecedented 108 seats in the House and 11 Senate positions. That election year also saw the first African American woman, Carol Moseley-Braun, take her place in the Senate. By the end of the 1990s, women comprised 11 percent of the United States Congress and held 25 percent of elective state offices.

Obstacles to female candidacy remain, however, including such factors as family demands, public perception of the incompatibility of the roles of mother and politician, sex and race discrimination, and perhaps most daunting, fund-raising difficulties. To encourage and assist women candidates, female political action committees (PACs) formed in the 1980s. EMILY's List, NOW PAC, Women in the Senate and House (WISH), and Republican Network to Elect Women (RENEW) contribute seed monies to help finance the campaigns of female candidates on the local, state, and national levels.

The presence of female lawmakers influences the introduction and progress of bills affecting women, as well as spending priorities (McGlen and O'Connor 1998, 90–91). The success of women's rights legislation, therefore, will continue to depend on increasing the proportion of women in elective offices at every level.

## THE HISTORY OF ECONOMIC AND EDUCATIONAL RIGHTS

### Economic Rights

"Women have always worked," as Alice Kessler-Harris (1981) noted in her book of the same title. Her history of working women in the United States records discriminatory pay, double shifts, exclusion from unions, and even deaths from dangerous working conditions. Women began organizing for better hours and wages almost upon the heels of their entrance into the wage labor market in the textile mills of Massachusetts in the 1820s. Historians Mary Beth Norton (1989) and Sara Evans (1989) trace the beginnings of female working-class activism to the Lowell mills, which experienced the first turnout to protest wage reductions in 1834 and 1836, and the first petition campaign, the Ten Hour Movement to reduce hours. By the time Lowell workers had organized the Female Labor Reform Association in 1845, however, mill owners were beginning to hire immigrant labor. This labor shift would intensify in the years after the Civil War and would result in the increased degradation of factory work and workers.

The invention of the sewing machine in the 1840s, together with succeeding waves of immigration, helped to transform the early garment industry in eastern urban centers into the horrors of tenement sweatshops by the turn of the twentieth century. Conditions at the Triangle Shirtwaist Company in New York at the time of the tragic fire in 1911, which took the lives of 146 women workers, were representative of the experiences of many women in the garment industry. Long hours, exploitative wages, and unsanitary and dangerous conditions, combined with the exclusion of women from the powerful American Federation of Labor and the relative ineffectiveness of the Women's Trade Union League, resulted in the deaths of these immigrant women, who were trapped by fire on the upper floors of an aging tenement. With stairwell doors locked, and inadequate fire escapes, their last choice in life was whether to burn or jump (Baxandall and Gordon 1995, 176–77). In the aftermath of this tragedy a state commission investigated labor abuses in the garment industry and recommended the passage of protective legislation in the spirit of the 1908 Supreme Court case *Muller v. Oregon*, which upheld the ten-hour day for women workers. Efforts to establish a minimum wage for female workers, however, were declared unconstitutional by the *Adkins v. Children's Hospital* decision in 1923. The Great Depression continued to defer women's attainment of equal economic rights, as many employers believed that men should receive whatever jobs were available, states passed laws barring married women from working, and the federal government prohibited the hiring of more than one person per family.

America's entrance into World War II presented working women with jobs and opportunities previously denied them. An unprecedented number of women, more than 6 million, found work in the paid labor market during the war. By 1944, they constituted 35 percent of the labor force and almost 22 percent of unions (Woloch 1996, 301–3). Black and white, married and single flocked to defense plants, where the need was greatest, the pay was highest, and the benefits most attractive. When the war ended, however, traditional attitudes about work and women's roles reemerged, and pressure was exerted to return women to their homes. Women were laid off, their jobs given to returning veterans who were given preference. Those who remained had their pay and benefits cut, were segregated on the job, and faced a society once again hostile to working women.

### Education

Women's educational advances fared little better by the beginning of the twentieth century. From the beginning, when Oberlin College became the first to admit females in the 1830s, education was race and class based. Only the daughters of the wealthy could afford to attend either the coeducational land grant colleges opened to them by the Morrill Act in 1862 or the elite, private women's colleges such as Vassar, Wellesley, Smith, Bryn Mawr, and Radcliffe founded in the 1870s and 1880s. By 1900, despite the fact that more than 15 percent of all college alumni in the country were female, the traditional professions of ministry, law, and medicine remained largely closed to women (Chamberlain 1988, 3–6).

Following World War II, despite their service to the country during the war, women were not eligible for G.I. benefits. Returning male veterans received tuition grants from the federal government and crowded into colleges throughout the 1950s, while the number of women in college dropped sharply. Although their numbers began to improve in the 1960s, most women students continued to major in such "women's" fields as teaching, social work, and nursing. Not until the 1980s did women outnumber men in institutions of higher learning and, even then, college-educated women would continue to swell the ranks of the typically female professions through the rest of the century (Solomon 1985).

### ECONOMIC AND EDUCATIONAL RIGHTS TODAY

The reemergence in the post–World War II years of an ethic of femininity and domesticity, with its excessive emphasis on motherhood, limited and constrained the lives of women from the working class to the educated, upper class. The publication in 1963 of Betty Friedan's *The Feminine Mystique* expressed this generalized sense of discontent among women as "the problem that has no name." This widely circulated book, coupled with a decade of women's activism in the social and political movements of the sixties, was a factor in the rebirth of the women's rights movement, announced in 1967 as the women's liberation movement. Undoubtedly the most significant spur to the creation of a new women's movement, however, was the passage of the Civil Rights Act of 1964. Title VII of this historic act contained a provision against sex discrimination in employment and established the Equal Employment Opportunity Commission (EEOC) to handle sex discrimination grievances. By 1966, however, it became clear that the EEOC, inundated with complaints, favored race discrimination cases and class action complaints over the cases of individual women. The National Organization for Women (NOW) was founded that year in response to this need for a civil rights organization and a political pressure group to push for "a fully equal partnership of the sexes" at home and in the workplace.

Title VII of the 1964 Civil Rights Act, prohibiting discrimination by employers or unions, was also the basis for affirmative action programs seeking to redress past inequities in the hiring of women and minorities. Executive Order 11375, issued by President Lyndon Johnson in 1967, specified that federal employers were required to take affirmative action to ensure that all employees, regardless of gender, race, color, or religion, were given equal treatment and opportunities. The Supreme Court further clarified affirmative action by ruling in 1987 in *Johnson v. Transportation Agency* that sex was to be considered as a factor in the hiring process, particularly in fields where women were traditionally underrepresented. Discrimination was permissible to end discrimination (McGlen and O'Connor 1998). By 1996, however, affirmative action was under attack in the United States. In that year the Republican Party platform called for an end to all affirmative action programs, and the state of California passed Proposition 209, which bars state and local governments from using race and gender preferences in hiring and education. A federal court ruling in 1997 affirmed that Proposition 209, ironically titled the California Civil Rights Initiative, is constitutional.

### Equal Pay and Family Leave Legislation

The Equal Pay Act of 1963 was the first legislative recognition of the wage gap that had existed between men and women workers since the nineteenth century. Because of the limitations of this act, requiring only equal pay for equal work, and failing to include professional and administrative workers, efforts to close the wage gap persisted throughout the remainder of the twentieth century. The 1981 Supreme Court case *County of Washington v. Gunther* supported the concept of "comparable wages" for work that is comparable in skill, effort, and responsibility (Goldberg and Kremen

1990, 30–31). The most recent legislation to address this inequity, the Fair Pay Act, was enacted by Congress in 1994 to prohibit wage discrimination in "equivalent" jobs. Regardless of the terminology used or the legislative efforts involved, women's wages continue to lag behind men's. As of 1999, overall, women were paid 75 percent of what men were paid, with black and Hispanic women earning approximately 84 percent of what white women were paid (McGlen and O'Connor 1998).

By the last decades of the twentieth century, a majority of mothers in the United States worked outside of the home. The availability of affordable, high-quality daycare for their children remains a major obstacle in the daily lives of working women. While women's rights groups lobbied Congress throughout the 1980s for federal legislation to make childcare more accessible to working mothers, groups that strongly oppose governmental regulation of childcare have largely succeeded in blocking such legislation. In 1990, however, Congress created the Childcare and Development Block Grant Program to provide money to the states for childcare programs. These funds have been earmarked for those low-income parents who most need assistance.

Another "family friendly" piece of legislation designed to ease the burdens of working women, the Family and Medical Leave Act, was introduced by Representative Patricia Schroeder (D-Colo.) in 1985. This proposal guaranteed family and medical leaves for working mothers, as well as paternity leaves for fathers. The bill made it through Congress in 1990, only to be vetoed by President George Bush. President Bill Clinton eventually signed the Family and Medical Leave Act into law in 1993, giving workers up to twelve weeks of unpaid leave to care for a newborn or to assist a family member with a serious health problem. These same workers are guaranteed their old job, or its equivalent, upon return to the workplace (McGlen and O'Connor 1998, 135–36).

Despite hard-won gains in the latter half of the twentieth century, working women continue to struggle against a host of problems. Many continue to crowd into female-dominated jobs and professions characterized by depressed wages and short career ladders. Women make up the majority of part-time workers, who are typically not eligible for benefits. Sex segregation and wage gaps, combined with childcare problems and women's "double shift" (Hochschild 1998), continue to create the situation where women work longer and harder for fewer rewards than men.

## THE HISTORY OF REPRODUCTIVE RIGHTS

The struggle for women's control over their own bodies and reproductive rights began in the United States in the early years of the twentieth century. Leftist radical and union organizer Emma Goldman was one of the first to speak in public about the need of poor women for some means of limiting the size of their families. She was jailed in 1916 for violating the 1873 Comstock Laws, which classified information about contraception as obscenity. However, it was Margaret Sanger whose name would become synonymous with this new movement. Inspired by Goldman and other Greenwich Village radicals, as well as by her own experiences as a public health nurse in the settlement houses in New York City, Sanger dedicated her life to the movement she called "birth control" (Baxandall and Gordon 1995, 188–89). As a socialist in the years before World War I, Sanger employed direct action techniques to challenge the law. In 1914 she began publishing her monthly magazine, the *Woman Rebel*, flaunting the Comstock Laws by disseminating birth control information through the postal system. She fled the United States under threat of arrest, and spent the year 1915 gathering information on contraceptive devices in Europe. Returning to this country in 1916, Sanger opened the first birth control clinic, in Brownsville, a working-class neighborhood in Brooklyn. She was jailed and the clinic closed within days of opening. However, the publicity was invaluable to the cause, particularly since suffrage leaders declined to support the birth control cause on grounds of public decency and feminine purity. "Your reform is too narrow to appeal to me," Carrie Chapman Catt wrote to Sanger in 1920, "and too sordid" (quoted in Chesler 1992). Not only suffrage leaders but also many other women's groups were offended by Sanger's movement and refused to endorse the Birth Control League. While the working-class National Women's Trade Union League publicly supported Sanger, the larger, more mainstream organizations such as the General Federation of Women's Clubs and the League of Women Voters found the topic of birth control too controversial to include in their agendas.

In the anti-socialist atmosphere of the country in the years following World War I, Sanger shifted the focus of the movement from a radical cause to an educational campaign. Her formation of the American Birth Control League also transformed the movement from its original working-class objective of limiting family size to a new middle-class ethic of liberation from "involuntary motherhood." By 1925 the league had succeeded in forging an alliance with physicians who then became the sole dispensers of birth control. Once the American Medical Association endorsed contraception to "cure or prevent disease," middle-class women became increasingly able to obtain contraceptive devices from their private physicians, while poor women, who needed it most, had the least access to contraception (Evans 1989, 227).

By the early 1960s, birth control pills were being marketed even though laws in such states as Connecticut and Massachusetts continued to prohibit the sale or use of birth control devices. To challenge these state laws, Planned Parenthood opened a birth control clinic in New Haven, Connecticut. The arrests and convictions that followed were appealed to the

Supreme Court, which in 1965 ruled in *Griswold v. Connecticut* that the constitutional right to privacy included the right of married couples to have access to birth control. *Eisenstadt v. Baird* extended that right of privacy to unmarried women in 1972. However, throughout the 1980s during the Reagan and Bush administrations, Congress passed legislation such as the the Adolescent Family Life Act to limit teenage girls' access to birth control by requiring parental notification in all federally funded clinics, and stressing abstinence in place of contraception.

## REPRODUCTIVE RIGHTS TODAY

### Abortion Rights

The fight for abortion rights chronologically parallels that of the birth control movement, but has been even more controversial throughout the twentieth century. State anti-abortion statutes were first enacted in the United States following the passage of the Comstock Laws at the end of the nineteenth century. Throughout the first half of the twentieth century abortions remained illegal except to save the life of the mother. Women of means could fly to Europe for an abortion. Others had to rely on secretive, clandestine, and dangerous arrangements for abortions performed outside of medical facilities, often by untrained practitioners. The first call for reform of the anti-abortion laws came from the American Law Institute, which advocated, in 1959, the decriminalizing of abortion in three circumstances: when the mother's health would be gravely impaired by the continuation of the pregnancy, when the child might be born with a serious defect, or when the pregnancy resulted from rape or incest. Public support for this type of reform began to build in the wake of a German measles epidemic that swept the country in 1963 and 1964, tragically resulting in the births of thousands of deformed babies. In 1967, at its first annual convention, NOW issued the first public demand for the repeal of restrictive abortion laws, claiming that a woman's control over her reproductive life was a basic civil right.

Joining NOW in this pro-choice movement were groups such as Planned Parenthood and the newly formed National Association for the Repeal of Abortion Laws (NARAL), which was renamed the National Abortion and Reproductive Rights Action League in 1994. These groups began lobbying state legislatures to repeal their abortion laws. In 1970, New York State became the first to pass more liberal abortion laws. As this battle was being waged on the state level, the United States Supreme Court agreed to hear a case involving abortion rights in December 1971, *Roe v. Wade.* A Texas woman, "Jane Roe," whose pregnancy was not life-threatening, was denied an abortion under Texas law. She could not afford to seek an abortion outside of her state, and her suit challenged the constitutionality of a law that deprived her of "the fundamental right to choose when and where to have children" (Weddington 1993).

Relying heavily on the earlier *Griswold v. Connecticut* decision, which had defined privacy rights, the Supreme Court ruled in January 1973 that a woman's right to privacy took precedence over a state's right to regulate abortions, invalidating nearly all existing state laws. Upon the heels of this landmark decision, however, the National Right to Life Committee (NRLC) was formed, in alliance with the Catholic Church, to lobby Congress for an amendment to ban abortions on the grounds of fetal right to life. Right to life groups pressured state legislatures into passing laws regulating clinics and placing restrictions on a woman's right to an abortion. By 1976, Congress had passed legislation, referred to as the Hyde Amendment, which withdrew federal funds, such as Medicaid, for abortions. Three challenges to the constitutionality of the Hyde Amendment were struck down by the Supreme Court in 1977 (Weddington 1993, 196–97).

Ronald Reagan's election in 1980 ushered in the Moral Majority and a continuation of the attack on abortion rights on the state level. In addition, Reagan packed the Supreme Court with anti-abortion justices, Antonin Scalia, Anthony Kennedy, and Byron White. William Rehnquist, who had dissented in *Roe*, was elevated to chief justice. During George Bush's administration, the abortion controversy in the country became even more public and contentious. A national right to life organization, Operation Rescue, began blocking access to clinics and women's health centers. Bush's appointment of two additional conservative justices, David Souter and Clarence Thomas, ensured that a majority of the Court was opposed to abortion. In 1991, *Rust v. Sullivan* imposed a gag order on clinics receiving federal funds, restricting them from discussing abortion, and *Planned Parenthood v. Casey* reversed *Roe*'s contention that a woman's right to an abortion was a fundamental right. *Casey* allowed states to place restrictions on abortions as long as they did not place an "undue burden" on a woman's right to an abortion (Woloch 1996, 364–65).

With the election of William Clinton in 1992 there was a change in administrative policy regarding abortion rights. Clinton repealed the gag order clinics had operated under since the Reagan administration, and appointed a pro-choice justice to the Supreme Court, Ruth Bader Ginsburg. In response to an escalation in violence by right to life groups, including clinic bombings and the shootings of physicians, Attorney General Janet Reno called for federal legislation to protect women and health care providers. The Freedom of Access to Clinic Entrances Act (FACE), passed in May 1994, made it a federal crime to block entrances to, or harass employees of, reproductive health clinics. Throughout the last decade of the twentieth century, states continued to pass laws restricting a woman's right to an abortion, such as withholding funding from clinics, imposing a twenty-four-hour waiting period, and requiring minors to have parental consent. Despite Clinton's veto of the Partial Birth Abortion Act, several states have passed such acts. As the century ended, birth control and abortion issues remained among the most controversial topics in the field of women's rights.

### Violence Toward Women

Another issue Americans became increasingly aware of and concerned about during the last decades of the century was the rising level of physical and sexual violence which threatened women in their private as well as public lives. Feminists such as Andrea Dworkin (1987) and Catharine MacKinnon (1994) drew direct correlations between the violence against women depicted throughout the culture in magazines, movies, and advertising, and the rising levels of rapes and domestic battering in society. Particularly targeted was the billion-dollar pornography industry. Proceeding under the belief that "[p]ornography is the theory; rape is the practice" (Morgan 1970), MacKinnon and Dworkin introduced a 1983 Minneapolis ordinance that classified pornography as a form of sex discrimination that violated the Civil Rights Act of 1964. Although the U.S. Court of Appeals struck down this ordinance in 1985 as a violation of freedom of speech, pornography remains an unresolved issue.

The 1986 Supreme Court case *Meritor Savings Bank v. Vinson* highlighted another form of aggressive discrimination against women, sexual harassment. With the *Meritor* decision, conduct that made submission to sex a condition for employment or advancement, or that created an "intimidating, hostile, or offensive working environment," was found criminal (Woloch 1996, 366). What constituted illegal conduct was based on the "reasonable woman" standard set in 1991 by the Ninth Court of Appeals in *Ellison v. Brady*. Sexual harassment, its definition, and its prevalence in the workplace continue to be controversial issues in American society.

## THE FUTURE OF WOMEN'S RIGHTS

The immediate future of women's rights in the United States will continue to include previous goals—equal wages and employment opportunities, reproductive freedom, increased representation in the political arena, and freedom from violence in society—as well as more recent controversies, such as legal recognition of same-sex marriages, domestic partnership laws, and adoption rights. Other issues for the "post-feminist" generation to address will be how to combat the forces of backlash launched in the 1990s against the feminist gains of the earlier decades (Faludi 1991), how to unite a movement historically divided along race and class lines, and how to redefine the movement to appeal to new generations of women who will continue the long tradition of struggle for women's rights in the United

States. One constant in what has become the longest lasting and most far-reaching civil and human rights movement in United States history is the intergenerational links of its participants. Feminists today are mindful that they stand upon the shoulders of past giants as they work for a better tomorrow.

## BIBLIOGRAPHY

Baxandall, Rosalyn, and Linda Gordon. 1995. *America's Working Women: A Documentary History*. New York: W. W. Norton.

Brinton, William M. 1996. *An Abridged History of the United States*. www.US-History.com.

Chamberlain, Miriam, ed. 1988. *Women in Academe: Progress and Prospects*. New York: Russell Sage Foundation.

Chesler, Ellen. 1992. *Woman of Valor: Margaret Sanger and the Birth Control Movement in America*. New York: Simon and Schuster.

Cott, Nancy F. 1977. *The Bonds of Womanhood*. New Haven: Yale University Press.

———. 1987. *The Grounding of Modern Feminism*. New Haven: Yale University Press.

Dworkin, Andrea. 1987. *Pornography: Men Possessing Women*. New York: Dutton.

Evans, Sara M. 1989. *Born for Liberty*. New York: The Free Press–Macmillan.

Faludi, Susan. 1991. *Backlash: The Undeclared War on American Women*. New York: Crown.

Flexner, Eleanor. 1975. *Century of Struggle: The Woman's Rights Movement in the United States*. Cambridge, MA: The Belknap Press of Harvard University Press.

Friedan, Betty. 1963. *The Feminine Mystique*. New York: Norton Press.

Goldberg, Gertrude Schaeffer, and Eleanor Kremen. 1990. *The Feminization of Poverty*. New York: Praeger.

Hochschild, Arlie. 1998. *The Second Shift*. New York: Viking Press.

Kalny, Cheryl Toronto. 1989. Daughters of Eve: Female Offenders and the Criminal Justice System, St. Paul, 1858–1929. Ph.D. dissertation, Marquette University.

Kessler-Harris, Alice. 1981. *Women Have Always Worked*. New York: Feminist Press.

———. 1982. *Out to Work: A History of Wage Earning Women in the United States*. New York: Oxford University Press.

Langley, Winston E., and Vivian C. Fox. 1994. *Women's Rights in the United States: A Documentary History*. Westport, CT: Greenwood Press.

Lunardini, Christine. 1986. *From Equal Suffrage to Equal Rights: Alice Paul and the National Woman's Party*. New York: New York University Press.

MacKinnon, Catharine A. 1979. *Sexual Harassment of Working Women*. New Haven: Yale University Press.

———. 1994. *Only Words*. Cambridge, MA: Harvard University Press.

McGlen, Nancy E., and Karen O'Connor. 1998. *Women, Politics and American Society*. Englewood Cliffs, NJ: Prentice-Hall.

Morgan, Robin, ed. 1970. *Sisterhood Is Powerful: An Anthology*. New York: Random House.

————. 1992. *The Beauty Myth.* New York: Anchor Books.

Norton, Mary Beth. 1989. *Major Problems in American Women's History.* Lexington, MA: D. C. Heath.

O'Neill, William L. 1989. *Feminism in America: A History.* New Haven: Yale University Press.

Schlafly, Phyllis. 1978. *The Power of the Positive Woman.* New York: Arlington House.

Sidel, Ruth. 1996. *Keeping Women and Children Last.* New York: Penguin Books.

Solomon, Barbara Miller. 1985. *In the Company of Educated Women.* New Haven: Yale University Press.

United States Government. 1999. *CIA Factbook.* www.odci.gov/cia/publications/factbook/us.html.

Weddington, Sarah. 1993. *A Question of Choice.* New York: Penguin Books.

Woloch, Nancy. 1996. *Women and the American Experience.* New York: McGraw-Hill.

# 15

# ZIMBABWE

## Women's Rights and African Custom

### Sita Ranchod-Nilsson

## INTRODUCTION

### Profile of Zimbabwe

Zimbabwe is located on a high plateau in central southern Africa and has a population of approximately 12 million people. The country shares borders with South Africa, Zambia, Mozambique, and Botswana. Zimbabwe attained independence from Great Britain and the rebel UDI (Unilateral Declaration of Independence) regime of Ian Smith's Rhodesia Front government in 1980 after a decade-long armed struggle. Since independence politics has been dominated, at times forcefully, by one party, the Zimbabwe African National Union (ZANU-PF), and its leader, Robert Mugabe. Opposition forces were not successful in breaking the one-party monopoly until the parliamentary elections in June, 2000, which were dominated by issues involving economic crises, land reform, and constitutional reform. Zimbabwe's economy is relatively diversified; agriculture is the dominant sector, followed by mining and small-scale manufacturing. Since 1991 the government has undertaken structural adjustments in an effort to create a more internationally oriented market economy. However, these efforts have led to high rates of unemployment and inflation as well as social and political unrest.

### A Case Study

In July 1997 Venia Magaya, a fifty-two-year-old seamstress, was evicted from her home in the Mabvuku subdivision of Harare by her younger half-brother. She had lived in this home with her parents until their death. Venia was the eldest child of her deceased father's first wife and had been designated as his heir by a community court. Her half-brother appealed this decision to the magistrate's court and won. Rita Makarau, a lawyer and a member of Zimbabwe's Parliament, appealed this decision on behalf of Venia Magaya to the Supreme Court and, in April 1999, lost. In a unanimous (5–0) decision, the Court ruled that under customary law, only men can inherit and all family members are subordinate to the male head of the family (Sayagues 1999). Writing on behalf of the Court, Justice Gibson Muchechetere stated that

women's status is therefore basically the same as that of a junior male in the family. . . . It must be recognized that customary law has long directed the way African people conducted their lives and the majority of Africans in Zimbabwe still live in rural areas and still conduct their lives in terms of customary law. (Quoted in Njanji 1999)

This decision set a legal precedent for customary law to erode legal gains made by women since independence in 1980; commenting on the decision, Welshman Ncube, one of Zimbabwe's leading legal scholars, said, "Basically, there's nothing left of the gains women's rights have made in the past 20 years. It's a full-bench decision, 5–0, by the Supreme Court. There is no appeal. They meant to settle this question once and for all" (quoted in Landsberg 1999).

Women's groups and human rights groups, both in Zimbabwe and internationally, have protested vehemently the Supreme Court's decision in this case. Following public protests in May, seven Zimbabwean women's groups—Women's Action Group, Musasa Project, Zimbabwe Women's Lawyers Association, Zimbabwe Women's Resource Centre and Network, Women in Law in Southern Africa, Women and Law in Development in Africa, and Young Women's Christian Association—sent a formal protest to Justice Muchechetere. In their letter the women's organizations stated that the decision had "set a very retrogressive precedent in erasing progress made in advancing the status and rights of women in independent Zimbabwe." They argued that the judgment had "heightened contradictions in Zimbabwe's own internal laws and had negated the country's international legal obligations" ("Supreme Court Hits Out at Women"). The women's organizations also suggested that "those who appointed senior judges should take account not only of their legal skills but also their grasp of the needs of modern society" (Njanji 1999).

This bold action by the women's organizations was indeed contentious. Writing on behalf of the Supreme Court, acting assistant registrar P. Nyeperayi warned the women's groups of the consequences of continued criticism of the Court: "[N]o action will be taken on this occasion, but a formal warning must be issued that registered legal practitioners especially, but others as well who indulge in gratuitous and unfounded insults to the judiciary, and in public demonstrations, will be dealt with under laws of contempt of court" (Sisterhood 1999). Even some sympathetic legal experts felt that the action taken by the women's groups was misplaced. Kevin Laue, a Harare-based human rights lawyer, said that by attacking the Supreme Court women "had fired at the wrong target" ("Supreme Court Hits Out at Women" 1999). According to human rights lawyer Pearson Nherere, "The decision is not palatable or desirable according to human rights, but it is correct according to jurisprudence." He suggested that the women's organizations should lobby Parliament to change the laws, not the Supreme Court (Sayagues 1999).

## Overview of Women's Rights Issues

The decision of Zimbabwe's Supreme Court in this case is only the latest development, though arguably the most devastating, in an ongoing struggle for women's rights in that country. As this case illustrates, the legal frameworks for women's rights are riddled with inconsistencies and contradictions originating in the historical development of the country's legal system under colonialism, but also involving contemporary gender struggles over African women's proper place in society. In 1980 the white settler regime in Southern Rhodesia turned over power to a popularly elected African government following a protracted armed struggle. In the two decades since then numerous laws have been enacted to improve the circumstances of women. Most significant among these was the 1982 Legal Age of Majority Act (LAMA), which guaranteed majority status to all Zimbabweans upon reaching the age of eighteen. This act was particularly important for women, who up until its passage were considered legal minors unable to vote, own property in their own names, or contract marriage without a guardian's consent. In addition the Zimbabwean government ratified three international agreements on women's rights: the Convention on the Elimination of All Forms of Discrimination Against Women (CEDAW), the United Nations Universal Declaration of Human Rights, and the African Charter on Human and People's Rights. Despite these public commitments, the government's support of women's rights can, at best, be described as half-hearted. Weak legislation, such as the 1997 Administration of Estates Amendment Act, which altered inheritance law to enable surviving spouses or children to inherit property in the absence of a will, and almost a decade of foot-dragging in producing its first report for CEDAW suggest that support for women's rights within the present government is limited.

Opponents of women's progress most often frame political struggles over women's rights in terms of "African culture" (see Ranchod-Nilsson 1998). Legal advances for women, they argue, undermine African culture by upsetting gender and generational hierarchies that are the very foundation of African social fabric. This leads not only to corruption of "authentic" African culture but also to a whole host of social problems such as prostitution, "baby-dumping" (the practice of women abandoning newborn infants), divorce, and domestic violence. In an interesting paradox, the parameters of "African culture" are established in legal terms by "African customary law," a legacy of the colonial era. Women's organizations in Zimbabwe have lobbied for an end to a legal system based on customary law because of the ways in which the codification of customary law disadvantaged women in terms of their legal status, property rights, and rights within marriage. Nevertheless, African "culture" and African "traditions" are powerful issues and, as the Supreme Court's decision in *Magaya v. Magaya* suggests, they gain political support at the expense of women's rights.

## HISTORY OF WOMEN'S RIGHTS

The legal system in Zimbabwe, like that of many other former colonies, is a legacy of the colonial era. During the period of colonial administration (1890–1980) the legal system in Southern Rhodesia was characterized by two separate and distinct bodies of law. On the one hand, the general law, derived from Roman-Dutch law, was applicable to all people, including European settlers and Africans. On the other hand, as part of their broader mission to establish their version of social order in the colonial territories, colonial authorities codified what they took to be "traditional" African customs or social practices into African customary law.

Although colonial authorities claimed that the codification of customary law accurately reflected indigenous social practices, there is considerable evidence to suggest that they viewed these social practices through gender biases, as well as through the moral and racial biases of Victorian England. Rather than understanding African customary law as local bodies of law that somehow survived colonial rule, scholars have highlighted the ways that colonial predilections shaped their understandings of indigenous societies throughout sub-Saharan Africa. Native commissioners initially interpreted African customary law with the assistance of local men, whom the commissioners recognized as local authorities. As a result of this process, "what had been guiding lines to the solution of disputes, aimed largely at conciliation, became the law administered by the courts, tempered by colonial perceptions and preconceptions as well as the manipulation of the situation (and the court) by the informant for his own reasons" (May 1987, 30). Not only was the new system of customary law more rigid than the social practices that preceded it, but the Africa men consulted by colonial officials also used their roles as informants in the codification process to bolster their own position vis-à-vis African women. For example, in her research on Goromonzi district, historian Elizabeth Schmidt illustrates how the coming of the colonial state and the parallel pressure of colonial capitalism created new opportunities for African women and young men, thus reducing the ability of elder men to control them. In the process of codifying African customary law, these elder men sought to regain control over women and young men through laws governing marriage, household property, inheritance, female mobility, and child custody (Schmidt 1991; also see Chanock 1982 and Ranger 1983). Thus, what is now known as customary law must be situated within the context of settler colonialism and the complex interaction between adjudicators and litigants (May 1987, 33).

In the process of codifying African customary law, European authorities, along with their African male collaborators, translated existing precolonial gender divisions into the status of legal minor for African women. This minority status not only overlooked areas of rights and responsibility enjoyed by African women, but as legal minors women had no contractual rights and remained under male guardianship for the duration of their lives. Customary law also altered social practices associated with marriage. In precolonial society the *lobola* transaction, the exchange of cattle and gifts for the rights to a woman's reproductive capacity and her labor, was a vital stage in a marriage process that created a broad network of reciprocal social relations that included a kind of safety net for women who had to leave bad marriages. Following the codification of customary law, the fluidity of these relations— and the social protections this meant for women—greatly diminished. The erosion of women's circumstances was further exacerbated by the use of cash in *lobola* transactions. Moreover, women were also severely disadvantaged in divorce cases after the creation of customary law. In the event of divorce or the death of a husband, the wife had no rights to the husband's property, with the exception of the cooking implements she brought to the marriage, and no rights to child custody. African women's legal status under customary law deteriorated during colonial rule because codification rendered it inflexible and unable to adapt to changing social circumstances such as land alienation, the growth of male labor migration, and severe rural impoverishment.

After independence this dual legal system remained, albeit in slightly different form. Now, the legal system that particular cases get tried under "largely depends on the individual circumstances of each case," although the structure of the court system, the choice-of-law rules, and women's general socioeconomic condition mean that most women still have their rights determined by customary law (Stewart et al. 1990, 167–68). African women continue to be most affected by the adjudication of cases under customary law in areas involving marriage, family, and related property relationships.

## Legal Reforms Affecting Women's Rights

After independence in 1980, the newly elected African government made what, at the time, appeared to be remarkable strides in supporting women's rights. The most visible change in the structure of the new government was the creation of a new Ministry of Community Development and Women's Affairs (MCDWA). The purpose of the MCDWA was to "facilitate the involvement of women in national development through the removal of all legal, cultural, and socio-economic barriers that hinder the full participation of women" (MCDWA 1983). The creation of the ministry was especially welcomed by those with high expectations that the new government held out opportunities for truly meaningful participation for women. Observing these changes in the early 1980s, Seidman pointed out that Zimbabwe appeared "to be unusual in the extent to which government leaders, especially women, have been willing to declare themselves committed to feminist goals" (1984, 431). Initially the ministry, in collaboration with women's organizations and the Ministry of Justice, introduced and helped to pass a series of legal reforms aimed at improving the circumstances of women. The new laws included the Legal Age of Majority Act (1982), which conferred adult legal status on all Zimbabweans at the age of eighteen; the Matrimonial Causes Act (1985), which gave women rights to property in marriage and changed the practice of automatically giving fathers child custody in the event of divorce; and the Labor Relations Act (1985), which contained provisions for paid maternity leave and for nursing mothers to feed their children during work hours. In addition the Customary Law and Primary Courts Act repealed the judicial authority of chiefs, headmen, and district commissions and amended the Maintenance Act to ensure financial support for deserted and divorced wives and their children under customary law.

On one level these laws were meant to end discrimination against women in the public realm of work and politics. However, these legal reforms also had implications for African customary law; more specifically, they promised gains for women in terms of laws governing marriage, inheritance, child custody, and divorce, areas where the colonial codification of African customary law had put them in disadvantaged positions. The struggle for women's rights has been waged over these so-called private issues and framed by opponents of women's rights as a struggle for the survival of authentic "African culture." This is clearly illustrated by the controversies that have surrounded LAMA since its inception.

LAMA has been one of the most controversial pieces of legislation since it was enacted in 1982, and has had the most far-reaching implications for African cultural practices. By making women legal majors at the age of eighteen, LAMA effectively ended African women's status as perpetual minors and gave them the right to vote, to own property, to contract a marriage without parental or family consent, to become the guardians of their own children, and to sue or be sued as individuals. The most enduring complaints about LAMA are that it allows women over the age of eighteen to get married without (male) parental involvement in *lobola* negotiations, and that it abrogates a father's right to sue a man for "seduction damages" for having sex with his daughter in contexts that are not socially sanctioned (e.g., prior to *lobola* negotiations or if the daughter is married). Concern over the potential impact of LAMA on parental rights in connection with *lobola* negotiations led to an uproar from men, and some women, who were concerned about the denial of their parental rights. According to a 1984 survey by the government-controlled daily paper the *Herald*, LAMA "was seen as 'corrupting and unafrican.' Interviewees disapproved in particular of girls becoming adults in their own right at the age of 18. Most fathers considered the age too young and felt that a girl still needed consent and guidance from her parents" (quoted in Batezat et al. 1988, 159). These complaints were not anticipated by the leadership of the Zimbabwe African National Union (Patriotic Front), or ZANU(PF), Zimbabwe's ruling party, who were initially more interested in the potential of new female voters to support the party.

In addition to the protests just described, the government acted in ways that directly contradicted women's rights as established by LAMA. Throughout the 1980s urban police, authorized by the national government, engaged in massive campaigns to round up prostitutes and vagrants. The initial campaign in 1983 was known as Operation Clean-up and targeted thousands of women, squatters, and vagrants who were detained under the vagrancy act. Detained women "who could not produce marriage certificates were sent to a resettlement area in the Zambezi Valley, deprived of courts and lawyers" (Geisler 1995, 557). Not only were the methods employed in this campaign, and subsequent campaigns, exceptionally brutal, but it was also clear that many of the women arrested were neither prostitutes nor vagrants. They were, however, independent women, outside the orbit of male control (Jacobs and Howard 1987).

Although LAMA has not been repealed as of this writing (April 2000), it continues to be a very controversial piece of legislation. In 1989, the ZANU(PF) party congress passed resolutions that, among other things, directed the government

to review the Legal Age of Majority Act so that it takes further account of our cultural background, with a view in particular to raising the age of majority to 21 years . . . to revise and amend the Maintenance Act to limit the number of children for which unmarried mothers can claim maintenance from different fathers . . . [and] to restore the powers of chiefs and headmen so that they can preserve and maintain rural family life, as well as control stock theft, deforestation and *other social evils*. (SAPEM March 1990, 24; emphasis added)

The vague mention of "social evils" here no doubt refers to social problems involving prostitution, baby dumping, and out-of-wedlock births, topics that are frequently addressed in the national press. In the late 1990s there continued to be widespread noncompliance among the population and, as suggested by the earlier account of *Magaya v. Magaya*, lack of support from the judiciary. As mentioned above, there are even examples of government policy that contradict this law. More than a decade after LAMA was enacted, few marriages take place completely outside the realm of customary law, without *lobola*. The Zimbabwe Women's Resource Centre and Network points out that the practice is highly commercialized. "*Lobola* charges increase with the bride's level of education and also with general inflation. Charges are as high as Z$5000 to Z$10000 per bride. Commercialized bride prices have given the wrong signal in some cases that women are just like any other piece of private property to men" (Getecha and Chipika 1995, 148). In February 1998 some parliamentarians called for the repeal of LAMA, again raising the concern that it allows eighteen-year-old women to marry without the consent of their guardians. Member of Parliament (MP) Livingstone Manhombo cited cultural differences in the appropriate role of children as his reason for wanting to scrap the law, and MP John Tsimba claimed that the act "had caused a lot of feuds between families" ("Zim Parliament Threatens Women's Rights").

The issue of legal reforms in the areas of marriage and inheritance was again raised in April 1993 when a coalition of women's groups brought their proposals for reforming the laws governing marriage and inheritance to the government. Their suggestions were circulated for debate in a government White Paper that included the proposals to incorporate the two marriage laws (customary and civil) into one that would include provisions for community property and inheritance, and for the banning of both *lobola* and polygamy. The White Paper rekindled debates about African culture, but unlike the early support for legal reforms that strengthened women's rights, this time President Mugabe and government representatives were far more conciliatory to those calling for protection of traditional cultural values. National newspapers featured stories that highlighted opposition from chiefs who claimed the proposals would "destroy the intrinsic cultural and family values while promoting divorce for personal gain" (*Sunday Mail* November 13, 1994), and from rural women who were "particularly incensed by the suggestions that lobola be abolished . . . such a move would destroy the family, as *lobola* bonds the family" (*Sunday Mail* November 20, 1994). Perhaps most revealing, however, was the outburst against "feminist extremism" by President Mugabe in response to a request from the National Association of Non-Governmental Organizations that property be registered in the names of both the husband and wife. Mugabe asked, "Where in the world have you ever seen such a division in the family?" and warned women not to listen to "terrible ideas" from abroad. One of the national papers described women in the audience and women's groups, who had been used to a certain level of support from the president, as "stunned," "shocked," and "disappointed" with his statements (*Chronicle* August 2, 1994). In August 1997 Parliament passed the Administration of Estates Amendment Act that provided for surviving spouses or children to inherit the property of deceased relatives regardless of the type of marriage. (Although this law was enacted prior to the Supreme Court's decision in *Magaya v. Magaya*, the decision stated that in this case Venia Magaya's parents died prior to the passage of the Administration of Estates Amendment Act. Therefore, it was not applicable. Critics from women's organizations argue that, regardless, the Court's decision in *Magaya v. Magaya* is a devastating blow to LAMA [Sayagues 1999].) Women's organizations were less than enthusiastic about the weak legislative response to their demands outlined in the 1993 White Paper. Instead of eliminating customary law, the new legislation merely elaborates on existing customary law by outlining provisions for inheritance in cases of customary marriage where the deceased spouse has no will. The legal officer of the Women's Action Group (WAG) described the law as falling far short of the goal of empowering women in inheritance cases (author interview at WAG in Harare, November 19, 1997).

In the period leading up to the June 2000 parliamentary elections, women's concerns about their legal rights spilled over into a broader political opposition movement. In 1999 the Constitutional Review Commission (CRC) came under fire from women's groups who pointed out that women had only 22 percent representation on the 395-member commission. Women's groups and other critics accused the CRC of being insensitive to gender issues and elitist (Moyo 1999). In February 2000 a national referendum was held on the new constitution that would have entrenched Mugabe's authority and allowed the government to take white-owned farms for redistribution to blacks without compensation. The referendum was resoundingly defeated opening the door for the opposition party, Movement for Democratic Change, to win 57 out of 119 elected parliamentary seats in the June 2000 elections.

Women's participation in Zimbabwe's liberation struggle—particularly their equal participation as armed combatants—was the catalyst for early government support for women's rights. However, since that time, the state's own discourse on legal reforms affecting women has changed significantly; from an initial concern with women's equality to the public debate preceding the 1997 Administration of Estates Amendment Act there has been a marked shift in government support for women's rights. Despite the recent public debates on the African cultural crisis and the role of women, those concerned with women's legal rights have had a significant influence on state politics in Zimbabwe.

## WOMEN'S RIGHTS TODAY

The complete turnaround in support for women's rights by Zimbabwe's government since independence has been discouraging for women's organizations. Indeed, some might argue that the low numbers of women in government (in 1994, 17 out of 150 MPs were women, no cabinet posts were held by women, and only 1 out of 22 mayors was a woman) are interpreted by some as an indication that women are indifferent to politics (figures from Getecha and Chipika 1995). However, anthropologist Gisela Geisler argues that "opting out of politics is not necessarily due to political apathy, as some African men would like to make us believe. Rather it is based on the experience that women enter politics on terms set by the male elite who use women's political energy for their own ends" (Geisler 1995, 546; also see Staudt 1986). Instead of taking their grievances to the realm of state politics, Geisler argues that "lacking other alternatives professional African women have instead retreated with their grievances into the non-governmental organizations (NGO) sector where women's groups and funding from international donors abound." She points out that in a number of places the NGO sector has assumed a more explicitly political character" (Geisler 1995, 546). This has certainly been the case in Zimbabwe, where women's organizations have been not only at the forefront of the continuing struggle for women's rights, but also at the forefront of the broader struggle for political transformation to end government corruption and the political control of the de facto one-party state.

The Women's Action Group (WAG) has undergone a transformation similar to that suggested by Geisler. The organization was founded quite spontaneously in response to the 1983 Operation Clean-up when women from across socioeconomic groups and racial groups came together to protest treatment of women during the campaign and the broader implication that women outside the realm of male control are "prostitutes." The presence of white, ex-patriate women led critics of the organization to charge that it represented only the views of "outside feminists," and not the views of local women. Despite the continuation of such criticism, WAG went on to become an NGO focusing on Zimbabwean women's issues such as maternal health care and AIDS, domestic violence, sexual harassment, and employment discrimination. Although WAG's members included urban professional women, they also had support from rural members. Indeed, much of the organization's activity during its first decade involved outreach efforts to educate a broad cross-section of women about legal reforms, health issues, and resources that were available in both urban and rural contexts.

Following the 1995 elections, however, WAG has become more critical of government policy on women's rights; perhaps even more important, it is a significant part of a broader social movement demanding meaningful political reform. The organization was inspired, at least in part, by Margaret Dongo's challenge to the ruling party, ZANU(PF). Margaret Dongo, an ex-combatant, was a rising star on President Mugabe's staff prior to her election to Parliament in 1990. There, she was appointed to the prestigious Central Committee. However, in 1994 her political success came to a grinding halt after she criticized the government's treatment of ex-combatants. In 1995 she stood for reelection in the Harare south district, where she enjoyed great popularity. After much political manipulation and harassment of her supporters, she lost the primary election. She continued to contest the election as an independent despite death threats. Intimidation and attacks by ZANU(PF) supporters continued through the election, which she narrowly lost amid charges of widespread voting irregularities. Subsequently the High Court overturned the election results and ordered a new election in the district, which Dongo won. Since then, she has been an outspoken critic of the government and a strong advocate for women's rights.

## THE FUTURE OF WOMEN'S RIGHTS

At the present time WAG is one of several NGOs that actively lobby Members of Parliament to support women's rights, to ensure that women's concerns are considered in all government initiatives, and to push for MPs to be more responsive to their constituents. WAG is not alone in these efforts—numerous NGOs focusing on women's issues, and explicitly women's rights, have proliferated in Zimbabwe. In addition to putting political pressure on the current government, NGOs have been active on the international front, often countering the government accounts of the women's situation with contradictory information. For example, in January 1998 the Zimbabwean government finally submitted its report on CEDAW, seven years after it ratified the international agreement. Rudo Kwaramba of the Musasa Project on Violence Against Women pointed out the contradiction as "Zimbabwe recently presented a flowery report to the international committee on CEDAW in New York, and then comes back home and wants to strip women of their rights." A group of NGOs, including the Musasa Project, wrote a "Shadow Report" to provide the CEDAW committee with independent information on the situation of women in Zimbabwe. According to Selina Mbengegwi, director of WAG, "It was our job as NGOs to highlight some of the issues that were left out" ("Zim Parliament Threatens Women's Rights").

The struggle for women's rights in Zimbabwe must be understood within the context of both the country's colonial history and its present political struggles. Framing women's rights in this way diminishes the power of arguments based on African cultural authenticity. Moreover, situating the struggle for women's rights within the framework of growing demands for far-reaching political transformation highlights both the centrality of gender politics and the importance of looking at multiple locations, in this case NGOs, as sites for carrying forward the struggle for women's rights.

## BIBLIOGRAPHY

Batezat, Elinor, Margaret Mwalo, and Kate Truscott. 1988. "Women and Independence: the Heritage and the Struggle." In *Zimbabwe Prospects*, ed. Colin Stoneman. London: Macmillan, 153–73.

Chanock, Martin. 1982. "Making Customary Law: Men, Women and Courts in N. Rhodesia." In *African Women and the Law: Historical Perspectives*, ed. Margaret Jean Hay and Marcia Wright. Boston: Boston University Papers on Africa VII.

*Chronicle*. August 2, 1994. Bulawayo, Zimbabwe.

Geisler, Gisela. 1995. "Troubled Sisterhood: Women and Politics in Southern Africa." *African Affairs* 94: 545–78.

Getecha, Ciru, and Jesiman Chipika. 1995. *Zimbabwe Women's Voices*. Harare: Zimbabwe Women's Resource Centre and Network.

Jacobs, Susie, and Tracy Howard. 1987. "Women in Zimbabwe: State Policy and State Action." In *Women, State and Ideology*, ed. Haleh Afshar. Albany: SUNY Press.

Landsberg, Michele. 1999. Posting to the Women's Studies List. WMST-L@ UMDD.UMD.edu. April 19.

May, Joan. 1987. *Changing People, Changing Laws*. Gweru, Zimbabwe: Mambo Press.

MCDWA (Ministry of Community Development and Women's Affairs). 1983. Community Action, no. 1, Harare: Government of Zimbabwe.

Moyo, Matilda. 1999. "Women Left Out of Zimbabwean Constitution Process." *Daily Mail and Guardian* (electronic version), Johannesburg, July 8.

Njanji, Susan. 1999. "Zim Women Fight for Lost Rights." *Daily Mail and Guardian* (electronic version), Johannesburg, June 10.

Ranchod-Nilsson, Sita. 1994. " 'This, Too, Is a Way of Fighting': Rural Women's Participation in Zimbabwe's Liberation War." In *Women and Revolution in Africa, Asia and the New World*, ed. Mary Ann Tétreault. Columbia: University of South Carolina Press.

———. 1998. "Zimbabwe: Women, Cultural Crisis and the Reconfiguration of the One-Party State." In *The African State at a Critical Juncture: Between Disintegration and Reconfiguration*, ed. Leonardo Villalón and Philip Huxtable. Boulder: Lynne Rienner.

Ranger, Terence. 1983. "The Invention of Tradition in Colonial Africa." In *The Invention of Tradition*, ed. Eric Hobsbawm and Terence Ranger. Cambridge: Cambridge University Press.

SAPEM (*Southern African Political and Economic Monthly*). 1990. Harare, Zimbabwe. March.

Sayagues, Mercedes. 1999. "Zimbabwe Court Hits Back." *Daily Mail and Guardian* (electronic version), Johannesburg, June 25.

Schmidt, Elizabeth. 1991. "Patriarchy, Capitalism, and the Colonial State in Zimbabwe." *Signs* 16, no. 4: 732–56.

Seidman, Gay. 1984. " 'No Freedom Without Women': Mobilization and Gender in South Africa, 1970–1992." In *Rethinking the Political: Gender, Resistance and the State*, ed. Barbara Laslett, Johanna Brenner, and Yesim Arat. Chicago: University of Chicago Press.

Sisterhood Is Global Institute. 1999. Urgent Action Alert. June 30.

Staudt, Kathleen. 1986. "Stratification: Implications for Women's Politics." In *Women and Class in Africa*, ed. Claire Robertson and Iris Berger. New York: Africana.

Stewart, J., W. Ncube, M. Maboreke, and A. Armstrong. 1990. "The Legal Situation of Women in Zimbabwe." In *The Legal Situation of Women in Southern Africa*, ed. Julie Stewart and Alice Armstrong. Harare: University of Zimbabwe Press.

*Sunday Mail.* 1994. Harare, Zimbabwe, November 13.

*Sunday Mail.* 1994. Harare, Zimbabwe, November 20.

"Supreme Court Hits Out at Women." 1999. *Zimbabwe Independent* (electronic version), Harare, June 18.

"Zim Parliament Threatens Women's Rights." 1999. *Daily Mail and Guardian* (electronic version), Johannesburg, February 12.

# APPENDIX 1: INTERNATIONAL COMPARISONS

| Country | Population (millions) 1997[a] | women /100 men 1995[b] | Life Expectancy at Birth (1997)[a] | | Total Fertility Rate 1997[a] | Infant Mortality (per 1000 live births, 1997)[a] |
|---|---|---|---|---|---|---|
| | | | Female | Male | | |
| Argentina | 35.7 | 102 | 78 | 71 | 2.6 | 21 |
| Bolivia | 7.8 | 102 | 63 | 60 | 4.4 | 69 |
| China | 1244.2 | 95 | 72 | 68 | 1.8 | 38 |
| Cuba | 11.1 | 99 | 78 | 74 | 1.6 | 7 |
| Denmark | 5.3 | 102 | 78 | 73 | 1.7 | 6 |
| Egypt | 64.7 | 97 | 68 | 65 | 3.4 | 54 |
| European Union[c] | 374.6 | 102 | 81 | 74 | 1.4 | 6 |
| India | 966.2 | 94 | 63 | 62 | 3.1 | 71 |
| Iran | 64.6 | 97 | 70 | 69 | 2.8 | 32 |
| Israel | 3.5 | 102 | 80 | 76 | 2.7 | 6 |
| Japan | 126.0 | 103 | 81 | 77 | 1.4 | 4 |
| American Indian[f] | 2.0[g] | 97 | 75 | 67 | 2.2[h] | 12 |
| Nigeria | 103.9 | 102 | 52 | 49 | 5.2 | 112 |
| U.S. | 271.8 | 105 | 80 | 73 | 2.0 | 7 |
| Zimbabwe | 11.2 | 101 | 45 | 44 | 3.8 | 53 |

| Country | Maternal Mortality (per 100,000 live births 1990)[a] | Women's (15+) Economic Activity Rate(%) 1997[a] | % of Women in Parliament 1999[a] | Year CEDAW in force[b] | Year Women Got the Vote[a] |
|---|---|---|---|---|---|
| Argentina | 100 | 25 | 23 | 1985 | 1951[i] |
| Bolivia | 650 | 30 | 10[j] | 1990 | 1952 |
| China | 95 | 58 | 22 | 1981 | 1949 |
| Cuba | 95 | 38 | 28 | 1981 | 1934 |
| Denmark | 9 | 51 | 37 | 1983 | 1915 |
| Egypt | 170 | 22 | 2 | 1981 | 1956 |
| European Union | | 57[d] | 27[e] | | |
| India | 570 | 29 | 8 | 1993 | 1950 |
| Iran | 120 | 16 | 5 | | 1963 |
| Israel | 7 | 34 | 8 | 1991 | 1948 |
| Japan | 18 | 43 | 9 | 1985 | 1947 |
| American Indian | 5 | 45 | 0 | | 1924 |
| Nigeria | 1000 | 28 | 3[i] | 1985 | 1957/76[j] |
| U.S. | 12 | 46 | 13 | | 1920 |
| Zimbabwe | 570 | 41 | 15 | 1991 | 1957 |

[a]World Bank. 1999. *Human Development Report.*
[b]United Nations. 1995. *The World's Women 1995, Trends and Statistics.* New York: United Nations.
[c]Eurostat. 1998. *Facts through Figures.*
[d]Eurostat. 1998. *Social Portrait of Europe,* data from 1996.
[e]Commission of the European Communities. 1998. *Equal Opportunities for Women and Men in the European Union,* data from 1998.
[f]Reddy, Marlita (ed.). 1993. *Statistical Record of Native North America.* Detroit: Gale Research Inc.
[g]American Indian Population data from 1990 U.S. Census.
[h]National Vital Statistics Report Supplements. 1989. 47(18):26.
[i]http://www.ipu.org/wmn-e/classif.htm.
[j]Data from chapter author.

# APPENDIX 2: DECLARATION OF SENTIMENTS

Adopted at the first U.S. women's rights convention at Seneca Falls, New York, in 1848.

When, in the course of human events, it becomes necessary for one portion of the family of man to assume among the people of the earth a position different from that which they have hitherto occupied, but one to which the laws of nature and of nature's God entitle them, a decent respect to the opinions of mankind requires that they should declare the causes that impel them to such a course. We hold these truths to be self-evident; that all men and women are created equal; that they are endowed by their Creator with certain inalienable rights; that among these are life, liberty, and the pursuit of happiness; that to secure these rights governments are instituted, deriving their just powers from the consent of the governed. Whenever any form of Government becomes destructive of these ends, it is the right of those who suffer from it to refuse allegiance to it, and to insist upon the institution of a new government, laying its foundation on such principles, and organizing its powers in such form as to them shall seem most likely to effect their safety and happiness. Prudence, indeed, will dictate that governments long established should not be changed for light and transient causes; and accordingly, all experience hath shown that mankind are more disposed to suffer, while evils are sufferable, than to right themselves, by abolishing the forms to which they are accustomed. But when a long train of abuses and usurpations, pursuing invariably the same object, evinces a design to reduce them under absolute despotism, it is their duty to throw off such government, and to provide new guards for their future security. Such has been the patient sufferance of the women under this government, and such is now the necessity which constrains them to demand the equal station to which they are entitled.

The history of mankind is a history of repeated injuries and usurpations on the part of man toward woman, having in direct object the establishment of an absolute tyranny over her. To prove this, let facts be submitted to a candid world.

He has never permitted her to exercise her inalienable right to the elective franchise.

He has compelled her to submit to laws, in the formation of which she had no voice.

He has withheld from her rights which are given to the most ignorant and degraded men—both natives and foreigners.

Having deprived her of this first right of a citizen, the elective franchise, thereby leaving her without representation in the halls of legislation, he has oppressed her on all sides.

He has made her, if married, in the eye of the law, civilly dead.

He has taken from her all right in property, even to the wages she earns.

He has made her, morally, an irresponsible being, as she can commit many crimes, with impunity, provided they be done in the presence of her husband.

In the covenant of marriage, she is compelled to promise obedience to her husband, he becoming, to all intents and purposes, her master—the law giving him power to deprive her of her liberty, and to administer chastisement.

He has so framed the laws of divorce, as to what shall be the proper causes of divorce; in case of separation, to whom the guardianship of the children shall be given, as to be wholly regardless of the happiness of women—the law, in all cases, going upon the false supposition of the supremacy of man, and giving all power into his hands.

After depriving her of all rights as a married woman, if single and the owner of property, he has taxed her to support a government which recognizes her only when her property can be made profitable to it.

He has monopolized nearly all the profitable employments, and from those she is permitted to follow, she receives but a scanty remuneration.

He closes against her all the avenues to wealth and distinction, which he considers most honorable to himself. As a teacher of theology, medicine, or law, she is not known.

He has denied her the facilities for obtaining a thorough education—all colleges being closed against her.

He allows her in Church as well as State, but a subordinate position, claiming Apostolic authority for her exclusion from the ministry, and with some exceptions, from any public participation in the affairs of the Church.

He has created a false public sentiment, by giving to the world a different code of morals for men and women, by which moral delinquencies which exclude women from society, are not only tolerated but deemed of little account in man.

He has usurped the prerogative of Jehovah himself, claiming it as his right to assign for her a sphere of action, when that belongs to her conscience and her God.

He has endeavored, in every way that he could to destroy her confidence in her own powers, to lessen her self-respect, and to make her willing to lead a dependent and abject life. Now, in view of this entire disfranchisement of one-half the people of this country, their social and religious degradation,—in view of the unjust laws above mentioned, and because women do feel themselves aggrieved, oppressed, and fraudulently deprived of their most sacred rights, we insist that they have immediate admission to all the rights and privileges which belong to them as citizens of these United States.

In entering upon the great work before us, we anticipate no small amount of misconception, misrepresentation, and ridicule; but we shall use every instrumentality within our power to effect our object. We shall employ agents, circulate tracts, petition the State and national Legislatures, and endeavor to enlist the pulpit and the press in our behalf. We hope this Convention will be followed by a series of Conventions, embracing every part of the country. Firmly relying upon the final triumph of the Right and the True, we do this day affix our signatures to this declaration.

# APPENDIX 3: THE UNIVERSAL DECLARATION OF HUMAN RIGHTS

Adopted and proclaimed by UN General Assembly resolution 217 A (III) of 10 December 1948.

## PREAMBLE

Whereas recognition of the inherent dignity and of the equal and inalienable rights of all members of the human family is the foundation of freedom, justice and peace in the world,

Whereas disregard and contempt for human rights have resulted in barbarous acts which have outraged the conscience of mankind, and the advent of a world in which human beings shall enjoy freedom of speech and belief and freedom from fear and want has been proclaimed as the highest aspiration of the common people,

Whereas it is essential, if man is not to be compelled to have recourse, as a last resort, to rebellion against tyranny and oppression, that human rights should be protected by the rule of law,

Whereas it is essential to promote the development of friendly relations between nations,

Whereas the peoples of the United Nations have in the Charter reaffirmed their faith in fundamental human rights, in the dignity and worth of the human person and in the equal rights of men and women and have determined to promote social progress and better standards of life in larger freedom,

Whereas Member States have pledged themselves to achieve, in co-operation with the United Nations, the promotion of universal respect for and observance of human rights and fundamental freedoms,

Whereas a common understanding of these rights and freedoms is of the greatest importance for the full realization of this pledge,

Now, Therefore THE GENERAL ASSEMBLY proclaims THIS UNIVERSAL DECLARATION OF HUMAN RIGHTS as a common standard of achievement for all peoples and all nations, to the end that every individual and every organ of society, keeping this Declaration constantly in mind, shall strive by teaching and education to promote respect for these rights and freedoms and by progressive measures, national and international, to secure their universal and effective recognition and observance, both among the peoples of Member States themselves and among the peoples of territories under their jurisdiction.

## Article 1.

All human beings are born free and equal in dignity and rights. They are endowed with reason and conscience and should act towards one another in a spirit of brotherhood.

## Article 2.

Everyone is entitled to all the rights and freedoms set forth in this Declaration, without distinction of any kind, such as race, colour, sex, language, religion, political or other opinion, national or social origin, property, birth or other status. Furthermore, no distinction shall be made on the basis of the political, jurisdictional or international status of the country or territory to which a person belongs, whether it be independent, trust, non–self-governing or under any other limitation of sovereignty.

## Article 3.

Everyone has the right to life, liberty and security of person.

## Article 4.

No one shall be held in slavery or servitude; slavery and the slave trade shall be prohibited in all their forms.

## Article 5.

No one shall be subjected to torture or to cruel, inhuman or degrading treatment or punishment.

## Article 6.

Everyone has the right to recognition everywhere as a person before the law.

## Article 7.

All are equal before the law and are entitled without any discrimination to equal protection of the law. All are entitled to equal protection against any discrimination in violation of this Declaration and against any incitement to such discrimination.

## Article 8.

Everyone has the right to an effective remedy by the competent national tribunals for acts violating the fundamental rights granted him by the constitution or by law.

## Article 9.

No one shall be subjected to arbitrary arrest, detention or exile.

## Article 10.

Everyone is entitled in full equality to a fair and public hearing by an independent and impartial tribunal, in the determination of his rights and obligations and of any criminal charge against him.

## Article 11.

(1) Everyone charged with a penal offence has the right to be presumed innocent until proved guilty according to law in a public trial at which he has had all the guarantees necessary for his defence.

(2) No one shall be held guilty of any penal offence on account of any act or omission which did not constitute a penal offence, under national or international law, at the time when it was committed. Nor shall a heavier penalty be imposed than the one that was applicable at the time the penal offence was committed.

## Article 12.

No one shall be subjected to arbitrary interference with his privacy, family, home or correspondence, nor to attacks upon his honour and reputation. Everyone has the right to the protection of the law against such interference or attacks.

## Article 13.

(1) Everyone has the right to freedom of movement and residence within the borders of each state.

(2) Everyone has the right to leave any country, including his own, and to return to his country.

## Article 14.

(1) Everyone has the right to seek and to enjoy in other countries asylum from persecution.

(2) This right may not be invoked in the case of prosecutions genuinely arising from non-political crimes or from acts contrary to the purposes and principles of the United Nations.

## Article 15.

(1) Everyone has the right to a nationality.

(2) No one shall be arbitrarily deprived of his nationality nor denied the right to change his nationality.

## Article 16.

(1) Men and women of full age, without any limitation due to race, nationality or religion, have the right to marry and to found a family. They are entitled to equal rights as to marriage, during marriage and at its dissolution.

(2) Marriage shall be entered into only with the free and full consent of the intending spouses.

(3) The family is the natural and fundamental group unit of society and is entitled to protection by society and the State.

## Article 17.

(1) Everyone has the right to own property alone as well as in association with others.

(2) No one shall be arbitrarily deprived of his property.

## Article 18.

Everyone has the right to freedom of thought, conscience and religion; this right includes freedom to change his religion or belief, and freedom, either alone or in community with others and in public or private, to manifest his religion or belief in teaching, practice, worship and observance.

## Article 19.

Everyone has the right to freedom of opinion and expression; this right includes freedom to hold opinions without interference and to seek, receive and impart information and ideas through any media and regardless of frontiers.

## Article 20.

(1) Everyone has the right to freedom of peaceful assembly and association.

(2) No one may be compelled to belong to an association.

## Article 21.

(1) Everyone has the right to take part in the government of his country, directly or through freely chosen representatives.

(2) Everyone has the right of equal access to public service in his country.

(3) The will of the people shall be the basis of the authority of government; this will shall be expressed in periodic and genuine elections which shall be by universal and equal suffrage and shall be held by secret vote or by equivalent free voting procedures.

## Article 22.

Everyone, as a member of society, has the right to social security and is entitled to realization, through national effort and international co-operation and in accordance with the organization and resources of each State, of the economic, social and cultural rights indispensable for his dignity and the free development of his personality.

## Article 23.

(1) Everyone has the right to work, to free choice of employment, to just and favourable conditions of work and to protection against unemployment.

(2) Everyone, without any discrimination, has the right to equal pay for equal work.

(3) Everyone who works has the right to just and favourable remuneration ensuring for himself and his family an existence worthy of human dignity, and supplemented, if necessary, by other means of social protection.

(4) Everyone has the right to form and to join trade unions for the protection of his interests.

## Article 24.

Everyone has the right to rest and leisure, including reasonable limitation of working hours and periodic holidays with pay.

## Article 25.

(1) Everyone has the right to a standard of living adequate for the health and well-being of himself and of his family, including food, clothing, housing and medical care and necessary social services, and the right to security in the event of unem-

ployment, sickness, disability, widowhood, old age or other lack of livelihood in circumstances beyond his control.

(2) Motherhood and childhood are entitled to special care and assistance. All children, whether born in or out of wedlock, shall enjoy the same social protection.

## Article 26.

(1) Everyone has the right to education. Education shall be free, at least in the elementary and fundamental stages. Elementary education shall be compulsory. Technical and professional education shall be made generally available and higher education shall be equally accessible to all on the basis of merit.

(2) Education shall be directed to the full development of the human personality and to the strengthening of respect for human rights and fundamental freedoms. It shall promote understanding, tolerance and friendship among all nations, racial or religious groups, and shall further the activities of the United Nations for the maintenance of peace.

(3) Parents have a prior right to choose the kind of education that shall be given to their children.

## Article 27.

(1) Everyone has the right freely to participate in the cultural life of the community, to enjoy the arts and to share in scientific advancement and its benefits.

(2) Everyone has the right to the protection of the moral and material interests resulting from any scientific, literary or artistic production of which he is the author.

## Article 28.

Everyone is entitled to a social and international order in which the rights and freedoms set forth in this Declaration can be fully realized.

## Article 29.

(1) Everyone has duties to the community in which alone the free and full development of his personality is possible.

(2) In the exercise of his rights and freedoms, everyone shall be subject only to such limitations as are determined by law solely for the purpose of securing due recognition and respect for the rights and freedoms of others and of meeting the just requirements of morality, public order and the general welfare in a democratic society.

(3) These rights and freedoms may in no case be exercised contrary to the purposes and principles of the United Nations.

## Article 30.

Nothing in this Declaration may be interpreted as implying for any State, group or person any right to engage in any activity or to perform any act aimed at the destruction of any of the rights and freedoms set forth herein.

# APPENDIX 4: CONVENTION ON THE ELIMINATION OF ALL FORMS OF DISCRIMINATION AGAINST WOMEN

Adopted by the UN General Assembly on December 18, 1979.
Articles 1–16 (omitted Articles 17–30 are on implementation)

## PART I

### Article 1

For the purposes of the present Convention, the term "discrimination against women" shall mean any distinction, exclusion or restriction made on the basis of sex which has the effect or purpose of impairing or nullifying the recognition, enjoyment or exercise by women, irrespective of their marital status, on a basis of equality of men and women, of human rights and fundamental freedoms in the political, economic, social, cultural, civil or any other field.

### Article 2

States Parties condemn discrimination against women in all its forms, agree to pursue by all appropriate means and without delay a policy of eliminating discrimination against women and, to this end, undertake:

(a) To embody the principle of the equality of men and women in their national constitutions or other appropriate legislation if not yet incorporated therein and to ensure, through law and other appropriate means, the practical realization of this principle;

(b) To adopt appropriate legislative and other measures, including sanctions where appropriate, prohibiting all discrimination against women;

(c) To establish legal protection of the rights of women on an equal basis with men and to ensure through competent national tribunals and other public institutions the effective protection of women against any act of discrimination;

(d) To refrain from engaging in any act or practice of discrimination against women and to ensure that public authorities and institutions shall act in conformity with this obligation;

(e) To take all appropriate measures to eliminate discrimination against women by any person, organization or enterprise;

(f) To take all appropriate measures, including legislation, to modify or abolish existing laws, regulations, customs and practices which constitute discrimination against women;

(g) To repeal all national penal provisions which constitute discrimination against women.

## Article 3

States Parties shall take in all fields, in particular in the political, social, economic and cultural fields, all appropriate measures, including legislation, to ensure the full development and advancement of women, for the purpose of guaranteeing them the exercise and enjoyment of human rights and fundamental freedoms on a basis of equality with men.

## Article 4

1. Adoption by States Parties of temporary special measures aimed at accelerating de facto equality between men and women shall not be considered discrimination as defined in the present Convention, but shall in no way entail as a consequence the maintenance of unequal or separate standards; these measures shall be discontinued when the objectives of equality of opportunity and treatment have been achieved.

2. Adoption by States Parties of special measures, including those measures contained in the present Convention, aimed at protecting maternity shall not be considered discriminatory.

## Article 5

States Parties shall take all appropriate measures:

(a) To modify the social and cultural patterns of conduct of men and women, with a view to achieving the elimination of prejudices and customary and all other practices which are based on the idea of the inferiority or the superiority of either of the sexes or on stereotyped roles for men and women;

(b) To ensure that family education includes a proper understanding of maternity as a social function and the recognition of the common responsibility of men and women in the upbringing and development of their children, it being understood that the interest of the children is the primordial consideration in all cases.

## Article 6

States Parties shall take all appropriate measures, including legislation, to suppress all forms of traffic in women and exploitation of prostitution of women.

## PART II

## Article 7

States Parties shall take all appropriate measures to eliminate discrimination against women in the political and public life of the country and, in particular, shall ensure to women, on equal terms with men, the right:

(a) To vote in all elections and public referenda and to be eligible for election to all publicly elected bodies;

(b) To participate in the formulation of government policy and the implementation thereof and to hold public office and perform all public functions at all levels of government;

(c) To participate in non-governmental organizations and associations concerned with the public and political life of the country.

## Article 8

States Parties shall take all appropriate measures to ensure to women, on equal terms with men and without any discrimination, the opportunity to represent their Governments at the international level and to participate in the work of international organizations.

## Article 9

1. States Parties shall grant women equal rights with men to acquire, change or retain their nationality. They shall ensure in particular that neither marriage to an alien nor change of nationality by the husband during marriage shall automatically change the nationality of the wife, render her stateless or force upon her the nationality of the husband.

2. States Parties shall grant women equal rights with men with respect to the nationality of their children.

## PART III

## Article 10

States Parties shall take all appropriate measures to eliminate discrimination against women in order to ensure to them equal rights with men in the field of education and in particular to ensure, on a basis of equality of men and women:

(a) The same conditions for career and vocational guidance, for access to studies and for the achievement of diplomas in educational establishments of all categories in rural as well as in urban areas; this equality shall be ensured in pre-school, general, technical, professional and higher technical education, as well as in all types of vocational training;

(b) Access to the same curricula, the same examinations, teaching staff with qualifications of the same standard and school premises and equipment of the same quality;

(c) The elimination of any stereotyped concept of the roles of men and women at all levels and in all forms of education by encouraging coeducation and other types of education which will help to achieve this aim and, in particular, by the revision of textbooks and school programs and the adaptation of teaching methods;

(d) The same opportunities to benefit from scholarships and other study grants;

(e) The same opportunities for access to programmes of continuing education, including adult and functional literacy programmes, particularly those aimed at reducing, at the earliest possible time, any gap in education existing between men and women;

(f) The reduction of female student drop-out rates and the organization of programmes for girls and women who have left school prematurely;

(g) The same opportunities to participate actively in sports and physical education;

(h) Access to specific educational information to help to ensure the health and well-being of families, including information and advice on family planning.

## Article 11

1. States Parties shall take all appropriate measures to eliminate discrimination against women in the field of employment in order to ensure, on a basis of equality of men and women, the same rights, in particular:

(a) The right to work as an inalienable right of all human beings;

(b) The right to the same employment opportunities, including the application of the same criteria for selection in matters of employment;

(c) The right to free choice of profession and employment, the right to promotion, job security and all benefits and conditions of service and the right to receive vocational training and retraining, including apprenticeships, advanced vocational training and recurrent training;

(d) The right to equal remuneration, including benefits, and to equal treatment in respect of work of equal value, as well as equality of treatment in the evaluation of the quality of work;

(e) The right to social security, particularly in cases of retirement, unemployment, sickness, invalidity and old age and other incapacity to work, as well as the right to paid leave;

(f) The right to protection of health and to safety in working conditions, including the safeguarding of the function of reproduction.

2. In order to prevent discrimination against women on the grounds of marriage or maternity and to ensure their effective right to work, States Parties shall take appropriate measures:

(a) To prohibit, subject to the imposition of sanctions, dismissal on the grounds of pregnancy or of maternity leave and discrimination in dismissals on the basis of marital status;

(b) To introduce maternity leave with pay or with comparable social benefits without loss of former employment, seniority or social allowances;

(c) To encourage the provision of the necessary supporting social services to enable parents to combine family obligations with work responsibilities and participation in public life, in particular through promoting the establishment and development of a network of child-care facilities;

(d) To provide special protection to women during pregnancy in types of work proved to be harmful to them.

3. Protective legislation relating to matters covered in this article shall be reviewed periodically in the light of scientific and technological knowledge and shall be revised, repealed or extended as necessary.

## Article 12

1. States Parties shall take all appropriate measures to eliminate discrimination against women in the field of health care in order to ensure, on a basis of equality of men and women, access to health care services, including those related to family planning.

2. Notwithstanding the provisions of paragraph 1 of this article, States Parties shall ensure to women appropriate services in connection with pregnancy, confinement and the post-natal period, granting free services where necessary, as well as adequate nutrition during pregnancy and lactation.

## Article 13

1. States Parties shall take all appropriate measures to eliminate discrimination against women in other areas of economic and social life in order to ensure, on a basis of equality of men and women, the same rights, in particular:

(a) The right to family benefits;

(b) The right to bank loans, mortgages and other forms of financial credit;

(c) The right to participate in recreational activities, sports and all aspects of cultural life.

## Article 14

1. States Parties shall take into account the particular problems faced by rural women and the significant roles which rural women play in the economic survival of their families, including their work in the non-monetized sectors of the economy, and shall take all appropriate measures to ensure the application of the provisions of this Convention to women in rural areas.

2. States Parties shall take all appropriate measures to eliminate discrimination against women in rural areas in order to ensure, on a basis of equality of men and women, that they participate in and benefit from rural development and, in particular, shall ensure to such women the right:

(a) To participate in the elaboration and implementation of development planning at all levels;

(b) To have access to adequate health care facilities, including information, counseling and services in family planning;

(c) To benefit directly from social security programmes;

(d) To obtain all types of training and education, formal and non-formal, including that relating to functional literacy, as well as, inter alia, the benefit of all community and extension services, in order to increase their technical proficiency;

(e) To organize self-help groups and co-operatives in order to obtain equal access to economic opportunities through employment or self-employment;

(f) To participate in all community activities;

(g) To have access to agricultural credit and loans, marketing facilities, appropriate technology and equal treatment in land and agrarian reform as well as in land resettlement schemes;

(h) To enjoy adequate living conditions, particularly in relation to housing, sanitation, electricity and water supply, transport and communications.

## Article 15

1. States Parties shall accord to women equality with men before the law.

2. States Parties shall accord to women, in civil matters, a legal capacity identical to that of men and the same opportunities to exercise that capacity. In particular, they shall give women equal rights to conclude contracts and to administer property and shall treat them equally in all stages of procedure in courts and tribunals.

3. States Parties agree that all contracts and all other private instruments of any kind with a legal effect which is directed at restricting the legal capacity of women shall be deemed null and void.

4. States Parties shall accord to men and women the same rights with regard to the law relating to the movement of persons and the freedom to choose their residence and domicile.

## Article 16

1. States Parties shall take all appropriate measures to eliminate discrimination against women in all matters relating to marriage and family relations and in particular shall ensure, on a basis of equality of men and women:

(a) The same right to enter into marriage;

(b) The same right freely to choose spouse and to enter into marriage only with their free and full consent;

(c) The same rights and responsibilities during marriage and at its dissolution;

(d) The same rights and responsibilities as parents, irrespective of their marital status, in matters relating to their children; in all cases the interests of the children shall be paramount;

(e) The same rights to decide freely and responsibly on the number and spacing of their children and to have access to the information, education and means to enable them to exercise these rights,

(f) The same rights and responsibilities with regard to guardianship, wardship, trusteeship and adoption of children, or similar institutions where these concepts exist in national legislation; in all cases the interests of the children shall be paramount;

(g) The same personal rights as husband and wife, including the right to choose a family name, a profession and an occupation;

(h) The same rights for both spouses in respect of the ownership, acquisition, management, administration, enjoyment and disposition of property, whether free of charge or for a valuable consideration.

2. The betrothal and the marriage of a child shall have no legal effect, and all necessary action, including legislation, shall be taken to specify a minimum age for marriage and to make the registration of marriages in an official registry compulsory.

# INDEX

# ABOUT THE EDITOR
# AND CONTRIBUTORS

ARACELI ALONSO is a Ph.D. candidate in anthropology at the University of Wisconsin–Madison, where she teaches in the Women's Studies Program. She has done extensive fieldwork in Cuba and research on women's issues. Her chapter in this volume is part of her ongoing "Cuban Women and Social Change" research project. Much of her current research focuses on the personal narratives of elderly Cuban women.

MANISHA DESAI is an Associate Professor of Sociology at Hobart and William Smith Colleges. Her main areas of research include the women's movements in India, the international human rights movement, globalization and transnational social movements, and international development. She is completing a book on the three generations of women's activists in India. She is also involved as an activist and consultant in women's and human rights groups in the United States and India.

CHAVA FRANKFORT-NACHMIAS is Associate Professor of Sociology at the University of Wisconsin, Milwaukee, where she teaches courses in research methods, statistics, and sex and gender. Born and raised in Israel, Professor Frankfort-Nachmias received her Ph.D. at the University of Oregon. She is the author of *Social Statistics for a Diverse Society* and numerous publications on ethnicity and development, urban revitalization, and science and gender.

SHARON K. HOM is Professor of Law at City University School of Law and supervising attorney in the Immigrant Refugee Rights Clinic. She was a Fulbright Scholar in China (1986–88) and is active in U.S.-China legal and women's studies exchanges and projects. Her most recent book publication is an edited collection, *Chinese Women Traversing Diaspora: Essays, Memoirs, and Poetry* (1999). She recently received an invitation from the Rockefeller Foundation for a residency at Bellagio to work on a collaborative civil/human rights project.

CHERYL TORONTO KALNY received her Ph.D. in American history from Marquette University. She is an activist-scholar, teaching women's studies courses at the University of Wisconsin–Green Bay, speaking on women's history, and working through a number of women's organizations for positive change. She is currently writing a biography of Elizabeth Smith Martin, an early pioneer to Wisconsin Territory, and working on an oral history of women in the paper industry. Her proudest and most engrossing project, however, is her fourteen-year-old daughter Abigail.

ZIBA MIR-HOSSEINI is a social anthropologist, working as an independent researcher and consultant. She is the author of *Marriage on Trial: A Study of Islamic Family Law in Iran and Morocco* (1993) and *Islam and Gender: The Religious Debate in Contemporary Iran* (1999) and co-directed the prize-winning documentary *Divorce Iranian Style* (1998).

MARYSA NAVARRO is Charles Collis Professor of History and chair of the Latin American Latino and Caribbean Studies Program at Dartmouth College. She is the author of *Evita* (1982) and numerous articles. She is co-author with Virginia Sánchez Korro of *Women in Latin America and the Caribbean: Restoring Women to History* (1999), and co-editor with Wilma Mankiller, Wendy Mink, Barbara Smith, and Gloria Steinem of *The Reader's Companion to U.S. Women's History* (1998).

LISA M. POUPART (WABISHKAGINWKE), is a member of the Lac Du Flambeau Band of the Lake Superior Ojibwe (Anishinabe). She is an Assistant Professor of American Indian Studies, Women's Studies, and Humanistic Studies at the University of Wisconsin–Green Bay.

SITA RANCHOD-NILSSON is Assistant Professor and Director of the International Studies Program at Denison University in Granville, Ohio. She has conducted research in Zimbabwe since 1988 and has written numerous articles on African women's participation in Zimbabwe's liberation war and gender politics.

MADELEINE SHEA received her doctorate in political science from the University of Maryland, Baltimore County. She is currently serving as Chief of the Evaluation Division of the Maryland State AIDS Administration. She is a comparative social policy analyst and has presented several papers on her European Union women's rights research conducted while living in Europe from 1995 to 1997.

BAHIRA SHERIF, who received her doctorate from the University of Pennsylvania, is Assistant Professor in the Department of Individual and Family Studies at the University of Delaware. She conducted field research in Egypt, and her research interests include gender and Islam, intergenerational relations, and the relationship between work and family life.

GRATZIA VILLARROEL SMEALL is Assistant Professor of Political Science and Coordinator of the International Studies Program at St. Norbert College in Wisconsin. Her areas of specialty include international organizations, third world politics, and women in politics.

VICTORIA B. TASHJIAN received her Ph.D. in African history from Northwestern University and is an Assistant Professor of History at St. Norbert College in De Pere, Wisconsin. Her research interests and publications are concerned with marriage, work, economic change, and "customary" law in West Africa, and she is the co-author with Jean Allman of *"I Will Not Eat Stone": A Women's History of Colonial Asante* (2000).

LYNN WALTER is Professor of Social Change and Development and Women's Studies at the University of Wisconsin–Green Bay. Her research in Ecuador and Denmark, focusing on ethnicity, feminist anthropology, social welfare, and women's movements, has appeared in *Ethnicity, Economy and the State in Ecuador* and in such journals as *American Ethnologist, Gender and Society, Feminist Review,* and *The Journal of Comparative Family Studies.*

LINDA WHITE is a feminist and mother of two children. Her doctorate is in anthropology from the University of Colorado at Boulder. She is an instructor at the University of Colorado, where she teaches courses on Japanese culture, gender, globalization, and popular culture.